Stress in Teachers:
Past, Present and Future

Stress in Teachers:
Past, Present and Future

**Edited by
Jack Dunham and Ved Varma**

Whurr Publishers Ltd
London

© 1998 Whurr Publishers Ltd
First published 1998 by
Whurr Publishers Ltd
19b Compton Terrace, London N1 2UN, England

British Library Cataloguing in Publication Data
A catalogue record for this book is available from the
British Library.

ISBN 1 86156 082 6

Printed and bound in the UK by Athenaeum Press Ltd,
Gateshead, Tyne & Wear

Contents

Jack Dunham:
An Appreciation

This edited book consists of 11 chapters written by well-known contributors in appreciation of Jack Dunham's research, conference and workshop contributions to the field of stress management in teaching. He carried out a substantial amount of the early research in this area and his more recent investigations were reported in his book *Stress in Teaching* (2nd edition 1992), which teachers and researchers have found most useful.

He has continued to work in this field and his stress publications have been based on his work as a consultant with special, primary and secondary schools in Germany, the UK and Ireland, consistently arguing for the recognition of the importance of the organisational aspects of stress in teaching. The concepts and skills essential for good management practice in the development of whole-school models of stress management for teachers and support staff have been presented in his book *Developing Effective School Management* (1994), which is based on the courses he ran from 1983 to 1993 for the Further Professional Studies Unit of Bristol University School of Education with middle managers in secondary schools.

Recently Jack Dunham was an expert witness for a teacher bringing an action against his former local education authority on account of occupational stress and his most recent workshops have been with the staff of the Avon Special Needs Service and with nursery nurses in Bristol.

He is a freelance management and stress management consultant in education and industry, an Associate Fellow and Chartered Psychologist of the British Psychological Society, a Fellow of the American Institute of Stress and the International Stress Management Association. He is a member of the Stress and Anxiety Research Association and has made presentations on whole school models of stress management to the STAR Annual Conferences in Cairo and Prague. Jack Dunham is also an Associate Member of the Royal Aeronautical Society and he is the Membership Secretary of the Royal Air Force Historical Society.

Ved Varma

Contributors

Vivien Bath was Deputy Head Teacher at Hayesfield Comprehensive School in Bath until she retired in July 1997. For some years she was Staff Development Co-ordinator at Hayesfield; as Head of Lower School, She had overall responsibility for the social and academic progress of pupils. She was the co-ordinator of the Careers and Personal and Social Education Programme.

Marie Brown is Senior Lecturer in Education in the University of Manchester School of Education. She lectures and researches in Educational Management and Administration and Education and the Mass Media and runs in-service courses for teachers and other professionals. She has researched and published extensively on the effects of stress on teachers.

Cary Cooper is Professor of Organisational Psychology at the Manchester School of Management, and Pro-Vice-Chancellor (External Activities) of the University of Manchester Institute of Science and Technology (UMIST). He is the author of over 70 books and has written over 250 articles for academic journals. A frequent contributor to national newspapers, TV and radio he is editor-in-chief of the *Journal of Organisational Behaviour* and co-editor of the medical journal, *Stress Medicine*. He is also a Fellow of the British Psychological Society and of the Royal Society of Arts.

Angela Creese has worked both as a researcher and lecturer at the Institute of Education, University of London for three years. Before that she taught in universities in Turkey and the USA. Her interests are in teacher collaboration, language planning and policy and applied linguistics.

Harry Daniels is Professor of Special Education and Education Psychology at the University of Birmingham. Together with Brahm Norwich, he has been involved in studies of the impact of teacher support teams in primary and secondary schools over the last four years.

He is also involved with research on the processes of gender differentiation in mainstream primary schools. He has published widely on many aspects of special education needs.

John Hinton is Honorary Senior Research Fellow at the University of Glasgow, directing the Stress-research Unit in the Psychology Department. He is President of the British Psychophysiology Society and a founder member of of the Society for the study of Psychophysiology in Ergonomics (PIE). He was the Senior Research Officer at a maximum security hospital heading a research team investigating biopsychological factors relating to psychopathy and violence. From 1983 he has been focusing on the development of a biopsychological theoretical model of psychological stress. Since 1993 he has been Project Leader on a British Council DAAD – sponsored ARC (Academic Research Collaboration) with the Work-Science Section for Dresden Technical University researching the psychophysiology of work-stress. He has more than 150 scientific publications, including an edited book and over 80 refereed articles in scientific journals.

Dr Chris Kyriacou is a Senior Lecturer in Educational Psychology at the University of York, Department of Educational Studies. He graduated in psychology, and then taught mathematics in a London comprehensive school before going on to complete a PhD on teacher stress. Since his move to York in 1979 he has published widely on teacher stress, and he regularly runs workshops in schools on coping with stress. He has also written widely on teaching methods in school, including two books *Effective Teaching in Schools* and *Essential Teaching Skills*.

Adrian Miles spent some seventeen years in the teaching profession, with a large proportion of this time spent working with young people with special needs. Indeed, it was seeing the enormous pressures under which colleagues were having to perform which prompted his initial interest in the field of stress. For the last ten years he has worked in a large Social Services Department, initially as a Performance Review Adviser and latterly as a Principal Officer. One of his key responsibilities in recent years has been concerned with the development of quality systems, performance improvement and more recently Best Value. A key dimension running through these areas is the importance of staff as a key resource.

Brahm Norwich has worked as a teacher and an educational psychologist. He is currently Professor of Special Needs Education and Head of the Psychology and Special Needs Group at the Institute of Education, London University. His interests include organisational and support systems for special educational needs.

Alistair Ostell is Senior Lecturer in Occupational Psychology at the University of Bradford Management Centre, where he is responsible for Executive MBA and DipBA programmes provided for senior and middle management of the British Broadcasting Corporation. He is a Chartered Psychologist whose main research interests and publications are in the fields of stress and coping, emotion management and health. His recent work has been concerned with advising and assisting companies in the assessment of stress and behaviour problems at work, both at the individual and organisational levels.

Sue Ralph is a Senior Lecturer in Education in the University of Manchester School of Education. She lectures and researches in Educational Management and Administration and Education and the Mass Media and runs in-service courses for teachers and other professionals. She has researched and published extensively on the effects of stress on teachers.

Elke Rotheiler is a Senior Lecturer in Occupational Psychology at the Caledonian University in Glasgow. Until 1983, when she came to Scotland and started work in the Psychology Department of Glasgow University, she worked in the GDR power supply industry. There she gained extensive experience as the chief work psychologist in the power supply industry of Dresden in the former GDR, and she published a definitive manual on work safety which was used throughout the country. In the last 15 years she has been actively researching in the field or work-stress and health, focusing on the application of psychological stress theory to the development of coronary heart disease. In this context she has collaborated with colleagues in Dresden University in the development and testing of new measuring instruments for assessing coronary-prone behaviours, and has a substantial number of scientific publications in this area.

Cheryl Travers is Lecturer in Organisational Behaviour and Human Resource Management at Loughborough University Business School. She has trained a large number of teachers in stress management and she has been the joint author with Professor Cary Cooper of a considerable number of publications on stress in teaching including a recent large scale investigation commissioned by the National Association of Schoolmasters and Union of Women Teachers (NASUWT).

Marion Tyler is the Managing Director of Living with Stress Ltd, a training company which specialises in stress management and associated lifestyle training. She provides training for many companies and organisations. She has a background in nursing and health visiting, from which she has developed her interest in stress management, winning a

Nurse of the Year award in 1989 for her pioneering work in providing stress management workshops within a Primary Health team. She has carried out considerable training in schools for pupils, as well as stress management training for teachers. She also provides stress management training for trainers themselves, having developed a basic training course, in conjunction with the RSA Examination Board, leading to a Certificate in Stress Management.

John Usher is the solicitor for John Walker, who suffered workplace stress and who, in a much publicised trial, became the first person successfully to sue his employers for damages. He is a partner with Thomsons, the UK's largest personal injury solicitors, who act for trade unions and those who have been injured. He has been responsible for many successful personal injury and employment law cases in the last 18 years of practice, several of which have been reported. He is often asked to speak on courses for trade union representatives or at conferences for the UK National Work-Stress Network, the National Association of Health Authorities and Trusts, the Association of Personal Injury Lawyers and the Personal Injury Claims Summit among others. He also contributes, at the request of the Law Commission, to various consultation papers particularly on issues relating to claims for damages.

Ved Varma was formerly a teacher in London and Middlesex and an educational psychologist with the Institute of Education, University of London, the Tavistock Clinic and the London Boroughs of Richmond and Brent. He has edited or co-edited more than thirty books in education, psychology, psychiatry, psychotherapy and social work, and is an international figure in the area of special needs.

Belinda Walsh is a Consultant Clinical Psychologist currently working in North Derbyshire where her work includes clinical work with a cognitive behavioural bias, interests in innovative therapies, links with a police welfare department, teaching in the University of Sheffield's Psychology Department and managing other psychologists. She also co-ordinates the staff support service for health service staff in North Derbyshire, so she is familiar with the problems of workplace stress and has particular interests in the management and treatment of the effects of traumatic incidents at work. She has recently been developing an alternative style of stress management training, which rather than focusing on training individuals to cope better, aims to enable managers to identify and control sources of stress for their staff.

Preface

The editors' understanding of stress in teaching is that it is a multidisciplinary concept broad enough to include physiological, psychological, organisational and legal approaches. Our main aim in inviting the distinguished contributors to *Stress in Teaching: Past, Present and Future* was to make their wide range of research and practical expertise available in one volume.

The editors believe that stress in teaching is an interactionist concept — a complex and sometimes precarious balance between perceived work pressures, coping strategies and stress reactions. The chapters by Chris Kyriacou, Marie Brown and Sue Ralph, Cheryl Travers and Cary Cooper, Alistair Ostell and John Hinton and Elke Rotheiler make important and original contributions to understanding the causes and costs of stress in teaching. Their collective conclusions are very worrying. The reader will find that these include:

- an alarmingly low level of job satisfaction;
- turnover intentions appear to be on the increase; a survey of 361 000 teachers has shown that 46 950 teachers in any one year are changing jobs.

These pessimistic conclusions are challenged by Harry Daniels, Angela Creese and Brahm Norwich, Marion Tyler, Jack Dunham and Vivien Bath who contribute more optimistic conclusions from their stress management and professional development workshops and research projects. A common theme of all these contributions is the danger of focusing stress research and management strategies on the individual rather than the organisation. The authors share the conclusion that initiatives at the organisational level can reduce some of the causes and costs of teacher stress. They report their 'hands-on' knowledge of the operations of teacher support teams and workshop and whole-school approaches to improving stress management strategies, training and career development.

The editors also believe that useful insights for workers in the education service can be gained from studies of workplace stress in other occupations. The view is strongly supported in Belinda Walsh's chapter, in which she has summarised a range of strategies that public service and commercial organisations have undertaken to tackle the problems arising from workplace stress such as absenteeism, ill-health, job dissatisfaction and turnover. Adrian Miles discusses his research project in which he attempted to bring about organisational change and reduce staff stress in a children's home and day nursery. John Usher, a solicitor in Leeds, has clearly delineated the meaning of 'the employer's duty of care', which has very important legal implications for teachers, school governors and local education authorities in the millennium.

The editors are most grateful to all of these distinguished and very busy authors who responded so gracefully to being invited to contribute to this volume and have been so friendly and warming in their communications throughout the project.

Jack Dunham

Chapter 1
Teacher Stress: Past and Present

CHRIS KYRIACOU

I first came across the notion of teacher stress when I was a teacher of mathematics at a comprehensive school in London in the mid-1970s. Teachers at the school where I taught received a salary enhancement to take account of the fact that the catchment area served by the school contained a relatively high proportion of pupils living in 'disadvantaged' circumstances. This payment was part of a government initiative to try to reduce the level of staff turnover in schools serving areas of urban deprivation. The technical term for this enhancement was a 'social priority allowance' but most staff in the school called it a 'stress allowance'. I was intrigued by this reference to stress. At the time I was interested in undertaking a higher degree and the idea of researching stress amongst schoolteachers seemed to be both intellectually interesting and a topic that might yield practical benefits.

When I started to look for writings on stress amongst schoolteachers I found that almost nothing had been published. There were a few references made to the pressures and difficulties faced by teachers in doing their work, particularly with reference to dealing with extremes of pupil indiscipline, but virtually no use of the specific term 'teacher stress'. A number of film portrayals and newspaper reports had focused on 'the blackboard jungle' and attempted to convey the difficulties faced by teachers in maintaining classroom order when challenged by disaffected pupils. However, none of these attempted to portray a wider picture of aspects of the teacher's work that might cause stress.

Nevertheless, there was a recognition that the teacher's job was a difficult one. One of the earliest references to this that I have come across is a report in *The Schoolmaster* of 6 December 1879 concerning the suicide of a headteacher as a result of pressure at work, whose circumstances have a striking resemblance to those commonly reported by headteachers in recent years:

> A most distressing case of suicide occurred recently at Woolwich. The headmaster of the Woolwich-Common Military College shot himself on Saturday last. His brother gave evidence to the effect that the deceased had often complained that the work was killing him, saying that the trouble of teaching did not affect him so much as the worry of management. The case gives rise to serious considerations. Every now and then we hear of a teacher, elementary or otherwise, committing suicide while suffering from temporary insanity. What is not so evident to the general public is the distressing state of mind in which a very large number carry on their work . . . The absurd anxiety to gain high percentages and outvie the other schools in their neighbourhood is the fruitful parent of many of the evils under which teachers groan. Overwork benefits neither teacher or pupil in the long run, however satisfactory may be the immediate results.

Another telling comment comes from the poet TS Eliot, who wrote:

> I have never worked in a coal mine, or a uranium mine, or in a herring trawler; but I know from experience that working in a bank from 9.15 to 5.30, and once in four weeks the whole of Saturday, with two weeks' holiday a year, was a rest cure compared to teaching in a school. (Eliot 1950)

In the mid-1970s, however, some of the teaching unions began to be concerned about the level of stress experienced by teachers, and started to produce reports on this. The first major report was entitled *Stress in Schools*, published by the National Association of Schoolmasters/Union of Women Teachers (NAS/UWT) in 1976. This report contained a seminal paper by Jack Dunham (Dunham 1976) on 'stress situations and responses', which in many ways can be regarded as the start of major research on teacher stress in the UK. Dunham's paper highlighted the stress for teachers resulting from role conflict, poor working conditions (which included communication difficulties within schools and dissatisfaction with the headteacher's style of leadership), and being involved in school reorganisation. The importance of Dunham's paper lies in its presentation of data from teachers (collected both orally and in writing), his categorisation of these in terms of major stress situations, and his portrayal of teachers' experiences of stress.

At the same time, Irene Caspari's (1976) book contained a very important chapter on 'stresses on the teacher at school', structured in terms of the following subheadings:

• The teacher's role.
• The teacher's concern about his knowledge of the subject matter.

- The teacher's concern about methods and ways of presentation.
- The complexities of keeping discipline.
- The importance of relationships within the staff group and between the staff and the school's management group.
- The importance of the communication system.
- Teachers and parents.
- The expectation of perfection in teachers.
- The consequences of these unrealistic expectations.
- The need to reduce stress.

In the next few years, other studies and reports began to appear, including my own questionnaire survey of stress amongst teachers in comprehensive schools (Kyriacou and Sutcliffe 1978), in which I identified four major groupings for sources of stress:

- pupil misbehaviour;
- poor working conditions;
- time pressures;
- poor school ethos.

This paper also attempted to obtain some indication of how widespread the experience of teacher stress was by asking the teachers to respond to the question 'In general, how stressful do you find being a teacher?' on a five-point scale labelled 'not at all stressful', 'mildly stressful', 'moderately stressful', 'very stressful' and 'extremely stressful'. Using this self-reported measure of teacher stress, about 20% of the sample rated being a teacher as either very or extremely stressful. This finding provided one of the first research-based indications of the prevalence of teacher stress in the UK.

The paucity of research on teacher stress was also evident in the United States. However, studies started to be published there too (Coates and Thoresen 1976; Phillips and Lee 1980). By 1980 the issue of teacher stress was well and truly on the research agenda. Only 10 years further on, at the start of the 1990s, teacher stress had become a major area of research throughout the world, with a huge published literature to its name, with concomitant in-service workshops for teachers devoted to it, and widespread public awareness (Cole and Walker 1989; Gold and Roth 1993; Schwab 1995).

Developing a definition and model of teacher stress

From the outset of research on teacher stress it became clear that there was a major problem with producing a definition. Much of the early writing on stress in general had led to a proliferation of different types of definition (Selye 1956; Lazarus 1966; Cartwright and Cooper 1997). It was thus not surprising that when writers tried to develop a definition of 'job stress' in general, or of 'teacher stress' in particular, this same proliferation would occur (Pithers 1995).

There are four major issues concerning the development of a definition of teacher stress. The first issue is whether to use the term 'teacher stress' to refer to the level of demands made on the teacher, or whether the term should refer to the emotional state engendered in a person in attempting to meet such demands. A second issue is whether stress should refer to all demands (both positive and negative), or only to negative ones, and/or to all emotional states (both positive and negative) or only to negative ones. In dealing with these two issues, I essentially took the view that the term teacher stress should refer to a negative emotional state engendered by aspects of the teacher's work (Kyriacou and Sutcliffe 1977). This appears to be the view adopted by most (but by no means all) writers on teacher stress. I have thus defined teacher stress as:

> the experience by a teacher of unpleasant emotions such as tension, frustration, anxiety, anger and depression, resulting from aspects of his or her work as a teacher. (Kyriacou 1997, p. 156)

The third issue involves the fact that teachers' emotional responses to their situation very much depends on their perception of the situation and on their perception of their ability to cope with the situation. This poses problems regarding how best to take account of both the objective nature of a teacher's circumstances and teachers' subjective appraisal of their circumstances. The fourth issue concerns how best to take account of the balance between the level of demands made on a teacher and the teacher's ability to meet such demands (objectively and/or subjectively). These two further issues have led to the development of quite sophisticated interactional or transactional definitions and models of teacher stress (Worrall and May 1989). What certainly seems to be the case is that any definition and model of teacher stress needs to take account of how teachers' own perceptions of their circumstances plays a major role in explaining their emotional experience.

My own definition seems to be broadly satisfactory, and broadly conceives of teacher stress as a reaction to excessive or difficult demands that need to be dealt with. However, there is one situation that still puzzles researchers. How does the definition and model of teacher stress explain why teachers experience stress when no major demands are made on them. For example, teachers may be very upset to hear they have not been allocated a particular teaching group they wanted. Since this situation requires no response by the teacher, how does the model account for the stress that results? I have tried to take account of this by arguing that any perception of threat to one's self-esteem or wellbeing can trigger the experience of stress. This normally occurs when excessive demands are made but it can also occur when the teacher perceives an insult or when their wishes are frustrated.

In more recent years models of teacher stress have developed using powerful statistical techniques to order the data collected on stress in a way that highlights those factors that appear to have a strong causal link to the experience of stress and other factors whose presence may inhibit or heighten the experience of stress without being a direct cause of the stress itself. For example, a study by Boyle, Borg, Falzon and Baglioni (1995) of primary school teachers in Malta indicated that 'poor colleague relations', which is cited as a source of stress in many studies, might actually be a by-product of the stress more directly caused by workload and student misbehaviour.

The prevalence of teacher stress

The wealth of research published on teacher stress over the last 20 years has indicated that most teachers experience some stress from time to time, and that some teachers (somewhere between a fifth and a quarter) experience a great deal of stress fairly frequently (Boyle et al. 1995; Chan and Hui 1995; Hart, Wearing and Conn 1995; Cockburn 1996; Travers and Cooper 1996).

Numerous studies have been reported that have looked at particular subgroups of teachers: primary school teachers, secondary school teachers, teachers of children with special educational needs, teachers of mathematics, teachers of vocational courses, student teachers, experienced teachers, teachers in State schools, teachers in independent schools, teachers in middle management, headteachers, and heads of pastoral care (eg Manthei, Gilmore, Tuck and Adair 1996; Capel 1997; Male and May 1997; Morton, Vesco, Williams and Awender 1997). Such studies, however, have not consistently shown that certain subgroups of teachers report higher levels of stress than other subgroups.

Studies comparing teachers with other professional occupations using a variety of measures (attitudinal, physiological, behavioural and medical) indicate that teaching is one of the high stress professions (Health Education Authority 1988; Travers and Cooper 1996; *Sunday Times* 1997). This is particularly the case when self-report measures are used, but less so for other measures. This difference would appear to be accounted for by the recuperative effects of the long holidays following a gradual build up of stress over the course of each school term, which leads to teachers having a slightly lower level of stress-related ill-health than their level of self-reported stress would predict (Esteve 1989; Salo 1995).

Measuring teacher stress

A major problem facing researchers has been the measurement of teacher stress (Hiebert and Farber 1984; Chan 1995). Self-reported stress questionnaires have been the most widely used approach. These differ a great deal in format and content. Some have included simple and direct questions, asking the teachers to report their overall level of stress on a response scale. Others asked teachers to report the frequency and intensity of either sources of stress and/or symptoms of stress and then computed an overall measure of the level of stress from these data. In addition to self-reported questionnaires, some studies have looked at physiological, behavioural and medical indicators of stress (such as absenteeism, leaving the profession, chronic levels of high tension and anxiety, sleeplessness, lowered sex drive and hormonal changes over the course of a working week). All measures of teacher stress have their strengths and weaknesses. The widespread use of self-reported questionnaires has been very successful in generating information about teacher stress, and has provided a suitable basis for model building and comparisons between subgroups. However, given the subjectivity involved in self-report, one must be very cautious about its use in providing information about a particular teacher's level of stress.

A number of researchers have focused on the term 'teacher burnout', which refers to a state of emotional, attitudinal and behavioural exhaustion that can occur following the experience of a high level of stress over a long period (Kremer-Hayon and Kurtz 1985; Gold and Roth 1993; Burke, Greenglass and Schwarzer 1996). The most pervasive symptoms of teacher burnout are taken to be a marked lowering of job commitment, a loss of enthusiasm and interest and feelings of disaffection and alienation. Measures of teacher burnout have also varied, although here again, a self-reported questionnaire format for collecting data has been the most widespread.

The main sources of stress

The voluminous literature on teacher stress has yielded a substantial amount of data on the sources of teacher stress (Borg 1990; Dunham 1992; Travers and Cooper 1996; Upton and Varma 1996). Such studies have not only indicated the main sources of stress facing teachers as a whole, but also how the main sources of stress vary to some extent from one subgroup to another. For example, teachers in independent schools often cite the intense pressure on them from parents to ensure their children achieve unrealistically higher levels of attainment; teachers of children with emotional and behavioural difficulties often cite the unpredictability of the behaviour they have to deal with; student teachers often cite having their teaching performance assessed by tutors and mentors.

Nevertheless, taken as a whole there are certain sources of stress that have been reported consistently across a wide range of studies. These sources of stress fall into six main categories:

- poor pupil behaviour, ranging from low levels of pupil motivation to overt indiscipline;
- time pressure and work overload;
- poor school ethos, including poor relationships with the headteacher and with colleagues;
- poor working conditions, including a lack of resources and poor physical features of the building used;
- poor prospects concerning pay, promotion and career development.

Coping with change

For some teachers in some schools, the need to deal with pupils who frequently challenge the teacher's authority and who overtly misbehave during lessons is a major source of stress. However, in addition to this, many teachers have reported that simply dealing with pupils who show little interest in schoolwork, but who can not in any way be regarded as misbehaving, is also a major source of stress. Indeed, some teachers have said that the continuous efforts they have to make to encourage pupils to work harder and show more interest in their work contributes more to their feelings of exhaustion at the end of a school day than any of the other demands with which they have to deal as a teacher.

Another major source of stress for teachers is simply that of having to deal with a heavy workload and time pressures. Even with the use of sound time management skills, there are a variety of tasks that teachers need to carry out (planning, teaching, marking, writing reports, meeting parents) that are very time consuming, and teachers often feel that the time available is insufficient for the work required of them.

Many teachers have a strong sense of camaraderie, and like to work in a positive atmosphere where they can feel they are collectively engaged in a worthwhile activity and where mutual support is available when the need arises. If a relationship between a teacher and his or her colleagues has become negative, this can be a major source of stress, in part because of the close dealings teachers need to have with each other on a daily basis. Part of the problem here lies in the fact that teachers are broadly speaking 'people focused'. By this I mean that teachers often see their dealings with others as being based on personal relationships. As such, when things go wrong, there is a danger that this can be interpreted personally and thereby undermine their feelings about their relationship with a colleague.

Another major source of stress relates to the worries and dissatisfaction teachers feel about their level of pay and their chances of promotion. This can be particularly acute during the middle years of teaching (typically when teachers are in their 40s) and they try to appraise their working life and compare their prospects with their initial expectations and those of their contemporaries in other jobs. Two fascinating studies to illustrate this have been reported by Cherniss (1995) in the United States and Huberman (1993) in Switzerland.

Finally, the need to cope with change is a major source of stress. Indeed, in recent years, frequent changes have occurred in the content and methods of teaching required in many countries, coupled with the introduction of greater accountability and public assessment of their performance. Often, such changes have occurred at short notice, and have not been linked with adequate programmes of in-service training. This has meant that teachers have often been expected to acquire new skills and become fully acquainted with new requirements at an unrealistic speed. Moreover, many changes have been introduced in a manner that criticised previous practice and made teachers feel they were under attack.

An aspect of change that has received particular attention because of its potentially traumatic effects on teachers has been that involved in the major reorganisation of schools. Examples of this include changing the composition of the type of pupils who will be attending the schools (in terms of age, ability and specialisms), which often results in the closure, relocation and amalgamation of many of the schools involved. In such circumstances, the teachers may be formally given notice of redundancy and have to apply for a post to commence after the reorganisation. Dunham (1976) likened the trauma for the teacher of having to leave a 'well-loved' school to a form of bereavement. Studies by Kyriacou and Harriman (1993) and McHugh and Kyle (1993) have both pointed to the extremely high levels of stress experienced by teachers who are involved in a major reorganisation, and instances of mental and physical ill-health generated by this.

These six areas have been consistently identified as the major sources of stress but it is important to recognise that each individual teacher has his or her own unique profile of sources of stress. Moreover, the makeup of this individual stress profile will change over time.

Despite the fact that studies of teacher stress have been reported in numerous countries throughout the world, few attempts have been made to undertake comparative studies of teacher stress. What comparisons have been reported (see Kyriacou 1996) indicate that, whereas there is a fair degree of consistency between countries regarding the major sources of stress that teachers report, there are also some interesting differences that relate to local circumstances and cultural factors. In addition, certain apparent similarities, for example, citing a particular source of stress such as 'a lack of adequate resources for teaching' may mean something entirely different when cited by teachers in a typical comprehensive school in London compared with when it is cited by teachers in a small rural school in Nigeria.

Coping with teacher stress

Much has also been written about how teachers cope with their own personal levels of stress and what schools can do to help reduce the levels of stress experienced by teachers in the school as a whole (Mills 1990; Rogers 1996; Dunham 1992).

Individual coping strategies fall into two main types: direct-action techniques and palliative techniques. Direct-action techniques refer to things that a teacher can do that eliminate the source of stress. This involves the teacher in first of all getting a clear idea of what the source of stress is, and then carrying out some form of action that will mean that the demands that are causing the stress can be successfully managed in future or changing the situation in some way so that the demands no longer occur. For example, if teachers are frequently anxious and worried by finding themselves unable to complete marking prior to lessons, one possible action is to allocate themselves more time for marking. Alternatively, it may even be possible to arrange to set tasks for classwork and homework where less marking is required or where some marking and feedback can occur within class time. Direct-action techniques may involve simply managing or organising oneself more effectively; they may involve developing new knowledge, skills and working practices; they may involve negotiating with colleagues, so that aspects of one's situation are changed or dealt with by others. Whatever the case, the essence of direct action is that the source of stress is now managed effectively, so that it no longer continues as a source of stress. In general, direct action is the best approach to dealing with stress, as the cause of the stress is resolved.

However, there are circumstances where the source of stress can not be managed effectively by direct action, either because various direct actions have not been successful or because direct action is not available. In these circumstances, palliative techniques come into play. Palliative techniques do not deal with the source of stress itself, but rather are aimed at lessening the feeling of stress that occurs. Palliative techniques can be mental or physical. Mental strategies involve the teacher in trying to change how the situation is appraised. For example, this may involve actively trying to put the source of stress in perspective, so that the anxiety is reduced by realising that the problem is not as great as first appears. Another powerful mental strategy is to try and see the humour in the situation. Physical strategies involve activities that help the teacher retain or regain a sense of being relaxed, but relieving any tension and anxiety that occurred. Physical techniques often occur at the end of the school day, when the teacher gets home. These may include having a hot bath while listening to some relaxing music, or taking part in recreational activities such as singing in a choir or playing squash. Some relaxation techniques can be learned that can be applied in school to help the body dissipate feelings of mental or physical tension by relaxing certain muscles and adopting a calmer pattern of breathing.

In a survey by Cockburn (1996) of coping strategies used by primary teachers to deal with stress, the 10 most effective strategies reported by the teachers were:

- ensuring that you understand the work you are about to teach;
- thorough lesson preparation;
- finding the humour in the situation;
- abandoning sessions that are not going well;
- discussing your concerns with other teachers in the school;
- getting to know your pupils as individuals;
- setting priorities;
- making lists;
- sharing your failures;
- chatting to colleagues about recreational interests, etc.

As well as individual coping actions, a number of studies have highlighted the importance of working in a school where a positive atmosphere of social support exists. This enables teachers to share concerns with each other, which can lead to helpful suggestions from a colleague that the teacher can implement, or action by colleagues that resolves the source of stress. Often, simply sharing problems or engaging in some social activity with colleagues during break periods can effectively help dissipate the feelings of stress. Research studies on the impact of social support, however, have not yielded consistent findings (Sheffield, Dobbie, Carroll 1994). This appears to be in large measure because a teacher's use of social support depends on its availability in the form desired by the teacher and because teachers differ in the role they may play in creating and activating such support.

Teachers and senior managers in schools also need to give thought to the way in which they may be creating unnecessary sources of stress through poor management. For example, an individual teacher or senior manager can set unrealistic targets for the completion of certain tasks, or fail to communicate adequately with others, and this then gives rise to avoidable problems.

A very important development in reducing teacher stress comes from the need to think more in terms of what characteristics make for healthy organisational functioning, and then to develop individual and organisational practices to come in line with these so that staff stress can then be reduced almost as a by-product of this (Cox, Boot and Cox 1989; Health and Safety Commission 1990).

Over the years a number of teachers have taken part in in-service workshops aimed at helping them to reduce their level of experienced stress (Seidman and Zager 1992). Such workshops typically focus on helping teachers to develop a mix of direct action and palliative techniques, and also helping teachers individually and the school as a whole to develop methods of working that will minimise the occurrence of unnecessary sources of stress. A common feature of such workshops is training in the use of relaxation exercises as a palliative technique. However, Roger and Hudson (1995) have argued that a key feature in prolonging the experience of stress is a tendency for emotional rumination, which serves to maintain the feelings of tension and upset engendered by the source of stress. They have thus pointed to the need to help individuals develop greater 'emotion control' by terminating such rumination and thereby enabling palliative techniques to be more effective. Similarly, Boekaerts (1993) has argued that such 'emotion control' can best be fostered by helping individuals to develop the ability to monitor their own behaviour when experiencing stress so that they can move from a 'coping mode' to a 'mastery mode' in dealing with the demands made on them. Certainly, one of the major challenges facing those working in the area of teacher stress is to develop more effective programmes in stress management.

Conclusions

Teacher stress has undoubtedly become an area of major interest to educationists and education policy makers throughout the world. On the basis of the research on teacher stress that has been published we now have a very good idea of the nature of teacher stress, its prevalence, the main sources of stress facing teachers, the coping actions used by teachers, and the features of successful intervention programmes designed to help teachers reduce stress.

Nevertheless the complexity involved in reaching a full understanding is clearly evident to those familiar with writings on teacher stress. This complexity in large measure stems from the way in which teacher stress is subject to marked individual differences and the way in which small and subtle changes in context can have a major influence on the type and nature of stress experienced.

Advances in our understanding of teacher stress in the future are most likely to come from

- studies of the influence of school organisation and climate on teachers' experience of stress;
- studies of the ways in which individuals appraise their situation, particularly in relation to how these influence their attempts to employ effective coping strategies; and
- studies of the extent to which intervention programmes aimed at enhancing teachers' skills to deal more effectively with work demands successfully reduce their experience of stress.

References

Boekaerts M (1993) Being concerned with well-being and with learning. Educational Psychologist 28: 149-67.

Borg MG (1990) Occupational stress in a British educational setting: a review. Educational Psychology 10: 103-26.

Boyle GJ, Borg MG, Falzon JM and Baglioni AJ (1995) A structural model of the dimensions of teacher stress. British Journal of Educational Psychology 65: 49-67.

Burke RJ, Greenglass ER and Schwarzer R (1996) Predicting teacher burnout over time – effects of work stress, social support, and self-doubts on burnout and its consequences. Anxiety, Stress and Coping 9: 261-75.

Capel SA (1997) Changes in students' anxieties and concerns after their first and second teaching practices. Educational Research 39: 211-28.

Cartwright S, Cooper CL (1997) Managing Workplace Stress. London: Sage.

Caspari IE (1976) Troublesome Children in Class. London: Routledge & Kegan Paul.

Chan DW (1995) Multidimensional assessment and causal modelling in teacher stress research: a commentary. British Journal of Educational Psychology 65: 381-6.

Chan DW and Hui EKP (1995) Burnout and coping among Chinese secondary school teachers in Hong Kong. British Journal of Educational Psychology 65: 15-25.

Cherniss C (1995) Beyond Burnout: Helping Teachers, Nurses, Therapists and Lawyers Recover from Stress and Disillusionment. London: Routledge.

Coates TJ, Thoresen CE (1976) Teacher anxiety: a review with recommendations. Review of Educational Research 46: 159-84.

Cockburn AD (1996) Primary teachers' knowledge and acquisition of stress relieving strategies. British Journal of Educational Psychology 66: 399-410.

Cole M, Walker S (eds) (1989) Teaching and Stress. Buckingham: Open University Press.

Cox T, Boot N, Cox S (1989) Stress in schools: a problem-solving approach. In Cole M and Walker S (eds) Teaching and Stress. Buckingham: Open University Press.

Dunham J (1976) Stress situations and responses. In NAS/UWT (ed.) Stress in Schools. Hemel Hempstead: NAS/UWT.

Dunham J (1992). Stress in Teaching (2 edn). London: Routledge.

Eliot TS (1950) The aims of education: the conflict between aims. In Eliot TS (1965) To Criticize the Critic and Other Writings. London: Faber & Faber.

Esteve J (1989) Teacher burnout and teacher stress. In Cole M and Walker S (eds) Teaching and Stress. Buckingham: Open University Press.

Gold Y, Roth RA (1993) Teachers Managing Stress and Preventing Burnout: The Professional Health Solution. London: Falmer Press.

Hart PM, Wearing AJ and Conn M (1995) Conventional wisdom is a poor predictor of the relationship between discipline policy, student misbehaviour and teacher stress. British Journal of Educational Psychology 65: 27-48.

Health and Safety Commission (1990) Managing Occupational Stress: A Guide for Managers and Teachers in the Schools Sector. London: HMSO.

Health Education Authority (1988) Stress in the Public Sector: Nurses, Police, Social Workers and Teachers. London: Health Education Authority.

Hiebert B, Farber I (1984) Teacher stress: a literature survey with a few surprises. Canadian Journal of Education 9, 14-27.

Huberman M (1993) The Lives of Teachers. London: Cassell.

Kremer-Hayon L, Kurtz JE (1985) The relation of personal and environmental variables to teacher burnout. Teaching and Teacher Education 1: 243-9.

Kyriacou C (1996) Teacher stress: a review of some international comparisons.

Education Section Review (of the British Psychological Society) 20(1): 17-20.

Kyriacou C (1997) Effective Teaching in Schools (2 edn). Cheltenham: Stanley Thorne.

Kyriacou C, Harriman P (1993) Teacher stress and school merger. School Organisation 13: 297-302.

Kyriacou C, Sutcliffe J (1977) A model of teacher stress. Educational Studies 4: 1-6.

Kyriacou C, Sutcliffe J (1978) Teacher stress: prevalence, sources and symptoms. British Journal of Educational Psychology 48: 159-67.

Lazarus RS (1966) Psychological Stress and the Coping Process. New York: McGraw-Hill.

Male DB, May D (1997) Stress, burnout and workload in teachers of children with special educational needs. British Journal of Special Education 24: 133-40.

Manthei R, Gilmore A, Tuck B, Adair V (1996) Teacher stress in intermediate schools. Educational Research 38: 3-19.

McHugh M, Kyle M (1993) School merger: a stressful challenge? School Organisation 13: 11-26.

Mills SM (1990) Stress Management for Teachers. Lancaster: Framework Press.

Morton LL, Vesco R, Williams NH, Awender MA (1997) Student teacher anxieties related to class management, pedagogy, evaluation, and staff relations. British Journal of Educational Psychology 67: 69-89.

Phillips BN, Lee M (1980) The changing role of the American teacher: current and future sources of stress. In Cooper CL and Marshall J (eds) White Collar and Professional Stress. Chichester: Wiley.

Pithers RT (1995) Teacher stress research: progress and problems. British Journal of Educational Psychology 65: 387-92.

Roger D, Hudson C (1995) The role of emotion control and emotional rumination in stress management training. International Journal of Stress Management 2: 119-32.

Rogers WA (1996) Managing Teacher Stress. London: Pitman.

Salo K (1995) Teacher stress processes: how can they be explained? Scandinavian Journal of Educational Research 39: 205-22.

Schwab RL (1995) Teacher stress and burnout. In Anderson LW (ed.) International Encyclopaedia of Teaching and Teacher Education (2 edn). Oxford: Pergamon.

Seidman SA, Zager J (1992). Teacher stress workshops. Work and Stress 6: 85-7.

Selye H (1956) The Stress of Life. New York: McGraw-Hill.

Sheffield D, Dobbie D, Carroll D (1994) Stress, social support, and psychological and physical wellbeing in secondary school teachers. Work and Stress 8: 235-43.

Sunday Times (18 May 1997) Stress at work: how your job rates (The Sunday Times Occupational Stress Register).

Travers CJ, Cooper CL (1996) Teachers Under Pressure: Stress in the Teaching Profession. London: Routledge.

Upton G, Varma V (eds) (1996) Stresses in Special Educational Needs Teachers. Aldershot: Arena.

Worrall N, May DS (1989) Towards a person-in-situation model of teacher stress. British Journal of Educational Psychology 59: 174-86.

Chapter 2
Workplace Stress: Some Findings and Strategies

BELINDA WALSH

Introduction

On the whole, work is good for us. It can motivate us, provide us with challenges and social contacts and give us opportunities to develop and use skills; it enhances our self-esteem and contributes to our identity. The absence of work, for example through unemployment or retirement, can result in the deterioration of health, both physical and mental.

On the other hand, there are aspects of work that can be harmful to our health. Many workplace hazards such as noise, dangerous machinery and toxic substances have a direct effect on health and are well recognised and addressed by legislation such as the Health and Safety at Work Act 1992. Those workplace hazards that have an indirect effect on health by creating stress and strain receive less attention.

There has been a considerable amount of research about those features of the workplace that pose a threat to health through stress and there is enough knowledge to enable jobs and workplaces to be designed so as to prevent unnecessary stress-related ill health. There is also an increasing body of research on the various strategies that may be employed to respond to and help workers who are at risk or who are experiencing strain at work.

This chapter will review some of the research literature concerning workplace stress and its prevention or management. First of all, the sources of stress are examined, looking at aspects of the job itself and the context of jobs such as relationships at work and the characteristics of the employing organisation. Secondly, strategies for reducing workplace stress are reviewed, with emphasis on the evidence for the effectiveness of counselling schemes, stress-management training and stressor reduction methods. Mention is also made of the stress that may result from a single, disturbing event at work, which is referred to here as traumatic stress. Finally the chapter draws some conclusions and recommendations about minimising stress-related ill health at work.

Although throughout the chapter I have used the terms stress and strain interchangeably, strictly speaking it is probably most useful to refer to the cause of the problem as a 'stressor', to use the word 'strain' to refer to the effect of the stressor on the individual and to regard the word 'stress' as a general term referring to the entire experience.

Sources of workplace stress

Work is experienced as stressful when workers realise that they are having difficulty coping with the demands of work and when coping is important to them. Thus defined, the experience of stress is a result of an interaction between workers and their environment. There are many characteristics of individuals that play a part in whether or how they experience stress but discussion of these is beyond the scope of this chapter. This review will concentrate on those aspects of the working environment that have been demonstrated to have the potential to be stressful and harmful to health.

Sources of stress at work can be broadly divided into two categories: physical and psychosocial. Physical sources include biological, chemical and mechanical features of the workplace whereas psychosocial sources of stress have been defined as 'aspects of job content, work organisation and management, and of social and organisational conditions which have the potential for psychological and physical harm' (Cox 1993). This review will focus on psychosocial sources of stress, as these are generally less familiar, although some physical sources will be mentioned initially.

It is important to remember that hazardous features of the workplace will often be tolerable, and although they will detract from the quality of working life they can usually be accommodated by individuals without causing harm. It is at extreme levels and under conditions of prolonged exposure that problems arise.

Physical sources of stress

Physical features of the workplace can, of course, have a direct effect on health although here we are interested in their indirect effects, that is, through a stress-mediated pathway. In reality both mechanisms may be operating and interacting. For example work with dangerous chemicals may have a direct effect on health by causing skin irritation and may have an indirect effect by causing worry and distress about harmful consequences.

A well-studied example of a physical source of stress is noise. High levels of noise directly damage the inner and middle ears whereas less severe noise interferes with communication and, if prolonged, may give rise to anxiety, irritability, tension, increased fatigue and impaired performance.

Noise levels correlate with accident frequency. The use of protective equipment not only protects the ears from damage but also reduces accident rates and the incidence of general medical problems (Cohen 1976).

Other potential physical sources of stress include the presence of danger, vibration, extreme temperature and humidity, dealing with infectious disease and poor equipment design. Not only are unpleasant working conditions stressful in themselves but they reduce tolerance to other stressors and adversely affect motivation, thus their impact is additive (Smith, Cohen, Cleveland and Cohen 1978).

Psychosocial sources of stress

Characteristics of the job itself

Demand

The demands of workload were one of the first aspects of work to be investigated as a source of stress and it is clear that both very low and very high demands can generate strain. For example, Cooper, Davidson and Robinson (1982) found that work overload was a significant source of strain for police officers. Margolis, Kroes and Quinn (1974) found that overload was related to poor motivation, low self-esteem, absenteeism and alcohol use. On the other hand, work that places a low demand on the individual is stressful if undertaken for long periods. Some machine-paced assembly lines are examples of underload and have been linked with high levels of strain (Smith 1985).

French and Caplan (1970) make a distinction between quantitative and qualitative workload. Quantitative workload refers to the amount to be done whereas qualitative workload refers to the difficulty of the work. The two dimensions are independent and it is possible to have work that involves, for example, quantitative overload and qualitative underload; short cycle repetitive assembly work may be of this nature. Both quantitative and qualitative overload were associated with high levels of anxiety and depression in a study by Cooper and Roden (1985) on British tax inspectors.

Clearly both psychological and physical work demands are important; workers can be overloaded or underloaded with intellectual or emotional demands as well as with practical ones.

Control

The issue of control, sometimes called job discretion, is a pervasive one throughout the stress literature. It refers to the extent to which people are able to make decisions, plan work and tackle problems themselves. At a wider level, it also concerns the extent to which employees can exert influence or participate in decision making in the workplace. Warr (1992) describes low job discretion as the most important single characteristic in terms of causing stress at work. People whose jobs have little discretion or control are likely to experience stress symptoms such as anxiety, depression, apathy, low self-esteem and low self-confidence (Ganster and Fusilier 1989). Several studies (for example Margolis et al. 1974; Spector 1986) report greater satisfaction, higher self-esteem, lower distress, improved performance and lower turnover where control is enhanced by opportunities for participating in decision making; non-participation is related to stress and poor physical health.

The importance of control is that it may also act as a buffer or mitigating factor for other sources of stress. There has been much investigation of how the amount of control workers have interacts with the level of demands placed upon them. Karasek (1979) hypothesised that high job demands were not necessarily harmful in themselves but when accompanied by low decision latitude would result in psychological strain. This theory has been developed as the demand-control model (Karasek and Theorell 1990) and Wall, Jackson, Mullarkey and Parker (1996) have found that control is a crucial factor interacting with demand in determining psychological strain (see Figure 2.1). When work demands are high but are accompanied by high levels of control, the job is considered to be an 'active' one that does not incur strain. Conversely, if high job demands are accompanied by low control, they result in strain and dissatisfaction. Jobs that are low in both demand and control are considered to be 'passive' jobs that offer little stimulation.

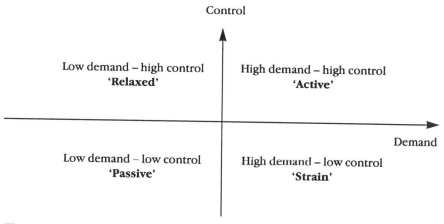

Figure 2.1: The interaction between control and demand producing different job characteristics. Source: Karasek (1979).

Theorell (1986) found that occupational groups that fell into the 'strain' category ran the highest risk of myocardial infarction. In the Framingham Heart Study in which 900 people were monitored over 10 years, those in high strain occupations were found to have a higher risk of developing heart disease (LaCroix and Haynes 1986).

It may be that increased control reduces the effects of other stressors by allowing individuals to face demands when they are best able to do so and in ways they find most acceptable. Control can thus provide the opportunity for individuals to adjust to demands according to their needs and circumstances.

Timing

The way that demand is perceived will depend on the amount of resources available to meet demands. Time in particular is an important resource. If there is little time available, or little control over time, this will contribute to strain. There is strong evidence that externally paced work is detrimental to health compared to work that is self-paced (Cox 1985). Feeling urgent time pressures is sometimes seen as a characteristic of the individual although in some cases the nature of the job can contribute to a sense of urgency. For example, Johansson and Aronsson (1984) have suggested that visual display terminal workers experience more time urgency in their work than do other occupational groups.

Skill use

It is repeatedly found that workers who have greater opportunity for skill use are mentally more healthy than colleagues with little opportunity. Cox (1985) has reviewed the health effects of semi-skilled and unskilled work and has concluded that repetitive and monotonous work with little chance of exercising skills is often associated with boredom, anxiety, depression, resentment and generally poor psychological health.

Task variety

Jobs that are deficient in variety can impair mental health. People engaged in boring work cannot learn anything new and have no challenges to give them a sense of achievement. This can happen both in low-level jobs and in any job where people have become locked into fixed and over-familiar routines where they experience little active involvement.

Uncertainty

McGrath (1976) has suggested that the concept of uncertainty represents a unifying theme in stress research that underpins many other variables. Uncertainty can occur at several levels. First, in the job itself, uncertainty can be generated by an absence of feedback about how well you are doing and what activities work best. Secondly, in the job context, there may be uncertainty about what should be prioritised, interactions with others may be unpredictable and there may be uncertainty about the flow of work. Thirdly, in the wider context, there may be uncertainty about the future, for instance in terms of career development or simply about whether the job is secure.

Work schedule

The two main issues here are shiftworking and long hours. There is considerable variation in reactions to shiftwork, with some workers adapting more readily than others. Where problems do arise it is thought to be because shiftwork disrupts the internal body clock that normally sends us to sleep at night. Hence, shift workers sleep less and have poorer quality sleep. Consequently they show a cumulative sleep deficit over successive night shifts, which is only partially restored on their rest days (Akerstedt 1985). Research on body rhythms and shift-work provides some guidance on alleviating problems by designing shift patterns to minimise problems and avoid the significant levels of physical and mental discomfort that can arise if shifts are not ordered correctly.

There is a firm link between working long hours and stress and ill health. Long hours of work, for example 12-hour days, and compressed working weeks, increase fatigue and reduce sleep and alertness. Mental and verbal performance, and vigilance in particular, are compromised although physical performance seems to be more resistant to impairment. Breslow and Buell (1960) found a relationship between the number of hours worked and death from coronary heart disease. Studies of junior doctors show that a significant proportion develop some degree of psychological ill health (Firth-Cozens 1987) and it is likely that sleep loss plays a part perhaps by increasing vulnerability to other sources of stress.

Control over work schedules is an important factor in job design. The perception of control has been shown to be significant by Ronen (1981) who reported that, although the introduction of flexitime does not substantially affect workers' behaviour with regard to arriving and leaving times, it does nevertheless have a positive effect on mental state.

Many of the job features described above are overlapping and it is clear that some are likely to be related. For example a job low in task variety is likely to be low on qualitative demand, and probably also low on skill use. It is in fact the presence of a combination of stressful job features that merits special attention when considering how hazardous a particular job is with regard to stress.

Organisational role

French, Caplan and Van Harrison (1982) have concluded that certain aspects of the workers' role in the organisation are among the most powerful predictors of psychological health. The two aspects of role considered here are role ambiguity and role conflict.

Role ambiguity occurs when workers do not have sufficient information about their work roles and when the consequences of their actions are unpredictable. This might include being confused about aims, having unclear expectations, being uncertain about scope and responsibilities and being unsure of the connection between performance and rewards. Numerous studies have consistently linked role ambiguity with high levels of psychological strain (for example O'Driscoll and Beehr 1994). French and Caplan (1970) found that role ambiguity was related to increased blood pressure and higher pulse rates as well as tension and anxiety. Other studies have found correlations with low job motivation and satisfaction, depression and low self-confidence (Kahn 1964; Margolis 1974).

The second role characteristic – role conflict – occurs when incompatible demands are made on a person or when a task conflicts with personal values. Effects of role conflict are seen on both psychological and physiological measures of strain and are related to cardiovascular ill health (French and Caplan 1970; O'Driscoll and Beehr 1994). Role conflict is an especially serious problem for individuals working at organisational boundaries, such as supervisors and those who deal with the public.

De Frank and Cooper (1987) cite several studies that identify conflict among roles and ambiguity over the content and responsibilities of these roles as sources of increased job stress and decreased job satisfaction.

Work relationships

Work should be designed to facilitate interaction between people; being able to develop relationships is an important part of work for many people although difficult relationships can be a source of worry and job dissatisfaction.

There has been considerable debate about whether the presence of social support at work can buffer the impact of a stressful work environment and there is some evidence that it may offset the negative effects of otherwise stressful environments (Cooper 1987). French and Caplan (1973) found that supportive relationships at work moderate the effects of job strain on blood pressure, glucose levels and cigarette use. Low levels of support at work have been associated with high anxiety, job tension and low job satisfaction and increased risk of cardiovascular disease (Motowidlo, Packard and Manning 1986).

The evidence, however, is mixed and the value of the support may depend on its nature. Some types of communication may serve to reinforce difficulties and problems rather than help to resolve them (Fenlason and Beehr 1994). Interpersonal demands and social pressures can in themselves be potent sources of stress.

Career development

We can consider two sources of stress in this area; firstly, lack of job security and fears of forced retirement and secondly, status incongruity – frustration at being at a career ceiling or being overpromoted or under-promoted. Concerns about promotion opportunities can be a primary source of job dissatisfaction. This is likely to lead to higher levels of strain for women and minority groups, who still encounter organisa-tional barriers to their career development. Career frustrations have been related to poor physical and psychological health (Margolis et al. 1974; Kasl and Cobb 1982).

Job insecurity and the threat of unemployment have already been mentioned as generators of uncertainty; older workers, for whom stability is important, will be especially vulnerable (Doering, Rhodes and Schuster 1983).

Organisational structure and climate

Worker well-being will be affected by the way in which the organisation treats its members. The culture and management style of an organisation may be responsible for causing some of the sources of stress already mentioned. For example, a hierarchical, bureaucratic structure is less likely to allow employees to participate in decisions affecting their work. In addition, communication may be poor resulting in increased uncer-tainty and inadequate feedback. On the other hand, a rigid organisation with formal procedures can reduce role ambiguity.

Studies of organisational climate (for example, Guzley 1992) have indicated that communication processes predict staff reactions to the job and employer. Organisational communications that focus on negative attributions, cynicism and self-interest induce feelings of unsupportiveness and mistrust in the workers.

Organisational style and culture is transmitted through the behaviour of managers and supervisors. Landy (1992) provides evidence that management behaviour and supervisory styles have an impact on the well-being of workers.

Direct care of others

High levels of contact with others, particularly in terms of dealing with crises or problems experienced by others, is thought to lead to a phenomenon known as 'burnout'. Freudenberger first observed this in 1974 in professions such as social work, nursing, teaching and police work and there have since been many studies (see Cordes and Dougherty 1993 for a review). Burnout is generally conceived to be a chronic response to extreme pressures and involves emotional exhaustion, feelings of low personal accomplishment and a depersonalisation of others in the work context – a tendency to treat them as objects rather than people. The attitudinal consequences have been studied systematically; for example, studies have demonstrated increased negative attitudes towards clients, co-workers, the job and the organisation (Cordes and Dougherty 1993), lowered commitment (Jackson, Turner and Brief 1987) and increased job dissatisfaction in teachers and intention to leave the profession (Shirom 1986). Many of the sources of job stress already mentioned in this chapter affect the development of burnout, although the critical characteristics are the frequency, duration and intensity of contact with the care group. Colligan, Smith and Hurrell (1977) looked at referrals to mental health services and found occupations involving continual contact with, and responsibility for, people were disproportionately represented. Most research has focused on job characteristics as determinants of burnout but there is evidence that organisational factors such as lack of support and low recognition of employee contributions, can also lead to emotional exhaustion and reduced personal accomplishment (Shinn, Rosario, Morch and Chestnut 1984).

Traumatic stress

Events in the workplace that may be considered to be traumatic have potentially deleterious effects on well-being. Such events may include death, injury, violence and situations where people experience a threat to life.

Clearly some occupations such as law enforcement, fire fighting and the military are to be considered high risk although there is increasing documentation of violence occurring in public service settings. It could be argued that workers who are not accustomed to dealing with potentially traumatic events are more at risk of developing psychological sequelae because of their unpreparedness, lack of training and unfamiliarity with these events.

Williams (1993) describes a pattern of emotional responses to traumatic events starting with shock, although this may be avoided in well-trained workers, followed by emotional distress. Fear, grief, nightmares, an exaggerated startle response and difficulty concentrating are all common subsequent symptoms. Trauma in work situations can also be accompanied by self-doubt and self-questioning, including concern about having done the right thing. Guilt and concern about responsibility may arise and low mood may ensue.

Many of the above reactions are considered to be normal responses to trauma, from which the majority of people will recover. A few will continue to experience major symptoms of hyperarousal, avoidance and re-experiencing for several months and would warrant the diagnosis of post-traumatic stress disorder, which can continue for months or even years unless treated.

The above is by no means an exhaustive list of all of the sources of workplace stress, although all of the aspects of work described have been demonstrated by research to be potential sources of ill health. How these job characteristics manifest themselves will depend on the nature of the job.

Stress-reduction strategies

Introduction

Cox, Leather and Cox (1990) describe three sets of objectives in managing work stress and its effects on health:

- prevention – using principles of good job design and worker training to reduce the likelihood of workers experiencing stress;
- timely reaction – improving the organisation's ability to recognise and deal with problems as they arise;
- rehabilitation – offering support and treatment to help workers cope with and recover from the effects of stress.

A further distinction may be made between interventions which focus on the organisation and those that focus on the individual and, as Figure 2.2 describes, interventions at each of these two levels could be placed in each of the three objectives.

Three types of interventions are commonly described in the literature: firstly, employee counselling; secondly, worker training in coping skills; and thirdly, methods which attempt to remove or reduce the sources of stress. The first two of these, counselling and training, are much more widely reported than interventions that tackle the sources of stress. The following is a review of some of the research in all three areas with the addition of current views on workplace trauma management.

Individual coping

Although this cannot be regarded as a strategy as such it is worth considering how individuals cope with job stress because, for the majority of workers, this is likely to be the only option for them. Much attention has been paid to the coping process and research has uncovered a variety of responses that people engage in when confronted by work-related

Level	Individual	Organisational
Prevention	To reduce the individual's risk factor or enable them to change the nature of the stressor	To remove the hazard or reduce employee's exposure to it or to reduce its impact on them
Reaction	To alter the ways in which individuals respond to the risks and stressors	To improve the organisation's ability to recognise and deal with stress-related problems as they arise
Rehabilitation	To heal those who have been traumatised or distressed at work	To establish programmes to help employees cope with and recover from problems at work

Figure 2.2: Stress management strategies at different levels of intervention. Adapted from Cox (1993).

stressors. A commonly used framework is Lazarus and Folkman's (1984) description of problem-focused versus emotion-focused strategies. Problem-focused strategies concentrate on direct action to remove the stressor whereas emotion-focused behaviours are those that attempt to minimise the psychological effects of a stressor. Edwards (1992) describes four mechanisms used by individuals:

- changing the situation, either objectively or subjectively;
- changing their expectations;
- making the problem less important or less central to well-being; and
- enhancing well-being by, for example diet, exercise or relaxation in order to buffer the effects of stress.

Coping is not only a response to stress but can also be a preventative strategy when used in anticipation of a forthcoming stressor. Murphy (1988) points out that this is the most effective coping method at work, given that most individual strategies tend to be relatively ineffective, probably because of the lack of worker control over many workplace factors.

Counselling schemes

An increasingly popular approach to reducing occupational stress is the provision of individual counselling to employees who are experiencing high levels of strain. Results from counselling and psychotherapy research indicate substantial and long lasting changes in psychological well-being (Firth and Shapiro 1986) and sickness absence (Allinson, Cooper and Reynolds 1989). Cooper, Sadri, Allinson and Reynolds (1992) evaluated the UK Post Office counselling scheme and found that counselling was effective in improving psychological health, sickness and absence from work but did not affect job satisfaction and organisational commitment.

The General Motors employee assistance programme in the United States, has been said to save the company $37 million per year (Feldman 1991). A study by the Paul Revere Life Insurance Company claims to show a saving of $4.23 for every dollar spent on employee counselling (Intidola 1991). Sutherland and Cooper (1990) cite the example of a copper corporation whose counselling programme produced a drop in absenteeism of nearly 60% in one year and a 55% reduction in medical costs.

It can be concluded that the provision of counselling to individual workers is often effective in improving mental health and can have a beneficial effect on absence rates. It must be borne in mind however that it is unlikely to affect the workplace sources of stress and may simply return workers to the same unsatisfactory conditions that caused the problem.

Stress-management training

Stress-management training is usually delivered to groups of employees and tends to be focused on white-collar and managerial workers rather than on manual workers. Broadly, they aim to teach skills that will enable workers to cope with stress and draw their technical content from four main areas: educational information, cognitive-behavioural strategies, arousal reduction methods and personal skills training. Commonly, stress-management trainers use a combination of all of these methods. The following is an overview of the different components and evidence of their effectiveness.

Educational information

This component usually includes an overview of current theories of stress, physiological information, and the causes and effects of stress and can also be used to present an introduction and rationale for other stress-management techniques. It is assumed that a conceptual framework will enable recipients to improve their understanding of stress and thereby improve their coping ability. However, West, Horan and Games (1984) found that one particular educational intervention did no better than a 'no treatment' control group on physiological and self-report measures of stress.

Cognitive behavioural strategies

Many of the techniques used in stress interventions have their origins in therapeutic methods such as cognitive therapy (Beck 1979), rational emotive therapy (Ellis 1962), stress inoculation, (Meichenbaum 1975) and anger management (Novaco 1975). Underlying many of these methods is the proposition that the way individuals interpret a situation or make attributions about it determines their emotional response. Cognitive-behavioural interventions aim to enable the participant to recognise, evaluate and, if appropriate, challenge their way of thinking about a situation. This technique, when combined with skills training, appears to be especially valuable for individuals experiencing high levels of strain (Kagan, Kagan and Watson 1995).

Arousal-reduction methods

Arousal-reduction strategies use relaxation methods that aim to lower physiological arousal and buffer the physical effects of stress. Examples include meditation techniques, progressive muscle relaxation, guided imagery and biofeedback. These methods have been shown to improve sleep patterns (Murphy 1984) and blood pressure (Higgens 1986) although combining arousal reduction with another component such as skills training or cognitive-behavioural methods is more effective than using arousal reduction methods alone (Kagan, Kagan and Watson 1995).

Personal skills training

The skills most often taught in stress-management training programmes are time management and relationship skills such as assertiveness and negotiation. These skills can then be used to prevent or reduce sources of stress, for example by delegating more effectively, by gaining more control in a relationship or by organising and planning a heavy workload. West, Horan and Games (1984) found coping skills training on an individual basis to be more effective on a variety of psychological and physical measures than either a 'no-treatment' control group or an educational programme.

The effects of stress-management training

It appears that combinations of techniques are more effective than a single approach. For example, in the study by Kagan, Kagan and Watson (1995) there was evidence that combining treatments was multiplicative rather than additive. They found that combining personal-skills training and cognitive-behavioural methods was superior to personal-skills training alone for depressed participants. Reynolds, Taylor and Shapiro

(1993), using a sessional analysis, demonstrated that different stress-management techniques have different effects. They found that cognitive strategies improved clarity of feelings and experiences, relaxation methods promoted relief and comfort and a session on dealing with stressful relationships promoted personal insight.

Stress-management training programmes have been shown to be effective on a variety of psychological and physical measures of stress. Murphy (1984) concluded that individuals benefited in a number of ways including reductions in physiological arousal levels, in tension and anxiety, in sleep disturbances and in somatic complaints. Many workers also reported an increased ability to cope with work and home problems. In some cases the effects of the training last for several months. One of the few studies to use organisational rather than personal outcome measures is that by Jones, Barge, Steffy, Fay, Kunz and Wuebker (1988) in which stress-management programmes were established in 76 hospitals. They resulted in a significant drop in average monthly medication errors and significantly fewer medical malpractice claims. Manuso, cited in Schwarz (1980), attempted a cost–benefit analysis of stress-management techniques. He concluded that every dollar spent on personal stress-management programmes might realise $5.52 in benefits for the organisation as a result of reduced symptoms and increased performance.

Criticisms of stress-management training

There is no doubt that stress-management training can be beneficial to workers in terms of improvements to their own health and well-being. Personal stress-management programmes also have some organisational advantages such as those described by Murphy (1984): they can be established quickly without major disruption, they can be tailored to workers needs and can link in to counselling schemes.

However, they can be criticised for failing to address the sources of stress in the workplace. They may be seen as attempts to change the worker rather than the workplace or as attempts to increase employee tolerance of noxious or unacceptable job characteristics. They do not eliminate or reduce sources of stress but only teach workers more effective coping strategies. Interventions aimed only at the individual imply that stress is solely a function of the individual and that sources of stress are found only in such factors as personality, family problems and lifestyle. They can promote the view that responsibility for change lies with the workers and that organisations are only responsible for providing services that assist the worker to change. This view of the experience of stress as an individual's inability to cope will contribute to stigma and result in problems being hidden rather than identified and tackled. Ganster, Mayes, Sime and Tharp (1982) argue that a more ethical form of intervention is to change the characteristics of the job and the environment that contribute to workers' experiences of stress. They propose that stress-management training should be used only in situations where environmental stressors cannot be modified, or should be offered in conjunction with the removal or reduction of environmental stressors from the workplace.

Stressor reduction

There are far fewer reports of strategies focusing on the workplace than strategies that focus on the individual. Although there is less evidence of the effectiveness of this type of approach, the evidence that is available is persuasive.

Elkin and Rosch (1990) have summarised a range of strategies that organisations can undertake. These include redesigning tasks, redesigning the work environment, role definition and clarification, establishing flexible work schedules, participative management, career development programmes, providing feedback and social support for employees and more equitable reward systems. Many of these serve to increase participation, autonomy and control.

Jackson (1983) reports a study of 25 UK hospitals in which health staff were given training and increased participation in decision making. Six months later staff reported significant reductions in perceived role ambiguity and role conflict.

Bunce and West (1996) describe an innovation promotion programme in which participants were encouraged to develop innovative responses to identified work-related stressors using group discussion and action planning. This intervention was more effective in reducing job-induced tension at a six-month follow-up than a multicomponent personal stress management programme. The training also increased the staff's propensity to innovate and make changes at work.

Stressor-reduction strategies at an organisational level have been described by MacLennan (1992). The First American Bank Corporation formed employee action teams that were trained in problem identification and problem solving. Employee membership rotated on and off the teams so that all staff had the opportunity to participate. Subsequent staff turnover was reduced from 50% to 25%. Other US banks have introduced strategies aimed at reducing conflicts between home and work such as homeworking, family sick leave and unpaid leave.

Murphy and Hurrell (1987) describe a reduction in worker strain following the establishment of a worker–management stress-reduction committee. The committee reviewed sources of stress identified at a workshop, planned interventions designed to address them and made recommendations to management.

In a four-year follow-up study of the effects of downsizing in a chemical manufacturing company, Parker, Chmiel and Wall (in press), found that the explicit company strategy of improving worker participation and control buffered the effects of the increased workload on employees. No reductions in well-being were found despite the considerable cutbacks in staff and increased demand on those remaining.

Pierce and Newstrom (1983) observed that flexible work schedules produced positive benefits for employees – including reductions in symptoms of stress.

Wall and Clegg (1981) conducted a longitudinal study of the effects of job redesign in which increases in work group autonomy were linked with significant improvements in employee mental health.

Burke (1993) summarised the effect of a range of organisational programmes. These included goal setting to enhance role definition and clarity, using problem-solving methods to resolve work-related difficulties, reducing conflict between job demands and family responsibilities and increasing communication and information sharing between management and employees. With the exception of the problem-solving groups, which were not actually implemented as planned, all these interventions appeared to yield benefits for employees.

Although there has been little systematic use of organisational interventions there is mounting evidence that job redesign interventions – especially those that increase employee control and autonomy, enhance the clarity of job descriptions and utilise performance feedback – can all enhance employee well-being and alleviate work-related strain. Research suggests that the initial costs, commitment and effort required from management will be offset by long-term benefits for individual employees and the organisation as a whole.

Incident trauma management

In contrast to the chronic nature of most workplace stress, a single traumatic incident can cause major organisational disruption and individual distress. Comprehensive management is required to maintain the function of both the organisation and the individual. However, there is little guidance on the most effective way of doing this as most of the literature on the management of workplace trauma is based on descriptive case studies rather than evaluative research reports.

Mitchell (1995) describes 'critical incident stress management', which is a comprehensive approach to the management of workplace trauma, developed for use with emergency-services personnel. Williams (1993) refers to primary, secondary and tertiary prevention in a model similar to Cox, Leather and Cox's levels of prevention, timely reaction and rehabilitation described above.

Ideally, post-trauma stress in the workplace should be prevented wherever possible by strategies to reduce the likelihood of incidents occurring in the first place. This approach represents Williams' first category of primary prevention and may, for example, take the form of security procedures to minimise violence, or equipment-maintenance policies to improve safety. Organisations whose staff regularly face repeated and predictable trauma should develop preventative procedures such as pre-trauma training and a crisis management plan that aims to minimise the impact on workers.

Secondary prevention refers to the employment of measures after a trauma that aim to reduce the likelihood of the development of significant emotional injuries. This is the basis behind the development and provision of critical incident stress debriefing (Mitchell 1995). Debriefing is a relatively formal and structured group meeting, held a day or two after the incident, which gives workers the opportunity to review their experiences in a controlled setting and provides information about likely reactions and ways of coping. It is conducted by trained and experienced professionals. Defusing is a briefer method of assisting workers more immediately after an incident; this is a procedure that aims to stabilise workers before they go home.

Tertiary prevention is concerned with providing continuing support or services to workers to address any residual symptoms of post-trauma stress and to aid recovery. This may be provided by a counselling service or occupational health programme and can usefully involve support for family members of workers.

There has been limited research on the effectiveness of workplace programmes to prevent or ameliorate reactions to trauma. Although there is often a high level of subjective satisfaction with the provision of debriefing (Hytten and Hasle 1989; Robinson and Mitchell 1993; Deahl, Gillham, Thomas and Searle 1994) there is at present no evidence that it does, in fact, help to prevent the development of post-traumatic stress disorder (Raphael 1995), which was one of the original claims made for it. However, there may be other advantages in its use in occupational settings. A preliminary study by Flannery and Penk (1996) suggests that a crisis intervention plan, which included debriefing for assaulted hospital staff, was successful in reducing staff turnover, sick leave and medical expenses.

Conclusions

It is clear from recent research that there are certain features of jobs that are implicated in causing stress at work. In addition, there is sufficient evidence on the effectiveness of stress-management interventions to support their use in the workplace. It makes intuitive and logical sense to offer a comprehensive programme of stress intervention aimed primarily at the sources of stress but providing additional help and training for individual workers. First, this might take the form of preventing harmful working conditions from arising wherever possible by applying principles of good job design. Secondly, where exposure to stressful conditions is unavoidable the evidence suggests that it is possible to mitigate the effects in a number of possible ways – for example by enhancing another aspect of work, by offering support, by training staff in coping skills, and by offering individual help such as counselling.

In practice, four main steps can be considered to reduce job stress:

- Identify the possible sources of stress by reviewing the job and environmental characteristics.
- Decide realistically what can and what cannot be changed, or what level of control to aim at. The options may include removing the stressor, reducing it, reducing the worker's exposure to it (by, for example, rotating people between roles so that no one person is exposed to the same stressor for long periods), protecting or buffering the worker against the harmful effects, or introducing moderating factors such as increasing worker control or making more support available.
- Take a problem-solving approach to the identified sources of stress. Stress-reduction strategies are likely to be concerned with such steps as increasing worker control, optimising demand, reducing uncertainty, making job roles clearer.
- Monitor the effects carefully ensuring that there are open communication systems and opportunities for feedback. Making changes at work can often have knock-on effects that can sometimes be unpredictable.

Implementing this type of stress-management strategy will have its difficulties. Many organisations may be willing to allow the provision of stress-management classes for their workers but will balk at modifying some of the sources of stress such as job design and managerial practices. Indeed, De Frank and Cooper (1987) point out that a key issue in occupational stress management is overcoming organisational resistance to change. Preventative stress-management strategies can appear to be more expensive and more difficult and disruptive to implement, although some of the examples described in this chapter suggest that this is not necessarily the case. Making changes at work can initially generate more stress, mainly in terms of increased uncertainty as people initially have inadequate skills and are unsure what to do. Hence there is a need for the period of change to be carefully planned, and for support and increased training so that people can acquire the necessary knowledge. The potential is for developing employee skills and increasing competence, self-confidence and job involvement. If the necessary changes can be worked through, both the employees and the organisation can become more confident and more effective as a result.

References

Allinson T, Cooper CL, Reynolds P (1989) Stress counselling in the workplace: the Post Office experience. The Psychologist 12: 384-8.

Beck AT, Rush AJ, Shaw BF, Emery G (1979) Cognitive Therapy of Depression. New York: Guilford Press.

Breslow L, Buell P (1960) Mortality from coronary heart disease and physical activity of work in California. Journal of Chronic Diseases 11: 615-26.

Bunce D (1997) What factors are associated with the outcome of individual-focused worksite stress management interventions? Journal of Occupational and Organisational Psychology 70: 1-17.

Bunce D, West MA (1996) Stress management and innovation interventions at work. Human Relations 49: 209-32.

Burke R (1993) Organisational-level interventions to reduce occupational stressors. Work and Stress 7: 77-87.

Cohen A (1976) The influence of a company hearing conservative program on extra-auditory problems in workers. Journal of Safety Research 8: 146-62.

Colligan MJ, Smith MJ, Hurrell JJ (1977) Occupational incidence rates of mental health disorders. Journal of Human Stress 3: 34-9.

Cooper C (1987) The experience and management of stress: job and organisational determinants. In Riley AW and Zaccaro SJ (eds) Occupational Stress and Organisational Effectiveness. New York: Praeger, pp. 53-69.

Cooper C, Roden J (1985) Mental health and satisfaction among tax officers. Social Science and Medicine 21: 747-51.

Cooper C, Davidson M, Robinson P (1982) Stress in the police service. Journal of Occupational Medicine 24: 30-6.

Cooper CL, Sadri G, Allinson T, Reynolds P (1992) Stress counselling in the Post Office. Counselling Psychology Quarterly 3: 3-11.

Cordes C and Dougherty T (1993) A review and integration of research on job burnout. Academy of Management Review 18: 621-56.

Cox T (1985) Repetitive work: occupational stress and health. In Cooper CL and Smith MJ (eds) Job Stress and Blue Collar Work. Chichester: Wiley, pp. 85-112.

Cox T (1993) Stress Research and Stress Management: Putting Theory To Work. Health and Safety Executive Research Report No. 61/1993. London: Health and Safety Executive.

Cox T, Leather P, Cox S (1990) Stress, health and organisations. Occupational Health Review 23: 13-18.

Deahl MP, Gillham AB, Thomas J, Searle MM, Srinivasan M (1994) Psychological sequelae following the Gulf War: factors associated with subsequent morbidity and the effectiveness of psychological debriefing. British Journal of Psychiatry 165: 60-5.

De Frank RS, Cooper CL (1987) Worksite stress management interventions: their effectiveness and conceptualisation. Journal of Managerial Psychology 2: 4–10.

Doering M, Rhodes S, Schuster M (1983) The Ageing Worker: Research and Recommendations. Beverley Hills: Sage.

Edwards J (1992) A cybernetic theory of stress, coping and well-being in organisations. Academy of Management Review 17: 238-74.

Elkin AJ, Rosch PJ (1990) Promoting mental health at work. Occupational Medicine: State of the Art Review 5: 739-54.

Ellis A (1962) Reason and Emotion in Psychotherapy. New York: Lyle Stuart.

Feldman S (1991) Today's EAPs make the grade. Personnel 68: 3-40.

Fenlason K, Beehr T (1994) Social support and occupational stress: effects of talking to others. Journal of Organisational Behaviour 15: 157-75.

Firth JA, Shapiro DA (1986) An evaluation of psychotherapy for job-related distress. Journal of Occupational Psychology 59: 111-19.

Firth-Cozens J (1987) The stresses of medical training. In Payne R and Firth-Cozens J (eds) Stress in Health Professionals. Chichester: Wiley.

Flannery RB, Penk WE (1996) Program evaluation of an intervention approach for staff assaulted by patients: a preliminary enquiry. Journal of Traumatic Stress 9: 317.

French J, Caplan R (1970) Psychosocial factors in coronary heart disease. Industrial Medicine 39: 383-97.

French J, Caplan R (1973) Organisational Stress and Individual Strain. In Marrow AJ (ed.) The Failure of Success. New York: Amacon, pp. 30-66.

French J, Caplan R, Harrison V (1982) The Mechanisms of Job Stress and Strain. Chichester: Wiley.

Ganster DC, Fusilier MR (1989) Control in the workplace. In Cooper CL, Robertson I (eds) International Review of Industrial and Organisational Psychology. Chichester: Wiley, pp. 235-80.

Ganster DC, Mayes BT, Sime WE, Tharp GD (1982) Managing organisational stress: a field experiment. Journal of Applied Psychology 67: 533-42.

Guzley R (1992) Organisational climate and communication climate: predictors of commitment to the organisation. Management Communication Quarterly 5: 379-402.

Higgens NC (1986) Occupational stress and working women: the effectiveness of two stress reduction programs. Journal of Vocational Behavior 29: 66-78.

Hytten K, Hasle A (1989) Fire fighters: a study of stress and coping. Acta Psychiatrica Scandinavica 80: 50-5.

Intidola B (1991) EAPs still foreign to many small businesses. National Underwriter 95: 21.

Ivancevich JM, Matteson MT (1986) Organisational level stress management interventions: review and recommendations. Journal of Organisational Behaviour and Management 8: 229-48.

Ivancevich JM, Matteson MT, Freedman SM, Phillips JS (1990) Worksite stress management interventions. American Psychologist 45: 610-14.

Jackson PR, Wall TD, Martin R, Davids K (1993) New measures of job control, cognitive demand and production responsibility. Journal of Applied Psychology 78: 753-62.

Jackson S (1983) Participation in decision making as a strategy for reducing job related strain. Journal of Applied Psychology, 68: 3-19.

Jackson S, Turner J, Brief A (1987) Correlates of burnout among public service lawyers. Journal of Occupational Behaviour, 8: 339-49.

Jones JW, Barge BN, Steffy BD, Fay LM, Kunz LK, Wuebker LJ (1988) Stress and medical malpractice: organisational risk assessment and intervention. Journal of Applied Psychology 73: 727-35.

Kagan NI, Kagan H, Watson MG (1995) Stress reduction in the workplace: the effectiveness of psychoeducational programs. Journal of Counseling Psychology 42: 71-8.

Karasek R (1979) Job demands, job decision latitude and mental strain: implications for job redesign. Administrative Science Quarterly 24: 285-306.

Karasek R, Thorell T (1990) Healthy Work: Stress, Productivity and the Reconstruction of Working Life. New York: Basic Books.

Kasl SV, Cobb S (1982) Variability of stress effects among men experiencing job loss. In LGoldberger and S Breznitz (eds) Handbook of Stress: Theoretical and Clinical Aspects. New York: Free Press.

LaCroix AZ, Haynes SG (1986) Gender differences in the stressfulness of workplace roles: a focus on work and health. In Barnett R, Baruch G, Biener L (eds) Gender and Stress. New York: Free Press.

Landy FJ (1992) Work design and stress. In Keita GP and Sauter SL (eds) Work and Well-Being: An Agenda for the 1990s. Washington DC: American Psychological Association.

Lazarus R, Folknam S (1984) Stress, Appraisal and Coping. New York: Springer Publications.

MacLennan BW (1992) Stressor reduction: an organisational alternative to individual stress management. In Quick JC, Murphy LR and Hurrell JJ (eds) Stress and Well-being at Work: Assessments and Interventions for Occupational Mental Health. Washington DC: American Psychological Association.

Management of Health and Safety at Work Regulations (1992) London: HMSO.

Margolis BL, Kroes WH, Quinn RP (1974) Job stress; an unlisted occupational hazard. Journal of Occupational Medicine 16: 652-61.

McGrath JE (1976) Stress and behaviour in organisations. In Dunnett MD (ed.) Handbook of Industrial and Organisational Psychology. Chicago: Rand McNally.

Meichenbaum DH (1975) A self-instructional approach to stress management: a proposal for stress inoculation training. In Spielberger CD, Sarason JG (eds) Stress and Anxiety, vol 1. New York: Halstead Press.

Mitchell JT, Everly GS (1995) Critical incident stress debriefing (CISD) and the prevention of work-related traumatic stress among high risk occupational groups. In Everly GS and Lating JM (eds) Psychotraumatology: Key Papers and Core Concepts in Post-traumatic Stress. New York: Plenum Press, pp. 267-80.

Motowidlo SJ, Packard JS, Manning MR (1986) Occupational stress: its causes and consequences for job performance. Journal of Applied Psychology 71: 618-29

Murphy LR (1984) Occupational stress management: a review and appraisal. Journal of Occupational Psychology 57: 1-15.

Murphy LR (1988). Workplace interventions for stress reduction and prevention. In Cooper CL, Payne R (eds) Causes, Coping and Consequences of Stress at Work. Chichester: Wiley.

Murphy LR, Hurrell JJ (1987) Stress management in the process of occupational stress reduction. Journal of Managerial Psychology 2: 18-23.

Novaco RW (1975) Anger Control. Lexington MA: Lexington Books.

O'Driscoll M, Beehr T (1994) Supervisor behaviors, role stressors and uncertainty as predictors of personal outcomes for subordinates. Journal of Organisational Behavior 15: 141-55.

Parker SK, Chmiel N, Wall TD (in press) Work characteristics and employee well-being within a context of strategic downsizing. Journal of Occupational Health Psychology.

Pierce JL, Newstrom JW (1983) The design of flexible work schedules and employee responses: relationships and processes. Journal of Occupational Behaviour 4: 247-62.

Raphael B (1995) Does debriefing after psychological trauma work? British Medical Journal 310 (June 10): 1479-81.

Reynolds S, Taylor E, Shapiro DA (1993) Session impact and outcome in stress-management training. Journal of Community and Applied Social Psychology 3: 325-38.

Robinson RC, Mitchell JT (1993) Evaluations of psychological debriefings. Journal of Traumatic Stress 6: 367-82.

Ronen S (1981) Flexible Working Hours; An Innovation in the Quality of Work Life. New York: McGraw Hill.

Schwartz G (1980) Stress management in occupational settings. Public Health Reports 95: 99-108.

Shinn M, Rosario M, Morch H, Chestnut D (1984) Coping with job stress and burnout in the human services. Journal of Personality and Social Psychology 46: 864-76.

Shirom A (1986) Does stress lead to affective strain or vice versa? A structural regression test. Paper presented at Twenty-first Congress of the International Association of Applied Psychology, Jerusalem. Cited in Warr P (ed.) (1996) Psychology at Work. London: Penguin.

Smith MJ (1985) Machine-paced work and stress. In Cooper CL and Smith MJ (eds) Job Stress and Blue Collar Work. Chichester: John Wiley and Sons.

Smith MJ, Cohen HH, Cleveland R, Cohen A (1978) Characteristics of successful safety programmes. Journal of Safety Research 10: 5-15.

Spector PW (1986) Perceived control by employees: a meta analysis of studies concerning autonomy and participation in decision making. Human Relations 39: 1005-16.

Sutherland VJ, Cooper CL (1990) Understanding Stress: A Psychological Perspective for Health Professionals. London: Chapman & Hall.

Theorell T (1986) Characteristics of employment that modify the risk of coronary heart disease. In Wolf S and Finestone A (eds) Occupational Stress. Health and Performance at work. Littleton, Mass: PSG.

Wall TD, Clegg CW (1981) A longitudinal study of group work redesign. Journal of Occupational Behaviour 2: 31-49.

Wall TD, Corbett JM, Martin R, Clegg CW, Jackson PR (1990) Advanced manufacturing technology, work design and performance: a change study. Journal of Applied Psychology 75: 691-7.

Wall TD, Jackson PR, Mullarkey S (1995) Further evidence on some new measures of job control, cognitive demand and production responsibility. Journal of Organisational Behavior 16: 431-55.

Wall TD, Jackson PR, Mullarkey S, Parker SK (1996) The demands-control model of job strain: a more specific test. Journal of Occupational and Organisational Psychology 69: 153-66.

Warr P (1992) Job features and excessive stress. In Jenkins R and Coney N (eds) Prevention of Mental Ill-Health at Work. London: HMSO.

West DJ, Horan JJ, Games PA (1984) Component analysis of occupational stress inoculation applied to registered nurses in an acute care hospital setting. Journal of Counselling Psychology 31: 209-18.

Williams T (1993) Trauma in the workplace. In Wilson JP and Raphael B (eds) International Handbook of Traumatic Stress Syndromes. New York: Plenum Press, pp. 925-33.

Chapter 3
The Identification of Stress in Teachers

MARIE BROWN AND SUE RALPH

Introduction

Stress and its effective management are high on the agenda of many primary, secondary and special schools in Britain today. When considering the impact of educational change and of teaching on teachers, one encounters a vast, often vaguely defined literature on such matters as teacher stress, burnout, morale, satisfaction and motivation. This literature has expanded with educational innovation and change in the period since the 1960s. These matters are also frequently the subjects of debate and discussion in the public arena, the media, in election campaigns and in teachers' salary disputes.

Over the past decade, the British education system has undergone a period of macro and micro policy swing shifts, resulting in enormous and rapid change in most teachers' lives. Nowhere in education has this been more keenly felt than at the 'chalkface'. All too often, classroom teachers have been left to cope with such change without adequate support. As a result, most teachers now find that they experience stress of one kind or another at some stage in their careers. Nor is this only a problem for the individual teacher. The recent High Court decision to award a social services officer very substantial damages following a stress-related breakdown has far-reaching implications for all managers in education. It means that, in common with other employers, local education authorities, school governing bodies and school senior management now have a clear obligation to take teachers' 'mental health' and safety into consideration, as well as their physical health and safety in the workplace (Griffiths 1995).

Stress has been identified as a major problem in nine out of 10 UK workplaces (Warren and Towl 1995) leading to rising absenteeism and low morale among staff. This is particularly true for schools. A raft of legislation, resulting from the Education Reform Act 1988, has advocated a locally managed approach to school governance as part of reform strategies intended to lead to improved student learning outcomes. Subsequent legislation (Education Acts of 1992, 1993 and 1994) and amendments to the national curriculum have meant that schools have been going through a period of continuous, government-imposed change. The consequence of all this change in schools is best summed up by the headteacher of an infant school in a research study that was conducted at the University of Manchester:

> My post as headteacher of an infant school has changed dramatically since the passing of the 1988 Education Act. Political legislation has transformed the nature and scale of my work, minimising my training experience whilst thrusting me rapidly forward into budgeting, computing, site management, risk management etc. – untrained and inexperienced.

Perspectives on stress

Teaching has been identified as one of the most stressful occupations in many countries today (Hunter 1977). Studies in the UK have found that, typically, approximately one-third of teachers surveyed have reported their job as stressful or extremely stressful (Borg, Riding and Falzon 1991; Kyriacou and Sutcliffe 1978). Studies in the US have found a similar situation (Coates and Thoresen 1976). In US, inner-city high school teaching is now ranked as the number one stressful job, ahead of occupations such as air traffic controller, medical intern and firefighter (*Men's Health* 1991). It is said that many teachers are being treated for symptoms similar to those that combat soldiers are likely to encounter (Bloch 1978). Studies undertaken in Australia and New Zealand have also found 'high' levels of stress (Otto 1982; O'Connor and Clarke 1990).

There is increasing concern and awareness among the teaching profession in the UK that its members are currently experiencing considerable stress. One of the major teaching unions, the Association of Assistant Masters and Mistresses (AMMA 1990, p. 9) points out that:

> Few would now dispute that teaching is a stressful profession, and it is widely acknowledged that the National Curriculum, LMS and other Education Reform Act developments are exacerbating an already tense situation.

Nattrass (1991), the Chair of the Health and Safety Executive's (HSE) Education Service Committee, at the launch of the HSE 1991 report, defined stress 'as the number one health problem amongst teachers'. He cited a survey of British teachers that revealed an increase of about 300% between 1979/80 and 1989/90 in the number of teachers leaving the profession through ill health. The importance of these comments can be contextualised more readily when one reads that in the 1980s and the 1990s the number of teachers leaving the profession through ill health nearly trebled (Dunham 1992). Retirements and dropouts (teachers leaving the profession) through ill health in the UK were 1617 in 1979 and 4123 in 1990, with steady yearly increases in the early 1980s and a big increase since 1988. The total annual cost of stress to the Education Service has been estimated to be as high as £230 million. This compares to a similar pattern of drop-out in the US where, in 1986, it was predicted that more than one million teachers would leave the profession in less than a decade, with the majority of these having been dedicated to teaching (McLaughlin, et al. 1986).

In the UK, stress or stress-related illness is often cited as a reason for teachers taking early retirement. Carvel and Macleod (1995) reported that recruitment to the profession is failing to keep up with increasing stress-related early retirement. Indeed research undertaken in the US in the late 1970s showed that teacher life expectancy was four years lower than the national average (Truch 1980). Anderson (1978) suggested that there is frequently a high amount of stress-related illness in groups of people who are responsible for the care of others while Watts and Cooper (1992, p. 49) state that the environment in which people work can have a direct effect on their stress levels:

> Until stress is recognised fully as a specific and detrimental influence on health, individuals will continue to hide the truth from themselves and their employers, going 'off sick' and adopting poor and potentially fatal coping strategies.

Teacher unions have become increasingly active in the identification and management of stress. A number of studies have been commissioned over the past decade by the major teaching unions (AMMA 1987 and 1990; National Union of Teachers 1990). These have highlighted the most common sources of stress in classrooms and schools. Other stress surveys conducted by Kelly (1988) and by Cox (1989) reinforced union stress survey results. Research has found that much of the stress reported by teachers can be attributed in general to the rapid rate of change in the education service in the 1980s and 1990s. Change, if it as rapid and continual as it has been over the last decade, is obviously a major stressor.

Occupational stress

Stress is blamed for a number of medical conditions and for exacerbating many others. As the stress currently facing the teaching profession appears to be without parallel, the consequent cost to schools of supply cover for stress-related illness and the heavy burden this places on staff remaining in school is rising at an alarming rate. It is important to take into account both personal and organisational factors in any consideration of teacher stress and its management. Therefore, before we consider how teachers and their managers might begin to identify sources of stress in school and other educational institutions, we need to define what exactly is meant by 'stress'.

There is no accepted definition of stress but it is generally seen as the consequence of a dynamic relationship between person and environment. It is often expressed as the response to something that happens to a person and that involves ambiguity, paradox or uncertainty. The effects of stress are generally seen in individual behaviour, mostly expressed in psychological or physiological changes. Definitions of stress can range from Selye's (1956) physiologically based demand–response model to definitions that are interactional in nature (Cox 1978). There are also definitions that view coping and control as integral factors in the perception of stress (Freeman 1986; Fisher 1986). For the purposes of this chapter, an individual's experience of stress is considered to be entirely subjective and therefore dependent on that person's interpretation and appraisal of a situation.

Occupational stress is an important issue in the teaching profession because of the health problems and reduction in work performance effectiveness that can result (Quick and Quick 1984). These can lead to poorer teaching performance, lowered self-esteem, poor job satisfaction, increased absenteeism, poor decision making and bad judgement (Quick and Quick 1984; Eckles, 1987). Schools can indeed be stressful places. Freeman (1986, p. 5), who evaluates school systems in terms of organisational role theory, writes that 'stress can be expected in all school organizations'. Weinstein (1979, p. 19) states: 'Nowhere but schools are large groups of individuals packed so closely together for so long yet expected to perform at peak efficiency on different learning tasks and to interact harmoniously'.

When looking at the wider question of stress, it is important to consider the point made by Freeman (1986) that stress is probably present and indeed inherent in all school organisations. We must, therefore, in the stress equation, consider both the individual and the school or other educational organisation in which he or she works. The AMMA (1987) report was concerned that both organisational and individual stress-handling strategies should be used in schools. If the school created an imbalance by inappropriate demands on staff, in terms of mismatch between teacher workloads and the abilities of individual teachers to meet them, stress reduction strategies would have to be implemented on the handling of stress in individual teachers. The report also suggested that, if teachers were given the skills necessary to manage their stress levels, both the individual and the school would benefit. Stressful situations may occur in a school because of:

- the organisation's culture;
- function;
- structure;
- the nature of its management procedures;
- poor recruitment/selection processes;
- teachers not trained sufficiently well or recently to meet changing demand;
- poor consultation and communication.

Identification of stress: the individual

Individuals differ in how they respond to stress. In particular, people interpret and evaluate successful situations in different ways depending, for instance, on their past experience, personalities, beliefs, vulnerabilities and resources. A situation perceived as threatening by one person may be seen as challenging or of no significance by another. Without some stress we cannot function properly as individuals. It is important that it does not get out of hand, however. Teachers need to be able to recognise situations in which they experience stress and to take steps to manage this. To do so they will need to be able to:

- know when they are experiencing stress;
- know they are experiencing stress;
- think about how they might manage it.

Recognising stress

Early identification of stress is very important and individuals respond to stress in different ways, so it is essential for the individual teacher to recognise and analyse the signs as soon as they become apparent (Brown and Ralph 1992). Some of the most common signs of stress are listed below.

Performance at work
- Frequently feeling like staying off work.
- Inability to manage time well.
- Inability to meet deadlines.

- Inability to concentrate.
- Having a heavy workload.
- Inability to delegate.
- Feelings of inadequacy related to performance at work.
- Job dissatisfaction.
- Taking work home more frequently.
- Low level of productivity.

Relationships with colleagues
- Increased feelings of irritation or aggression.
- Becoming increasingly introverted.
- Inability to relate to colleagues.
- Unwillingness to cooperate.
- Frequent irrational conflicts at work.
- Cynical, inappropriate humour.
- Demotivation.
- Withdrawing from supportive relationships.
- Lying.
- Role ambiguity.
- Role conflict.

Behavioural and emotional indicators
- Loss of appetite.
- Reduced self-esteem.
- Increased use of alcohol, tranquillisers, coffee, cigarettes, etc.
- Insomnia, bad dreams or nightmares.
- Being unduly fussy.
- Feelings of alienation.
- Loss of confidence.
- Too busy to relax.
- Frequent colds, influenza or other infections.
- Vague aches or pains.
- Accident prone.
- Persistent negative thoughts.
- Palpitations.

Responses to stress can vary, both between individuals and over time. Some people may primarily experience physical symptoms whereas others may experience psychological disturbance (Education Services Advisory Committee 1990, p. 5). A teacher under stress may well induce stress in students and among other colleagues. Teachers under stress may exhibit changes in behaviour that may seriously affect and disrupt the learning of children in individual classrooms. On a larger scale, if several teachers in any one school have high levels of stress, the entire school could be affected in a potentially negative manner.

Stress-prone personality factors

Meyer Friedman and Ray Rosenman (1975) in their book *Type 'A' Behaviour and Your Heart,* identified two principal types of behaviour patterns; Type 'A' and Type 'B'. They found that coronary patients whom they had studied exhibited similar behaviour patterns. Type 'A' behaviours were the high-risk ones.

Type 'A' behaviour characteristics

- Extremely busy.
- Very ambitious.
- Emphasising key words in ordinary speech in an explosive manner.
- Preoccupation with competition.
- Self-confidence.
- Aggression, hostility and impatience.
- Moving, walking and eating rapidly.
- Guilty about relaxing.

A number of research studies have looked at people who exhibit the characteristics of Type 'A' behaviour in different situations. The following is a summary of the major findings of these studies. These people were more inclined to:

- Pack more things into a shorter space of time.
- Work longer hours.
- Spend more time on school-related work (teachers).
- Sleep for fewer hours.
- Spend less time in relaxational and recreational activities.
- Communicate less with close relations, friends etc.
- Experience more breakdowns in relationships.
- Have little desire to socialise.

Type 'B' behaviour characteristics

Unlike Type 'A' people, Type 'B' people adopt a more realistic view of work and life and are not inclined to take on more than they can cope with. They do not always like to work to deadlines and are better at delegating to those who work for them. They are secure in themselves and in what they do and always maintain a sense of balance in their lives. In most respects their behaviour is almost a mirror image of that of Type 'A' people.

Identifying the causes

The following two case studies illustrate the importance of recognising

stress signals while they are at manageable levels and also the importance of the headteacher's or other support dimension.

Case study A

Ms B aged 45 and divorced, is a history teacher in an urban comprehensive school. She is very conscientious and well liked by both pupils and
staff. She felt herself being increasingly overwhelmed by the demands of
the national curriculum and the rapid rate of change in the education
service. She noticed that her intake of alcohol was on the increase and
began to experience loss of confidence and self-esteem. This led to
further feelings of depression and demotivation. She felt sufficiently
concerned to seek professional help and in a series of counselling interviews was encouraged to draw up a personal stress profile and develop
ways of managing her stress levels.

Case study B

Mr G, aged 32 and married, is a year three teacher in a suburban primary
school. He is a generally competent and capable teacher. He began to
experience feelings of increased irritability and aggression towards his
colleagues. He frequently came into open conflict with the headteacher
and this was having a very disruptive effect on the class that he taught.
He became very unpopular in the staff room due to his cynical and
caustic comments on education in general and the school in particular.
At this point the headteacher intervened sensibly and effectively by
encouraging Mr G to attend a stress management course run by the local
authority educational psychologist. This course helped him to identify
his own stressors and to work out an action plan.

Personal stress audit

It is possible to audit individual stress levels by means of a questionnaire. There are many examples of questionnaires designed to measure
stress in teachers, but questionnaires are notoriously difficult to design
and their reliability and validity is questionable.

Identification of stress: the school

It is not sufficient just for individual teachers to identify and devise
management strategies for themselves; the whole organisation of the
school needs to recognise the symptoms of stress in itself and provide an
impetus for its identification. It is important, therefore, that a whole-
school approach to stress identification should be adopted. Senior
managers have an obligation to their staff to help them identify and

manage their stress. Too many highly stressed members of any school staff can seriously affect the performance of the school.

How schools can identify stress

This will involve senior management identifying the sources of stress in their own schools. It is very important that this is done so that plans can be drawn up to alleviate the situation as soon as possible. It is essential that all staff members are fully involved in the identification of school stressors and the drawing up of an action plan to alleviate them. Stress levels are very much dependent on the individual teacher and the individual school. What is stressful for one teacher in one school is not stressful for another teacher in another school. A useful starting point in the identification of whole school stressors may lie in a consideration of the concepts of organisational climate and health. Schools, like other organisations, have climates that can have very powerful effects on the individuals working in them without them being aware of this. Ideas of climate need to be understood because a poor school climate can often be the cause of stress amongst its teachers. Knowing about the climate of your school can help you as a staff member to move towards taking steps to developing a whole-school approach to the management of stress. Anyone who has visited a number of schools will have been struck by their different 'feel'. Some schools are characterised by bright faces and one suspects that they are optimistic and happy workplaces, whereas in others there is the equally subjective impression that there is a dark, tense and threatening atmosphere with the staff and pupils conveying a melancholy air of resignation. It is reasonable to assume, then, that an open, happy and healthy work environment leads to a less stressed staff. The climate and health of a school, therefore, are important concepts in the identification of school stress.

Openness

What is meant by an open climate? Hoy, Miskel and Kotcamp (1991) identified critical aspects of teacher–teacher and teacher–headteacher interactions in American schools. They constructed the organisational climate descriptive questionnaire (OCDQ), which attempted to map and measure the climates of primary and secondary schools along an open-to-closed continuum. The four areas of open-to-closed climate that arise from this questionnaire are as follows:

- Supportive headteacher behaviour. This is shown when the headteacher is helpful, genuinely concerned with teachers and attempts to motivate them by using constructive criticism and setting an example through hard work.

- Directive headteacher behaviour. This is characterised by rigid and domineering control. The headteacher closely monitors all teachers and school activities down to the smallest detail.
- Engaged teacher behaviour reflects a climate in which teachers are proud of their school, enjoy working with each other, are supportive of their colleagues and committed to the success of their students.
- Frustrated teacher behaviour. This describes a teaching staff that feels itself burdened with routine duties, administrative paperwork and excessive assignments unrelated to teaching. It is where the teacher as a person is ignored.

This questionnaire does not explain: it merely describes. It measures how teachers in schools interact with the headteacher and each other. It does, however, reveal the foundations for organisational self-analysis and as such may be a powerful instrument for identification of school stress. Open schools are likely to be schools where the issue of stress is debated at all level whereas in closed schools it is not likely to be on the agenda at all.

School health

Organisational health is another framework for looking at the general atmosphere of a school. It refers to teachers' perceptions of their work environment. A healthy school is protected from unreasonable community and parental pressures. The governors successfully resist all narrow efforts of vested interest groups to influence policy. The headteacher is a dynamic leader, is supportive of teachers, yet provides and expects high standards of performance. The teachers are committed to both teaching and learning. Teachers set high but achievable standards for their pupils and promote a serious and orderly learning environment. Classroom resources are always available. Teachers are proud of their school, with which they readily identify, and have a lot of trust in one another both personally and professionally. Organisational health can be measured by the Organisational Health Inventory (OHI). The dimensions of organisational health that are measured by the OHI are as follows:

At the institutional level
- Institutional integrity can be seen in a school that has integrity in its educational curriculum. The school is not vulnerable to narrow, vested interests of community groups; indeed teachers are protected from unreasonable community and parental demands. The school is able to cope successfully with outside forces.

At the managerial level
- Initiating structure. This is where the headteacher makes his or her attitudes clear to the teaching staff and maintains definite standards of performance.

- *Consideration*. This is defined as headteacher behaviour that is friendly, supportive and collegial. The headteacher looks out for the welfare of the staff and is open to their suggestions.
- *Headteacher influence*. This is defined as the headteacher's ability to affect the actions of superiors. The influential headteacher is persuasive, works effectively with superiors yet demonstrates independence in thought and action.
- *Resource support*. This refers to the issue of whether adequate classroom supplies and teaching materials are available and whether extra materials can be obtained easily.

At the technical level
- *Morale*. This is defined as the sense of trust, confidence, enthusiasm and friendliness among teachers. Teachers feel good about each other and, at the same time, feel a sense of accomplishment from their jobs.
- *Academic emphasis*. This refers to the school's drive for achievement. High but achievable goals are set for students; the learning environment is orderly and serious; teachers believe pupils can achieve and pupils work hard and respect those who do well (Hoy et al. 1991).

The questionnaires on climate and health will give some idea of the staff culture of schools and may help to describe the complicated interpersonal processes at work in highly stressed school staff. Hoy et al. (1991) say that the staff culture of an 'inadequate' school may show many of the characteristics of an 'inadequate' or insecure person. These are:

- projection of individual teachers' deficiencies on to the children or their parents as excuse for ineffectiveness;
- 'cling-ons' of past practice (we've always done it this way);
- defences, whereby teachers have built walls round themselves to keep out threatening messages from outsiders;
- fear of attempting change because it may fail – this is associated with a reluctance to take risks;
- the fantasy that change is someone else's job;
- the 'safety in numbers' ploy, whereby the staff retreat into a ring-fenced mentality.

Many of the above are defensive mechanisms that are sometimes employed by highly stressed school staff to protect themselves from outside influences.

School climate and health may be very important factors in the identification of sources of whole school stress but they are not the only factors to take into account. Union and other stress reports have revealed the following problems in schools and have highlighted many that they perceive to be important sources of stress:

- *Lack of resources.* Teachers currently suffer from a lack of resources, or perceive that they suffer a lack of resources, largely due to government policies since 1988. This will have important implications for the teachers' working environment, as they will not do a good job if they feel that they are being deprived of the tools of their trade.
- *Lack of administrative support.* This seems to be particularly problematic in primary schools where much of the headteacher's time is often taken up with bureaucratic duties. Increased administrative duties for all teachers leads to lack of preparation time and increased workloads.
- *Poor working environment.* Torrington and Weightman (1989) in *The Reality of School Management* have highlighted the issue of poor working conditions in schools, particularly the appalling state of some of the staff rooms in some secondary schools and the lack of staff rooms in some primary schools. Teachers need somewhere to relax and switch off as well as the provision of a quiet working area. They also need to be confident that the teaching rooms in which they work and other staff facilities are clean and well maintained.
- *Teacher workloads.* Teachers are now reporting much more intensive workloads than ever before due to the demands of the national curriculum and its associated assessment procedures.
- *School staffing.* Some schools may not be as well staffed as they have been previously because of financial constraints and budget decisions and this may add to already stressful situations.
- *Time constraints.* Administrative duties have also increased since the Education Reform Act 1988. This may result in less contact time for teachers due to the increased bureaucratic nature of their jobs. Extra demands are frequently made on teachers, which result in them having to work even more at home and leads to even more stress.
- *Poor management of schools at all levels.* This was also a finding of the Torrington and Weightman study and is frequently mentioned by teachers as a major dissatisfier.
- *Poor communication.* Staff frequently perceive a divide between 'them' and 'us' and report feelings of being devalued, ignored and poorly motivated. Poor communication systems in schools are also frequently quoted as a major source of stress.

University of Manchester research findings

In an extensive piece of research conducted by the authors with teachers in the School of Education at the University of Manchester the findings indicated that certain work-related factors emerged as common, even though the causes of stress might be different for each individual teacher or group of teachers. These factors were as follows:

Teacher/pupil relationships
- Class size and ability mix.
- Lack of discipline as perceived by teachers.
- Changes in pupil motivation and attitude.
- Anxiety over test and examination results.

Relationships with colleagues
- Uneven distribution of work loads.
- Personality clashes/differences.
- Poor systems of communication at every level.
- Lack of community spirit.
- Little or no social or academic interaction between different staff groupings.

Relationships with parents and the wider community
- Parental pressure to achieve good results.
- The threat of performance management systems.
- Poor status and pay.
- Biased media coverage.
- Being obliged to accommodate unrealistic expectations.
- General societal cynicism about the role of teachers.

Innovation and change
- Apparent lack of rationale behind constant demands for change.
- Feelings of powerlessness and of failure.
- Lack of resources and information to facilitate change.

School management and administration
- Little real involvement in the decision-making process.
- Poor overall school organisation.
- Poor models of communication
- Lack of appropriate training to meet new job demands.
- Poor technical and administrative support.
- Poor staff facilities – for cxample, lack of personal work spaces and storage areas.

Time factors
- Increasing variety and number of tasks.
- Additional work demands outside the normal school hours, which could lead to conflict with family and friends.
- Frequency and ineffective organisation of meetings.

Our study confirmed the importance of considering both organisational and personal factors in any examination of teacher stress. It also revealed that it is the relationship among the above factors that explains why many teachers find it difficult to address what they increasingly perceive to be the stigma of stress. Most teachers say that organisational needs must be met before personal ones. They prefer to operate at the surface level, tinkering with and modifying traditional practices until school organisations give them the appropriate recognition and support. Teachers say they become more able to manage stress, even in the face of organisational constraints, if they have a substantial voice in deciding and initiating stress-management strategies. School senior management also shares this concern.

Our intention in this research into the identification of stress in teachers was to present the missing voice (Schratz 1993) of teachers with the clarity necessary for others to recognise their very real concerns. We felt the need to emphasise the individual perspectives of teachers as their voices are often ignored or have become silent in the turbulent environments that are a common characteristic of most schools today. As part of our research we asked teachers to reflect in writing on the issues raised. A number of teachers chose to make their voices heard in this way and we replicate some individual comments.

Peggy, a primary school headteacher in an urban area, reported the following:

> My attempts to alleviate stress are as follows . . . firstly, I blocked up one of three doors into my very small office . . . to reduce the three pronged attack! Secondly, I attended a stress management course at Manchester University which helped me to plan my time more effectively and to regain control of my working life. I counsel myself to value myself and my life. Fortunately, we have a life-saving support group of headteachers within our area. We meet for two hours once a month – and laugh (the best therapy of all). We have decided on two residential courses a year, each based on a project to benefit all our schools e.g. all schools share a 'Good Behaviour Book' so that the same rules apply in all our schools, and we are working on a cross-phase policy at present. The greatest support is to know that you are not alone and can turn to a colleague who will understand your anxieties.

Change issues emerged as a very significant factor in determining and contributing to stress levels. Teachers, for instance, say that a lack of time, professional development opportunities and funding can limit their interest in even thinking about change. Demands for change under these circumstances can result in excessive stress for teachers. Mary, a teacher with some 10 years' experience in a city centre school, had this to say:

> The current political situation and the insistence on getting back
> to traditional [Victorian!] values in teaching have greatly
> contributed to levels of stress among my colleagues in school.
> Some of the changes which have been introduced since 1988 have
> looked positive at a superficial level and yet the overall result has
> been the deskilling of many of my teacher colleagues and has led
> to feelings of powerlessness and alienation in my school.

Contraction in school budgets has meant reduced opportunities for
personal and professional growth for teachers. Appointment to a senior
post in a school would usually be associated with expectations of change
and growth, not with cutbacks and downsizing. The following report
from Eric, a senior teacher in an urban secondary school, echoes the
comments of many other teachers in our survey:

> When I became a senior teacher I expected to be given the oppor-
> tunity to be proactive and to introduce new ideas to the school. I
> expected to have some time for creative thinking, to engage in
> philosophical discussion with colleagues and to read educational
> journals and literature. Budget cuts, at both national and local
> levels interfered with my plans. I was unable to develop myself or
> my colleagues and I found this very frustrating. I lost all enjoyment
> in my job and am now looking forward to taking early retirement.

Since the introduction of the Education Reform Act 1988, teachers'
workloads have increased enormously. Some of our sample teachers, in
order to survive, have had to learn time management and assertiveness
skills. Pat, a male teacher in an urban school, is a typical survivor:

> As a teacher I find the major source of stress to be workload. Not only
> is the volume of what one is expected to do increasing continuously,
> but also what one is expected to do and when. Many additional
> demands come in the form of administrative tasks to be completed at
> short notice as a matter of relative urgency. While managers perceive
> such work as important, it is not by me, as it is not teaching.
>   Coping with stress requires refusal, prioritisation and subver-
> sive socialising. When I can say 'no' to extra work I do so – if it is
> not part of my job description, I will not do it. The work I must do,
> I attempt to prioritise, tackling important and urgent work first.
> Finally, I indulge in a good gripe with close colleagues as often as
> possible. This typically takes the form of contrasting the work
> required of us by managers in a limited time, with that required of
> them in more, and better-paid, time. Pointing up the hypocrisy
> and incompetence of those 'in charge' is very therapeutic.

David, a teacher of some four years' experience in an inner-city secondary school, achieved an excellent first degree and is currently in his first job. Like many others in our sample, he is finding it difficult to cope, and even more difficult to express these feelings and fears with his colleagues. He says:

> I hate getting up in the morning. The thought of having to face the fourth year yet again fills one with despair. I cannot control them. They do not want to learn. I am terrified that my colleagues will hear the noise and call me a failure. I can't sleep at night and count the days to the end of term. I think it would help to talk to somebody about my stress, but I think then I would be labelled as incompetent. There is so much stigma attached to admitting that you are stressed. It's an admission that you can't cope. If I said this and lost my job, where would I get another one?

Discussion and conclusion

One theme above all has resonated through education internationally since the 1960s and that is change. Change is, of course, a natural part of life and there is no reason why educational employees, institutions or systems should be immune to, or protected from, change. However, what is perhaps problematic about change in education is the often-conflicting motives and pressures for change and the various outcomes of attempts to facilitate change – outcomes that are not always positive for teachers and schools. Changing education must inevitably mean changing teachers, or at least more pressure being placed upon teachers to change both themselves and their practices. Rather than achieving 'educational ends', these changes have in many cases been promulgated in order to facilitate both 'economic regeneration' and the rebuilding of 'national cultures and identities' (Hargreaves 1994), such attempts occurring within a context of greater criticism of education and tighter economic constraints. Hargreaves has noted the 'twin realities of change' as being 'ideological compliance' and 'financial self-reliance' (1994). A third reality, in many cases, is undoubtedly greater workloads to meet the demands of change. These three realities are mirrored in our findings.

Having listened to teachers describe those factors that contribute to stress in schools at both personal and organisational levels, we found that conflicting views about the nature and intensity of stress factors were common. Teachers repeated the words 'stressed', 'tired', 'exhausted', 'frustrated' and 'alienated' over and over again when talking about teaching and stress. What we found most strongly expressed in the many self-reports and interviews was that there appears to be a major stigma attached to the idea that individual teachers suffer from stress. Often our respondents were afraid to discuss this for fear that it might indicate to colleagues and superiors that they were not up to the job. For example, we noted that teachers were concerned to conceal attendance at stress-management courses from others. We feel that there is still a reluctance on the part of some teachers even to admit to themselves that they are experiencing stress. One of the central issues to emerge is that individuals need to recognise and analyse signs and causes of stress at work openly for themselves, thus removing the real or imaginary stigma attached to it. They then need to decide upon appropriate strategies for its management. These themes lead to a focus on the importance of teacher voice as a bridge between organisational and personal stress reduction policies. These voices need to be heard at the whole-school level and senior management teams need to adopt a considered approach to the management of staff stress. Only an organisational approach can provide the appropriate help for all teachers (NUT 1990). This approach will have implications for those who lead schools, as they, too, need to recognise that the acknowledgement of stress in teachers is not a sign of laziness, weakness or incompetence. Ordinary teachers need to be reassured that they will not lose professional esteem or promotional opportunities by admitting to stress. What schools need is a coherent strategy that recognises the importance of stress as a crucial personnel management issue and thus incorporates stress-related issues into the school strategic development plan. There can be no instant 'cure' for the high levels of stress that we find in many primary and secondary schools today.

However, it is apparent that teaching staff are increasingly feeling inadequate in the face of the rising expectations and greater responsibilities being placed upon them. Commensurate with this situation is the perception that the general community does not value or appreciate, in both senses of the word, what teachers and schools do. To some extent, teachers have been handed an impossible task, being expected to be the miracle workers of modern society – an unrealistic expectation that ultimately results in guilt and strain when teachers and schools cannot deliver all that is demanded of them. It seems imperative that there be a reassessment and redefinition of teachers' work and school responsibility, not least because of what appears to be a looming teacher shortage in many countries (Dinham 1996). Others within the community must reassume responsibility for some of the expectations currently being shifted to schools and teachers.

School managers must develop strategies to prevent staff stress and burnout. These should include staff development activities and better procedures in the general organisation and management of the school, making sure that staff have the appropriate training and resources to implement new initiatives, and consulting staff on any changes about to take place. They should also help in the identification of burned-out teachers and take steps to provide a supportive atmosphere to allow staff to be helped to overcome or eliminate stress successfully. There should be an active endeavour by all senior managers to break down communication barriers in schools. Feeling able to talk over problems with colleagues is a big step towards the identification and reduction of work stress and the mutual sharing of experience breaks down feelings of isolation.

Those involved with initial training and with continuing professional development also have an important part to play in the identification, prevention and reduction of teacher stress by helping teachers and managers prepare for problems they are likely to face and by suggesting possible ways of solving these problems. They need to encourage teachers to recognise factors that can cause stress and provide them with strategies and stress-reducing mechanisms from which they can select those most appropriate to the school context in which they find themselves. Central government and local education authorities also have a vital role to play in school stress elimination. Over-stressed teachers will not be effective in their jobs and the consequences of this will be a burden for other staff and children. Such teachers are likely to be absent for long periods of time and may ultimately leave the school or the profession entirely. Steps need to be taken at both national and local levels to reduce the amount of change that teachers are going through at any one time. Full consultation on any new changes should be undertaken and teachers' efforts and achievements should be recognised and celebrated. Research could be undertaken to determine the causes of stress in schools linked to particular national or local policies, and on the relative effectiveness of different stress-management strategies.

Being able to identify and deal with stress is an essential skill for educational managers. Individual battles can be won (in terms of helping individuals suffering from stress) but that is only a matter of cure rather than prevention. Prevention is much more effective in the long run. Root causes must be recognised and eliminated wherever possible. Effectively identifying and managing occupational stress in educational institutions has important implications for the efficient conduct of the establishment apart from the very important human concerns. Stress will have a knock-on effect related to the continuous improvement of teaching, learning and achievement and will place financial burdens on the institutional budget.

The problem of stress, therefore, needs to be tackled from as many different fronts in education as possible. Cole and Walker (1989) tell us that unique solutions to the unique causes and manifestations of stress in any one teacher can be managed effectively if there is recognition of the problem and meaningful co-operation at all levels of the profession. Likewise, with such collaboration, it should be possible for educational managers to reduce or indeed eliminate the incidences of stress in their schools. Many enlightened school managers have now reached the conclusion that the identification and prevention of stress is far cheaper than dealing with the consequences. Benefits to the school will include less absenteeism, greater retention of staff and a healthier and happier working environment. As the *Times Educational Supplement* (1997) suggests this should surely be the goal of all managers in education.

Those responsible for managing the education service at a local level may have an added role to play in the co-ordination of programmes to help teachers identify and manage their stress. Our research suggests that most of the work that has been done thus far has concentrated on dealing with the symptoms rather than removing the causes of stress. We would welcome more emphasis placed upon the encouragement of teachers to formulate action plans, supported by the necessary follow-up by school or local education authority, in the pursuance of stress-reduction policies. Identifying and managing stress is, in our opinion, a whole-school issue, and may well require a modification of culture and attitudes in many schools and local education authorities.

References

Anderson RA (1978) Stress Power. New York: Human Services Press.

Association of Assistant Masters and Mistresses (AMMA) (1987) Teacher Stress: Where Do We Go From Here? London: AMMA.

Association of Assistant Masters and Mistresses (AMMA) (1990) Managing Stress. Guidelines for Teachers. London: AMMA.

Bloch AM (1978) Combat neurosis in inner city schools. American Journal of Psychiatry 135: 189-92.

Borg MG, Riding R, Falzon JM (1991) Stress in teaching: a study of occupational stress and its determinants, job satisfaction and career commitment among primary school teachers. Educational Psychology: An International Journal of Educational Psychology 11: 59-75.

Brown M, Ralph S (1992) Towards the identification of stress in teachers. Research in Education 48: 103-10.

Carvel J, Macleod D (1995) Ministers face teachers' shortage time bomb. Guardian (12 December).

Coates TJ, Thoresen CE (1976) Teacher anxiety: a review with recommendations. Review of Educational Research 46: 159-84.

Cole M, Walker S (1989) Teaching and Stress. Milton Keynes: Open University.

Cox T (1978) Stress. London: Macmillan.

Cox T (1989) Teachers and Schools: a Study of Organisational Health and Stress. London: National Union of Teachers.

Dinham S (1996) In loco grandparentis? The challenge of Australia's ageing teacher population. International Studies in Educational Administration 24(1): 16-30.

Dunham J (1992) Stress in Teaching. London: Routledge.

Eckles RW (1987) Stress – making friends with the enemy. Business Horizons (March-April): 74-8.

Fisher S (1986) Stress and Strategy. London: Lawrence Erlbaum Associates.

Freeman A. (1986) Coping in Schools. Unpublished Dissertation, University of Sheffield.

Friedman M, Rosenman R (1974) Type A Behaviour and Your Heart. Fawcett: Greenwich Publications.

Gold Y, Roth RA (1993) Teachers Managing Stress and Preventing Burnout. Washington DC: Falmer Press.

Griffiths A (1995) Work related stress and the law: the current position. Journal of Employment Law and Practice 2(4): 93-6.

Hargreaves A (1994) Changing Teachers. Changing Times. London: Cassell.

Health and Safety Executive (1991) Managing Occupational Stress: A Guide for Managers and Teachers in the Schools' Sector. London: HMSO.

Hoy W, Miskel J, Kotcamp R (1991) Open Schools: Healthy Schools. London: Sage.

Hunter M (1977) Counter Irritants to Teaching. Paper presented at the American Association of School Administrators Annual Meeting, Las Vegas, NV, February.

Kelly MJ (1988) The Manchester Survey of Occupational Stress in Headteachers and Principals in the United Kingdom. Manchester: Manchester Metropolitan University.

Kyriacou C, Sutcliffe J (1978) Teacher stress: prevalence, sources and systems. British Journal of Educational Psychology 48: 159- 67.

Marshall G, Rossman G (1989) Designing Qualitative Research. Newbury Park: Sage.

McLaughlin MW, Pfeifer RS, Owens-Swanson D, Yee S (1986) Why teachers won't teach. Phi Delta Kappen 67(6): 420-6.

Men's Health (1991) (July/August).

National Union of Teachers (1990) Teachers, Stress and Schools. London: NUT.

Nattras S (1991) Beating stress. Teacher's Weekly 138: 7.

O'Connor PR, Clarke VA (1990) Determinants of teachers' stress. Australian Journal of Education 34: 41-51.

Otto R (1982) Occupational Stress Among Teachers in Post-primary Education: A Study of Teachers in Technical Schools and Some Comparative Data on High School Teachers. Bandoora: Department of Sociology, La Trobe University.

Quick JC, Quick JD (1984) Organisational Stress and Preventative Management. New York: McGraw-Hill.

Schratz M (1993) Qualitative Voices in Educational Research. London: Falmer.

Selye H (1956) The Stress of Life. New York: McGraw-Hill.

Stake RJ (1986) Foundations of Program Evaluation: Theories of Practice. Newbury Park: Sage.

Times Educational Supplement (2 May 1997) Deep sighs of relief. p. 8.

Torrington D, Weightmann J (1989) The Reality of School Management. Oxford: Blackwell.

Truch S (1980) Teacher Burnout. San Francisco, California: Therapy Publications.

Warren E, Towl C (1995) The Stress Workbook. London: The Industrial Society.

Watts M, Cooper S (1992) Relax: Dealing with Stress. London: BBC Books.

Weinstein C (1979) The physical environment of the school: a review of the research. Review of Educational Research 49: 577-610.

Chapter 4
Increasing Costs of Occupational Stress for Teachers

CHERYL TRAVERS AND CARY L COOPER

Introduction

John was a 28-year-old teacher when he experienced his first anxiety attack. Having been in teaching for two years, he was teaching in a school for special needs with pupils exhibiting particularly severe behavioural problems. It was not uncommon for pupils to 'kick off' in the class, swear, become violent, or steal from John. The support within the school when he entered teaching was not great as it seemed that the majority of senior teachers were 'burnt out'! John was of a very positive disposition, had a number of relaxing hobbies, felt reasonably positive about his job but the pressure had been mounting – in particular he often felt that he was not able to utilise all of the skills that he had. John had obtained a reputation for being able to transform a class as he was popular with the pupils. His experience, therefore, was that he was given a new intake to 'break in' and this class was then passed on to the deputy head who had been off ill with stress on a number of occasions. One day, whilst at lunch with a colleague, he complained that he felt 'rather strange'. He could not quite explain what it was but he could feel his chest tightening. Later in the classroom, having been given yet another new class to 'break in', he suffered severe pains to his chest, felt as if he was going to collapse, and became hot and shaky and unable to breathe. He was rushed to hospital where he was tested and told that he had suffered a major anxiety attack. Still shaken, he was prescribed mild tranquillisers for a fortnight – and told to take two weeks off school to recover. His feelings of unease took a number of months to pass, he revealed that it felt as if a number of tremors were passing through his body, and that he had done 10 rounds with

Mohammed Ali. His confidence took a beating. Throughout the two weeks in which he was absent, the headteacher attempted to bring work home for John – so that they would not all get behind.

The above description is of a real situation experienced by a real teacher. It is alarming when we focus on the costs that this teacher has endured so early on in his career.

In the last few years, the incidence of stress among teachers has received a considerable amount of attention, particularly by the press, teacher unions and academics (for example Kyriacou and Sutcliffe 1979; Phillips and Lee 1980; Travers and Cooper 1991, 1994, 1996) – so much so that those who are involved in education are recognising that attention needs to be paid to its alleviation. In an international review of teacher stress and burnout, Kyriacou (1987a) refers to the occurrence and consequences of stress in the teaching profession in countries as widespread as Great Britain, the United States, Israel, Canada and New Zealand. Due to the findings from these studies and the public display by teachers and their unions, teaching has become characterised as high ranking amongst the high-stress occupations (Milstein and Golaszewski 1985).

A major difficulty for researchers attempting to obtain information about the extent of the problem is that often many victims fear that to report stress may be seen as a weakness. However, over the last 10 years there have been many changes that have resulted in disillusioned teachers expressing their concerns and bringing the issue of teacher stress under the spotlight.

The extent of the problem

Estimates of the percentage of teachers actually experiencing high levels of perceived stress have varied considerably, with reports concluding that the figure could be from 30% to 90% (Hawkes and Dedrick 1983; Laughlin 1984). British research has revealed that between one-fifth and one-third of teachers report experiencing a great deal of stress (Pratt 1978; Dunham 1983) with more teachers than ever before experiencing severe stress (Dunham 1983). The most effective way to measure the impact of teacher stress is to compare teachers with other highly stressed occupational groups. By doing this the authors of this chapter found that UK teachers were suffering from poorer mental health and lower job satisfaction than doctors, tax officers and nurses.

Teacher stress, however, is not just a British phenomenon and over the years American teachers have been found to be showing high levels of perceived stress (Coates and Thoresen 1976; Sparks 1983). A study by the Chicago Teachers' Union (1978) discovered that 56% of the teachers reported suffering physical illness and 26% were suffering mental illness that they related to stress on the job. A survey by the National Education Association also gave evidence of the major sources of teacher stress (McGuire 1979). In Western Australia, Tunnecliffe, Leach and Tunnecliffe (1986) revealed that teachers believed that they were working under considerable stress. The researchers claimed that 'the problem of teacher occupational stress and the search for effective ways of stress management remains chronic'.

However, findings are not conclusive. Researchers have obtained varying levels of stress response in the teachers under scrutiny to the extent that Hiebert and Farber (1984) emphasise the need for caution when proclaiming teaching a 'stressful' occupation, as it may set up an 'expectancy' of being stressed.

As previous chapters in this book have outlined, although certain causes of stress may present themselves in the teacher's environment, the extent to which these become a problem will depend upon the reaction of the individual teacher. Fimian (1982) explains: 'the frequency with which stressful incidents occur and the strength of their occurrence vary from teacher to teacher'.

A multitude of factors including the biographical characteristics of the individual (such as age), situational demands (intensity and duration) and past experiences (coping strategies), as well as differences in the way that the individual teacher assesses or appraises the situation that they may find themselves in will turn a potential stressor into an actual stressor. This chapter will describe the costs of stress for teachers as a whole.

How are teachers responding to stress?

At a general level, occupational stress has been found to have a variety of manifestations – psychological, physiological and behavioural. The long-term effects of stressors have also been well documented (Cooper and Payne, 1988). Individuals who are unable to cope effectively with environmental demands that they perceive to be threatening, soon begin to show distress through:

- emotional manifestations – feelings of undefined anxiety, dissatisfaction, depression, fear and frustration and low self-esteem with a possible extreme result being burnout;
- behavioural manifestations – behavioural problems such as appetite disorders, excessive smoking and alcohol and/or drug abuse, violence, inability to sleep and withdrawal (absence and resignations from the profession);
- physiological manifestations – heart disease, psychosomatic illness, fatigue and depleted energy reserves (Milstein and Golaszewski 1985).

Fimian and Santoro (1981) claim that emotional manifestations are often precursors for behavioural and physiological manifestations of stress in teachers, and so these should never be seen as discrete in nature.

The following sections present research evidence, where available, relating specifically to teachers. In some cases, where teacher research is not available, evidence relating to other occupational groups will be presented.

Mental ill health and teachers

Tinning and Spry (1981) suggest that in excess of 40 million days are lost per year due to psychological disorder (such as poor mental well-being, nervous debility, tension, headaches) in the general population of workers. Poor mental well-being can be directly related to unpleasant working conditions, the necessity to work fast, expenditure of physical effort and inconvenient hours (Argyris 1964; Kornhauser 1965). A review by Miner and Brewer (1976) suggests that 'certain stresses in the occupational sphere can be a source of emotional disorder'.

There have been a number of studies that have highlighted a positive relationship between self-reported teacher stress and overall measures of mental ill health (for example Pratt 1978; Galloway et al. (1982); Tellenback, Brenner and Lofgren 1983). Kyriacou and Pratt (1985) emphasise, however, that it might be more beneficial to examine more specific mental symptoms in order to consider appropriate coping strategies as a purely 'overall' indicator may not be precise enough (Beech, Burns and Sheffield 1982; Fletcher and Payne 1982). Emotional reactions may take the form of depression, anxiety, helplessness, insecurity, vulnerability and inadequacy, general uneasiness, irritability, emotional fatigue, resentment towards administration, negative self-concept and low self-esteem. The authors of this chapter in a study of UK teachers found that almost a quarter were suffering from levels of free floating anxiety, somatic anxiety and depression comparable with those seen in psychoneurotic outpatients (Travers and Cooper 1996). Levels of mental ill-health in teachers in their sample were found to be higher than all other comparable occupational groups (for example tax officers, nurses and doctors).

Dunham (1976) has identified the two most common types of reactions to teacher stress: frustration and anxiety. Frustration can be seen to be associated with the physiological symptoms of headaches, sleep disturbances, stomach upsets, hypertension and body rashes and, in severe cases, depressive illness, whereas anxiety can be linked to loss of confidence, feelings of inadequacy, confusion in thinking and sometimes panic. In severe cases, anxiety can lead to the physiological psychosomatic symptoms of a nervous rash, twitchy eye, loss of voice and weight loss. In prolonged cases, a nervous breakdown may result.

Burnout in teachers – an extreme reaction to stress

A more extreme result of long-term effects of teacher stress is total emotional exhaustion (Hargreaves 1978). This state of 'burnout' may lead to out-of-school apathy, alienation from work and withdrawal into a number of defensive strategies. Burnout might be identified as a type of chronic response to the cumulative long-term negative impact of work stress (Blase 1982). It varies with the intensity and duration of the stress but usually results in workers becoming emotionally detached from their jobs (Daley 1979). This is different to short-term acute stress, is far more intense, and refers to negative working conditions, when job stress seems unavoidable to an individual and sources of satisfaction or relief appear unavailable (Moss, 1981). Since it was first identified by Freudenberger in 1974, it has been identified as a separate phenomenon from stress (although research into the two has inevitably overlapped) achieving an increasing amount of attention since the mid-1970s (Gillespie 1983).

Certain studies have identified the conditions that precipitate burnout. It would appear that it is most experienced by those professionals who deal with other people (such as lawyers, accountants, managers, nurses, police officers, social workers and in particular, teachers). Another view expressed by Harvey and Brown (1988) is that those who experience job burnout as a result of job-related stress are those who are professionals and/or self-motivating achievers seeking unrealistic or unattainable goals. As a consequence of this, they cannot cope with the demands of their job and their willingness to try drops dramatically.

The actual symptoms that result from burnout are perhaps of greatest concern. Pines (1982a) has identified high emotional exhaustion, high depersonalisation and low personal accomplishment. Of major concern to the teaching profession is the fact that 'burnout' can detract from the quality of teaching. Mancini, Wuest, Clark and Ridosh (1982) and Mancini, Wuest, Vantine and Clark (1984) have shown that 'burned-out' teachers give significantly less information and less praise, show less acceptance of their pupils' ideas and interact less frequently with them.

What causes teachers to burnout?

Studies into burnout in teachers have shown that it is largely a result of excessive work stress over extended periods of time (Blase 1982) and relentless work demands (Begley 1982). A study of 33 teachers of emotionally disturbed children by Lawrenson and McKinnon (1982) revealed that a way of preventing burnout was to be aware of the stressful nature of the job. Nagey (1982) found that type A personality, workaholism and perceptions of working environment were individual factors that contributed to burnout. However, none of these were good predictors of its occurrence.

A teacher's personality can also play its part. Teachers with a negative attitude towards students, an external locus of control (see later sections of this chapter) and intolerance of ambiguity are reported to have higher levels of burnout than other teachers in a study by Fielding (1982). A further finding was that a school with a negative work climate exhibited a greater 'burnout-personality' relationship, than one with a positive work climate. A study of 100 teachers in the USA by Zabel and Zabel (1982) revealed that young, less-experienced teachers exhibited higher levels of burnout. A clue to prevention of burnout was also revealed in this study by the finding that less burnout was experienced by those receiving more support from administrators, fellow teachers and parents. If we look back to the case that opened this chapter we can see that it is not so surprising that John was starting to suffer from burnout symptoms – but was luckily caught in time.

Woodhouse (1985) and Schwab (1981) have shown that role conflict and role ambiguity were significantly related to teacher burnout. A study of 40 American teachers by Cooley and Saviki (1981) concluded that individual, social psychological and organisational factors were all strongly associated with the burnout response, and that it was important, therefore, to study all of these factors together to be able to understand the relative importance of these factors.

Lowenstein (1975) found that burnout was also a product of a lack of social recognition, large class sizes, lack of resources, isolation, fear of violence in the classroom, control role ambiguity, limited professional opportunities and lack of support. These are all factors that Britain's teachers are reporting as causing them stress at present (Travers and Cooper 1996).

Job dissatisfaction

One of the major significant manifestations of the experience of stress at work is low job satisfaction. A study of UK teachers by Fletcher and Payne (1982) of 148 teachers found that the majority of this sample actually liked their job but at the same time felt a considerable amount of pressure. However, a comparison of teachers' experience compared with participants in the University of Michigan's (Institute for Social Research) Quality of Employment Survey in 1977, revealed that teachers were less satisfied with their jobs than other professionals (Cooke and Kornbluh 1980). This study did show that levels of job satisfaction varied from school to school. A study by Moracco, D'Arienzo and Danford (1983) discovered a high level of dissatisfaction with teaching as a career, with stress being seen as a major contributory factor.

More detailed analysis of the issues relating to this job dissatisfaction reveals that factors such as salary, career structure, promotion opportunities and occupational status are involved (Tellenback et al. 1983).

Kyriacou and Sutcliffe (1979a) in a study of 218 teachers from mixed comprehensive schools in England found that self-reported teacher stress was negatively correlated with job satisfaction. However, they found that there was no significant difference in terms of age, length of experience and position held in school.

Needle, Griffin, Svendsen and Berney (1980) also found that teachers reporting higher levels of job stress reported greater job dissatisfaction. Kyriacou and Sutcliffe (1979a) found that job satisfaction was significantly negatively correlated to the following job stressors:

- poor career structure;
- individual misbehaving pupils;
- inadequate salary;
- inadequate disciplinary policy of school;
- noisy pupils;
- difficult classes;
- trying to uphold/maintain standards;
- too much work to do.

In addition, other studies have discovered that the older, more experienced teachers tend to express higher levels of job satisfaction.

The authors of this chapter found that teachers' job satisfaction was significantly lower than other comparable occupational groups (for example doctors, nurses, tax officers) and that the major predictor of this was the pressure they experience from the management and structure of the schools in which they teach. The lack of recognition that teachers currently perceive also has a part to play in what is acknowledged as an alarmingly low level of job satisfaction.

One of the complexities of teaching as a profession, however, is that teachers can be suffering from occupational stress but still gain job satisfaction from other aspects of the job. Indeed Hart (1994) has revealed that if we reduce negative experiences in the teaching environment this may reduce stress but will not necessarily enhance satisfaction. Moreover, if we enhance the positive aspects this may lead to greater job satisfaction, but it might not necessarily reduce psychological distress – they are not mutually exclusive.

Behavioural responses to stress

Many changes in behaviour may result from stress: impulsive behaviour, excitability, restlessness, emotional outbursts, excessive eating or loss of appetite, drug taking (including excessive drinking and smoking), absence from work and unstable employment history (Cox 1985). Many of these have direct and indirect consequences for the health and well-being of the individual.

Although there is little evidence with regard to stress in the teaching population and smoking and drinking, we may suppose that teachers will be as vulnerable to these responses to stress as any other occupational group. Examples of evidence on a more general level suggest that the level of smoking displayed by an individual does largely depend upon the working environment and social acceptability. In addition to social pressures and personality, work environment and exposure to stress is also an important factor that influences smoking behaviour. Russek (1965) found that 46% of men in high-stress occupations were smokers, compared to only 32% in low-stress jobs.

Caplan, Cobb and French (1975) found that an inability to stop smoking was linked to high demand (quantitative overload; too much to do; time urgency). It is also linked to tension and anxiety (McCrae, Costa and Bosse 1978) and it appears that increased smoking under stress is proportional to the number of stressors within a given period of time (Lindenthal, Myers and Pepper 1972). O'Connor (1985) suggests that perhaps it is important to understand why an individual smokes. For example, under high stress it may be a secondary activity and a minor distraction from the task; in a low activity–low stimulation situation, it might be associated with changing affective states to escape unpleasant situations, or to help overcome distraction and maintain a state of relaxation.

It is generally believed that alcohol is consumed in order to help relieve stress and 'help' the individual to manage a crisis, but in reality alcohol renders the distressed person less able to cope. Social influence and social pressure have a great impact on alcohol use and abuse. Plant (1979) suggests that one's occupation may be the most influential factor in determining drinking habits. Margolis, Kroes and Quinn (1974) and Hurrell and Kroes (1975) found that those individuals experiencing high job stress drank more than those in low-stress occupations, although it is not understood why some individuals under stress control their alcohol intake whereas others become alcoholics. The authors in a study of UK teachers found that a large proportion of the sample was drinking above the recommended weekly average. In a longitudinal study of teachers in London it was found that the presence of alcohol indicators in their blood increased as the term progressed (Travers and Cooper 1994).

Withdrawal from teaching as a response to stress

Another set of symptoms associated with teacher stress is absenteeism, intention to leave and early retirement – all forms of withdrawal. These are perhaps the options teachers take when they find themselves in intolerably stressful situations.

In general terms, behavioural responses to stress in the form of alcohol abuse and cigarette smoking are in part responsible for high levels of absenteeism in the industry, although there are a host of other causes. Miner and Brewer (1976) found that poor health, especially poor mental well-being, is a major cause of absenteeism. Research in a more general sense has suggested that there is a positive relationship between stress levels at work and frequency and duration of absenteeism, and the tendency for progression from absenteeism to labour turnover (Muchinsky 1977) and job satisfaction, job context and personality factors have been shown to relate to turnover (Grunberg and Oborne 1983).

More specific findings reveal that dissatisfaction with pay, failed expectations, inconsiderate leadership, lack of autonomy and poor social support from colleagues leads to high turnover along with certain personality variables (for example high anxiety, ambition, aggression and emotional insecurity) and age and tenure (young and job hoppers) (Porter and Steers 1973).

So how are teachers responding to stress in terms of withdrawal behaviours?

Methods of escape as ways of dealing with stress

Turnover of teachers is increasing, the profession is failing to attract young people and most resignations are in key subjects, according to a survey published today. The survey by local authority employees and teacher unions shows that in one Greater London borough, about a third of staff resigned last year. A spokesman for the National Union of Teachers said that the survey showed a picture of a profession under stress. (*Independent*, 18 September 1990)

The Health and Safety Commission yesterday urged every education authority to draw up a policy for dealing with stress among teachers. It is seeking to reduce absenteeism and cut staff turnover in schools. The costs of reduced productivity and loss of trained teachers add up nationally to several million pounds each year. (*Financial Times*, 17 November 1990)

Recent years have witnessed a problem with regard to absenteeism, turnover and early retirement in teaching, leading in some areas of the country to the phenomenon of 'teacherless classes'. As the above comments imply, the loss of well-trained teachers is far too costly to be neglected and many experts believe that the problem is a direct manifestation of teacher stress.

Turnover in teaching

A turnover rate in any profession of between 7–8 % may be seen as healthy, but in teaching the rate is far greater.

According to the survey of 8,500 schools, in England and Wales, the largest of its kind, the resignations rate went from 9.4% in 1987 to 13% in 1989. (*Independent*, 18 September 1990)

The resignations would appear to be affected by both the subject area in which teachers teach, the type of school and the sector. In a study by local authority employers and teacher unions (*Independent* 8 September 1990), it revealed that higher rates were found in foreign language, business, commercial and music teachers. Other findings suggest that Greater London has been worse hit, and evidence reveals that teachers within the primary sector may be the most likely to 'escape' from the profession:

Greater London has a higher regional rate of resignations (in primary 17.1% in 1985 compared to 23.5% in 1989) and other regions show a dramatic increase (in primary in the West Midlands 6.7% in 1985 compared with 12.1% in 1989). (*Independent*, 18 September 1990)

This results in an unexpectedly older workforce in primary schools. The same survey discovered that half of all primary teachers were over 40 and very few are under 30.

Early retirement and teachers

The number of retirements due to ill health increased from 1,617 in 1979/80 to 4,123 in 1989/90, with a large jump in 1988 when the Education Reform Act brought in the National Curriculum. (*Independent*, 25 January 1991)

In addition to the problems of absenteeism and turnover, a large number of teachers are looking for early retirement as a way out of teaching. This is not to say that for the vast majority this is not legitimate on the grounds of ill health, but for many this is the only way they see to get away from the job that is causing them excessive pressure. This means the education system and society as a whole are losing a large proportion of their experienced workforce. Many have explained that this desire to leave early is indeed a reaction to the stress of the job. Estimating that about a third of headteachers are retiring early due to stress, David Hart of the National Association of Headteachers remarked:

There is an urgent need to raise the morale of and to provide motivation for the most senior members of the profession. Better training, more administrative support for heads and more resources are essential. (*The Times*, 16 November 1990)

A report in *The Times* recalled:

> A younger primary school teacher said he was leaving teaching
> after only three years because of the amount of work he had to
> take home with him, which he said, left him without a life of his
> own. (*The Times*, 16 November 1990)

It has been suggested that the shortage of teachers in Britain's classrooms is being exacerbated by the government's inability to control a
surge of these early retirements (Hughes 1990). Financially, the costs of
such early retirements were outlined by John Bown, the Controller and
Auditor General in a report to Parliament on the superannuation
accounts for teachers for England and Wales, published by the National
Audit Office (October 1990). This showed that the Department of
Education and Science (DES) were urgently looking for a reduction in
early retirement seekers, due to the excessive costs incurred. The DES
had set aside £287 million, but this was insufficient to meet demand:

> Between 1987/88 and 1989/90 the numbers of teachers taking
> early retirement rose from 7,594 to 12,343 at a time when pupil
> numbers were rising, and shortages becoming more intense.
> Meanwhile, the department had to dip into its contingencies fund,
> and a supplementary £170 million was raised to meet the short-
> fall. By the end of last March there were 40,000 teachers still under
> the normal retiring age receiving pensions accounting for a little
> more than one fifth of the pension sums being paid out.
> (*Independent*, 5 November 1990)

Not only is this costly at a national level, but it affects the local authorities in that they incur the additional costs of recruitment and training on
an ongoing basis.

Sickness absence in teachers

Simpson (1976) has suggested that sickness absence is a way in which
teachers can allow themselves time to temporarily withdraw from stress
at work without having to make a definite break. It is believed that this
then allows teachers to continually readjust to stressful work situations
by such occasional withdrawals, and at the same time develop skills
necessary to deal with the sources of stress that they face. A problem with
this interpretation, however, lies with the fact that it is difficult to distinguish between somewhat 'voluntary' absenteeism related to psychological causes (such as depression) and stress-related physical illness.

In a study of 218 secondary schoolteachers, Kyriacou and Sutcliffe
(1979a) investigating an association between self-reported teacher

stress, job satisfaction, absenteeism and intention to leave the teaching profession, found that significant associations existed between stress and satisfaction, total days absent and intention to leave teaching. But as the level of correlation suggests, the size of these relationships is not as large as has been implied in previous discussion.

The author's own research into teacher absenteeism revealed that most days off sick were due to stress-related causes, such as persistent virus, anxiety and depression, bowel and stomach disorders.

Intention to leave the profession

A study by the authors found, in their large nationwide study, that 66% of teachers had actively considered leaving the profession in the five years prior to the survey (1996). This is an alarming rate and one that merits further examination to attempt to determine how many of these teachers will actually leave and what factors will help them make this decision.

It is not always possible to make turnover predictions unless factors from the both inside and outside of the immediate work environment are considered, because negative reactions do not always result in quitting. Other factors (such as education and availability of alternative employment) can also affect intention to leave (Martin 1979), or actual quitting itself (Spencer, Steers and Mowday 1983). Other factors affecting the decision will be those associated with the immediate job context or organisation (for example, valuable investment outcomes or accumulated gains). This means that even if teachers are very dissatisfied with their jobs, they might still endure them if they weigh up the advantages and disadvantages and believe that they have too much to lose. It is not always possible to transfer such accumulated gains from one organisation to another (for example Steers and Mowday 1981).

Some intentions do not come to fruition and some resignations are of an impulsive nature (Mobley 1982). However, as teacher turnover intentions appear to be on the increase, it is important to be able to understand what factors have the most disruptive impact.

What factors influence teachers' intentions to leave the profession?

The most frequently cited predictors of withdrawal have been those of intrinsic and extrinsic rewards (Bridges 1980). Studies into teachers' intentions to leave have come to different conclusions regarding the effects of these two features of the working environment. Intrinsic rewards (recognition, sense of accomplishment, fulfilment, advancement) have been found by some to play a more important role than extrinsic rewards (working conditions, management policies) in the process of withdrawal. As teachers are in the service sector, motivation is assumed to be linked with intrinsic rather than extrinsic rewards (Spuck 1977). Size of classes, administrative and teaching loads, availability of teaching aids, social and work relations have all been found to be related to teachers' affective reactions, stress and turnover intentions (D'Arienzo et al. 1982).

A study by Coughlan (1969) distinguished four main dimensions:

- management (including policy, procedures, administration, conditions);
- interpersonal relations (staff and students);
- school functioning (for example, curriculum, student development, teaching load);
- teachers' self-actualisation (professional autonomy and recognition).

A study by Lachman and Diamont (1987) proposed that

> Teachers' perceptions of their work environment lead to an affective reaction to the job, which in turn influences their intentions to leave. Specifically, it is hypothesised that self-actualisation, interpersonal relations, management and school functioning directly influence teachers affective reactions to their job, which in turn influences their turnover intentions.

These turnover intentions have been found to be exacerbated by structural characteristics of the job and lack of extrinsic and intrinsic rewards but reduced by group support, social co-operation and good work relations (Golembiewski, Munzenrider and Carter 1983).

The presence of reactions also has an impact. Studies have suggested that burnout leads to turnover intentions and affects withdrawal behaviours (Burke, Shearer and Deszca 1984). In the study by the authors it was found that by far the greatest predictor of intention to leave was the poor level of mental health being reported by the teachers in the sample (Travers and Cooper 1996). This could be interpreted as indicating that teachers are intending to 'get out' in a final act of self-preservation and awareness.

What factors stop teachers from wanting to leave?

The longer teachers hold a particular job or are employed within a particular school, the more benefits and privileges they accrue and these are not transferable. Some individuals will be psychologically constrained from leaving because of this. Steers and Monday (1981) suggest that the following will enhance a teacher's choice to stay:

- individually tailored work conditions;
- financial rewards, such as pension plans;

- specialised information and skills;
- familiarity with organisational work procedures;
- seniority privileges;
- personal reputation, social standing or power.

Specific restraining factors in the school environment are the status within the particular school and the specificity of teacher training that the teacher has received.

Lachman and Diamont (1987) tested this model on a sample of 239 high school teachers in Israel and found differences between male and female teachers in terms of the restraining effects on the intention to resign in both groups. However, the assumption that affective work reactions mediate between the work environment and the intent to leave were found for male teachers only.

Nias (1985) has pointed out that consolidation and extension of a teaching career does not necessarily depend upon age or experience but largely relies on luck. In a study of 99 postgraduate certificate in education (PGCE) students, she followed their career by means of extended and extensive interviews over a period of nine years. From periods ranging from three months to two years, the probationers saw teaching as a 'status passage necessarily marked by suffering'. For a number of members of the group, this continued for as long as four years. Some of these left teaching but a number of others kept on trying. Nias discovered that the factors that influenced their decision to stay or leave the profession were complex, but mainly rested on support or lack of support from colleagues, superiors, family and friends. Nias drew no major conclusions but she emphasised the probationers' view of themselves as teachers (which they had chosen to be) and successful people (which they hitherto had been academically), and highlighted the probationers' dependence on pupils for recognition and validation of their role as a teacher.

What are the implications of teacher stress in a wider context?

It is hard to gauge the impact that the problem of teacher stress is having on our schools without costly (in both money and time) longitudinal analysis but it is not difficult to hypothesise the impact that it will have on the way a school runs either indirectly or directly. Impacts due to withdrawal are easier to realise:

> On average a school is having to recruit 10 new teachers a year. In one borough in Greater London 25 or more teachers are changing in one year. (*Independent,* 18 September 1990)

This turnover will have an effect on the climate of the school affecting relationships between staff, and between staff and pupils, as Nigel De

Gruchy, General Secretary of the NAS/UWT said of a survey by the local authority and teacher unions:

> This is a survey of 361,000 teachers, about 46,950 teachers in any one year are changing jobs. This is a remarkable amount of turbulence that must damage the stability of schools. (*Independent*, 18 September 1990)

Other problems facing schools are the decisions involved with losing staff through the introduction of school-based budgeting, as many schools are having to shed posts to match their budgets.

Conclusion

The costs of stress in the teaching profession are incalculable but if we are to manage the pressure we must all contribute to the process of stress reduction.

As Kyriacou (1981) suggests:

> many schools are proud to think of themselves as a caring community for their pupils. It is time to put more effort into providing a mutually caring community for their staff.

References

Argyris C (1964) Integrating the Individual and the Organization. New York: Wiley.

Beech HR, Burns LE, Sheffield BF (1982) A Behavioural Approach to the Management of Stress. Chichester: Wiley.

Begley D (1982) Burnout Among Special Education Administrators. Paper presented at the Summer Convention of the Council for Exceptional Children, Houston TX.

Blase JJ (1982) A social-psychological grounded theory of teacher stress and burnout. Educational Administration Quarterly 18(4): 93-113.

Bridges EM (1980) Job satisfaction and teacher absenteeism. Education Administration Quarterly 16: 41-6.

Burke RJ, Shearer J, Deszca G (1984) Correlates of burnout phases among police officers. Group and Organizational Studies 9: 451-66.

Capel SA (1987) The incidence of and influences on stress and burnout in secondary teachers. British Journal of Educational Psychology 57: 279-88.

Caplan RD, Cobb S, French JPR (1975) Relationships of cessation of smoking with job stress, personality and social support. Journal of Applied Psychology 60(2): 211-19.

Chicago Teachers' Union (1978) Chicago Union Teacher (Special Supplement) (March).

Coates TJ, Thoresen CE (1976) Teacher anxiety: a review with recommendations. Review of Educational Research 46(2): 159-84.

Cooke R, Kornbluh H (1980) The General Quality of Teacher Worklife. Paper presented at the Quality of Teacher Worklife Conference, University of Michigan, Ann Arbor.

Cooley E, Laviki V (1981) Preliminary Investigations of Environmental and Individual Aspects of Burnout in Teachers. Paper presented at Oregon Education Association, Otter Rock OR.

Cooper CL, Payne R (eds) (1988) Causes, Coping and Consequences of Stress at Work. Chichester and New York: Wiley.

Coughlan RJ (1969) The Factorial Structure of Teacher Work Values. American Educational Research Journal 6: 169-89.

Cox T (1985) The nature and management of stress. Ergonomics 23: 1155-63.

Daley MR (1979) Burnout: smouldering problem in protective services. Social Work 24(5): 375-9.

D'Arienzo RV, Moracco JC, Krajewski RJ (1982) Stress in Teaching. New York: University Press of America Inc.

Dunham J (1976) Stress Situations and Responses. In NAS/UWT (ed.) Stress in Schools. Hemel Hempstead: NAS/UWT.

Dunham J (1983) Coping with stress in schools. Special Education: Forward Trends 10(2): 6-9.

Fielding JE (1982) Personality and Situational Correlates of Teacher Stress and Burnout. Doctoral Dissertation, University of Oregon. Dissertation Abstracts International, 43/02a

Fimian MJ (1982) What is teacher stress? Clearing House 56(3): 101-5.

Fimian MJ, Santoro TM (1981) Correlates of Occupational Stress as Reported by Full-time Special Education Teachers. I Sources of Stress. II Manifestations of Stress. Educational Information Research Centre, No 219-543.

Financial Times (17 November 1990) Policies Urged to Combat Teacher Stress.

Fletcher B, Payne RL (1982) Levels of reported stressors and strains among school teachers: some UK data. Educational Review 34(3): 267-78.

Freudenberger HJ (1974) Staff-burnout. Journal of Social Issues 30: 159-65.

Galloway D, Ball T, Blomfield D, Seyd R (1982) Schoola and Disruptive Pupils. London: Longman.

Gillespie DF (1983) Understanding and Combatting Burnout. Monticello IL: Vance Bibliographies.

Golembiewski RT, Munzenrider R, Carter D (1983) Phases of progressive burnout and their worksite covariates. Journal of Applied Behavioural Sciences 19: 461-81.

Grunberg MM, Oborne DJ (1983) Industrial Productivity. A Psychological Perspective. London: Macmillan.

Hargreaves D (1978) What teaching does to teachers. New Society 9: 43: 540-3.

Hart PM (1994) Teacher quality of work life: integrating work experiences, psychological distress and morale. Journal of Occupational and Organisational Psychology 67: 109-32.

Harvey DF, Brown DR (1988) OD Interpersonal Interventions. In Harvey DF and Brown DR (eds) An Experiential Approach to Organizational Development (3 edn). Englewood Cliffs NJ: Prentice-Hall International.

Hawkes RR and Dedrick CV (1983) Teacher stress: phase II of a descriptive study. National Association of Secondary School Principals' Bulletin 67(461): 78-83.

Hiebert BA, Farber I (1984) Teacher stress: a literature survey with a few surprises. Canadian Journal of Education 9(1): 14-27.

Hughes C (1990) Early retirement trend 'inflaming teacher shortage'. Independent (5 November p. 7).

Hurrell JJ, Kroes WW (1975) Stress Awareness. Cincinnati OH: National Institute for Occupational Safety and Health.

Independent (18 September 1990) Resignations causing turbulence in schools.

Independent (18 September 1990) Cracks appear at the chalkface.

Independent (5 November 1990) Early retirement trend inflaming teacher shortage.

Independent (25 January 1991) Teachers retiring because of stress.

Kornhauser A (1965) Mental Health of the Industrial Worker. New York: Wiley.

Kyriacou C (1981) Social support and occupational stress among schoolteachers. Educational Studies 7(1): 55-60.

Kyriacou C (1987) Teacher stress and burnout: an international review. Educational Research 29(2): 146-52.

Kyriacou C, Pratt J (1985) Teacher stress and psychoneurotic symptoms. British Journal of Educational Psychology 55: 61-4.

Kyriacou C, Sutcliffe J (1978a) Teacher stress: prevalence, sources and symptoms. British Journal of Educational Psychology 48: 159-67.

Kyriacou C, Sutcliffe J (1978b) A model of teacher stress. Educational Studies 4: 1-6.

Kyriacou C, Sutcliffe J (1979a) Teacher stress and satisfaction. Educational Research 21(2): 89-96.

Kyriacou C, Sutcliffe J (1979b) A note on teacher stress and locus of control. Journal of Occupational Psychology 52: 227-8.

Lachman R, Diamant E (1987) Withdrawal and restraining factors in teachers' turnover intentions. Journal of Occupational Behaviour 8: 219-32.

Laughlin A (1984) Teacher stress in an Australian setting: the role of biographical mediators. Educational Studies 10(1): 7-22.

Lawrenson GM, McKinnon AJ (1982) A survey of classroom teachers of the emotionally disturbed: attrition and burnout factors. Behavioural Disorders 8: 41-8.

Lindenthal J, Myers J, Pepper MP (1972) Smoking, psychological status and stress. Social Science and Medicine 6: 583-91.

Lowenstein L (1975) Violent and Disruptive Behaviour in Schools. Hemel Hempstead: National Association of Schoolmasters.

McCrae RR, Costa PT, Bosse R (1978) Anxiety, extroversion and smoking. British Journal of Social and Clinical Psychology 17: 269-73.

McGuire W (1979) Teacher burnout. Today's Education: 68.

Mancini V, Wuest D, Clark E, Ridosh N (1982) A Comparison of the Interaction Patterns and Academic Learning Time of Low-burnout and High-burnout Physical Educators. Paper presented at Big Ten Symposium on Research on Teaching, Lafayette IN.

Mancini V, Wuest D, Vantine K, Clark E (1984) Use of instruction and supervision in interaction analysis on burned out teachers: its effects on teaching behaviours, level of burnout and academic learning time. Journal of Teachers in Physical Education 3(2): 29-46.

Margolis BL, Kroes WJ, Quinn RP (1974) Job stress: an unlisted occupational hazard. Journal of Occupational Medicine 1(16): 654-61.

Martin TN Jr (1979) A contextual model of employee turnover intention. Academy of Management Journal 22: 313-24.

Milstein MM, Golaszwski TJ (1985) Effects of organisationally-based and individually-based stress-management efforts in elementary school settings. Urban Education 19: 4.

Miner JB, Brewer JF (1976) Management of ineffective performance. In Dunette MD (ed.) Handbook of Industrial and Organizational Psychology. Chicago: Rand McNally.

Mobley WH (1982) Employee Turnover: Causes, Consequences and Control.. Reading MA: Addison Wesley.

Moracco JC, D'Arienzo RV, Danford D (1983) Comparison of perceived occupational stress between teachers who are contented and discontented in their career choices. The Vocational Guidance Quarterly: 44-51.

Moss L (1981) Management Stress. Reading MA: Addison Wesley.

Muchinsky PM (1977) Employee absenteeism: a review of the literature. Journal of Vocational Behaviour 10: 316-40.

Nagey S (1982) The Relationship of Type A Personalities, Workaholism, Perception of the School Climate and Years of Teaching Experience to Burnout of Elementary and Junior High School Teachers in Northwest Oregon School District. Unpublished Doctoral Dissertation, University of Oregon, Aegean OR.

Needle RH, Griffin T, Svendsen R, Berney C (1980) Teacher stress: sources and consequences. Journal of School Health 50(2): 96-9.

Nias J (1985) A more distant drummer: teacher development as the development of self. In Barton L and Walker J (eds) Education and Social Change. Beckenham: Croom Helm.

O'Connor K (1985) A model of situational preferences amongst smokers. Personality and Individual Differences 6 (2): 151-60.

Phillips BL, Lee M (1980) The changing role of the American teacher: current and future sources of stress. In Cooper C and Marshall J (eds) White Collar and Professional Stress. Chichester: Wiley.

Pines A (1982) Helper's motivation and the burnout syndrome. In Wills TA (ed.) Basic Processes in Helping Relationships. London and San Diego: Academic Press.

Plant MA (1979) Occupations, drinking patterns and alcohol-related problems: conclusions from a follow-up study. British Journal of Addiction 74(3): 267-73.

Porter LW, Steers, RM (1973) Organisational work and personal factors in employee turnover and absenteeism. Psychological Bulletin 80: 151-76.

Pratt J (1978) Perceived stress among teachers: the effects of age and background of children taught. Educational Review 30: 3-14.

Russek HI (1965) Stress, tobacco, and coronary disease in North American professional groups. Journal of the American Medical Association 192: 189-94.

Schwab RL (1981) The Relationship of Role Conflict, Role Ambiguity, Teacher Background Variables and Perceived Burnout Among Teachers. Doctoral Dissertation, University of Connecticut. Dissertation Abstracts International 41 (09-a), (2) 3823-a.

Simpson J (1976) Stress, sickness, absence and teachers. In NAS/UWT (ed.) Stress in Schools. Hemel Hempstead: NAS/UWT, pp. 11-18.

Sparks DC (1983) Practical solutions for teacher stress. Theory into Practice 22(1): 33-42.

Spencer D, Steers R, Mowday R (1983) An empirical test of the inclusions of job search linkages in Mobley's turnover decision model. Journal of Occupational Psychology 56: 603-9.

Spuck DW (1977) Rewards structure in the public high school. Educational Administration Quarterly 18-34.

Steers R, Mowday R (1981) Employee turnover and post decision accommodation process. In Staw B and Cummings I (eds) Research in Organizational Behaviour 3. Greenwich: JAI Press.

Taylor JK, Dale IR (1971) A Survey of Teachers in Their First Year of Service. Bristol: University of Bristol.

Tellenback S, Brenner SO, Lofgren H (1983) Teacher stress: exploratory model building. Journal of Occupational Psychology 56: 19-33.

The Times (16 November 1990) Classroom stress takes its toll on teachers.

Tinning RJ, Spry WB (1981) The extent and significance of stress symptoms in industry – with examples from the steel industry. In Corlett E and Richardson J (eds) Stress, Work Design and Productivity. Chichester: John Wiley.

Travers CJ, Cooper CL (1991) Stress and status in teaching: an investigation of potential gender-related relationships. Women in Management Review and Abstracts 6(4): 16-23.

Travers CJ, Cooper CL (1994) Psychophysiological responses to teacher stress: a move towards more objective methodologies. European Review of Applied Psychology 44 (2): 137-46.

Travers CJ, Cooper CL (1996) Teachers Under Pressure: Stress in the Teaching Profession. London: Routledge.

Tunnecliffe MR, Leach DJ, Tunnecliffe LP (1986) Relative efficacy of using behavioural consultation as an approach to teacher stress management. Journal of School Psychology 24: 123-31.

Woodhouse DA, Hall E, Wooster AD (1985) Taking control of stress in teaching. British Journal of Educational Psychology 55: 119-23.

Woods P (1979) The Divided School. London: Routledge & Kegan Paul.

Zabel R, Zabel MK (1982) Factors in burnout among teachers of exceptional children. Exceptional Children 49: 261-3.

Chapter 5
Stress, Anger and Headteachers

ALISTAIR OSTELL

Background

Anger is a relatively under-researched emotion. Psychologists have tended to focus primarily upon anxiety and depression as emotions that are very often dysfunctional for a person's well-being, relationships and work performance (Williams, Watts, MacLeod and Mathews 1988). Yet anger is the emotion that employees identify as the one they experience most commonly at work when confronted by situations that prove 'stressful' (Keenan and Newton 1985; Oakland 1991). Anger and the attitudinal orientation of hostility (Williams, Barefoot and Shekelle 1985) not only affect work behaviour adversely but can also be damaging to psychological and physical health (see Chesney and Rosenman 1985), destructive of relationships and the precursor to emotions such as anxiety and depression (Ostell 1992).

As anger is such a significant emotion it is important in occupational contexts to identify the kinds of work circumstances that lead to this emotion, those people who are most prone to experience anger, how it is generated and what can be done to better manage or pre-empt anger and its effects. This chapter draws upon a study of how headteachers coped with the changes following the introduction of the Education Reform Act 1988 (ERA) (Oakland 1991; Ostell and Oakland 1995) to explore these issues.

Most recent research into stress in education has focused on government-inspired changes to the educational system and their impact upon classroom teachers. The ERA, however, not only brought about enormous changes to education in general but to the role of headteachers in particular. Under this legislation many of a head's traditional powers over the curriculum and school standards were taken over by government. In return, heads were given new managerial and financial powers for which, as educationalists, they had little, if any, training.

Soon after the introduction of the ERA there was regular media coverage about the negative impact of these changes on headteacher recruitment and the numbers of heads taking early retirement on grounds of stress and ill-health greatly increased (Earley and Baker 1989). Thus, at the time of this research, headteachers were a particularly relevant group to study as they attempted to cope with the considerable and continuing change imposed on their working lives. The findings arising from the research are equally valid today and are an important contribution to the relatively small amount of research into headteachers (c.f. Sihera 1989; Cooper and Kelly 1993).

Before examining the study in more detail it will be useful to clarify the meanings of and relationships between stress and anger and the role of absolutist thinking in promoting these states.

Stress and anger

The concept of 'stress' is a broad one. It has consequently been defined in various and often conflicting ways (Cox 1978). The prevailing view is that psychological stress is best understood as an interactional or trans-actional concept. That is, it refers to the processes of relating to circum-stances and events, or to private experience, which result in a person becoming psychologically and physically distressed. Put more formally for the purposes of this chapter: *a person is in a state of psychological stress when that person perceives and reacts to circumstances and events, whether real or imagined, internal or external, in such a way as to tax unduly, or exceed, their resources for coping.*

The ensuing psychological distress is manifest as disturbances in thought, emotion and behaviour that are disruptive to normal functioning but are normally not sufficiently serious or enduring to be considered mental illnesses. In other words, these disturbances, sometimes known as stress reactions or stress responses (e.g. anxiety or depressive states, post-traumatic stress, protracted grief, preoccupation with failure), are not indications of organic disease processes but of the failure of people to cope adequately with their work, social, domestic or personal circumstances. A basic premise of the interactional approach is that most situations are not intrinsically stressful; rather, people distress themselves by the ways they perceive and react to situations.

Figure 5.1, adapted from Ostell 1996b, illustrates this view with three overlapping circles. The largest circle represents a person who is the central point of reference in this model. The circle on the left portrays the situations to which that person has to react. They can arise from external circumstances or events (of work, social or domestic origin, for example), or from within the person (an individual's thoughts, feelings, state of health) – hence the overlap of these circles. Situations are not taken at face value but are appraised in terms of their significance for the

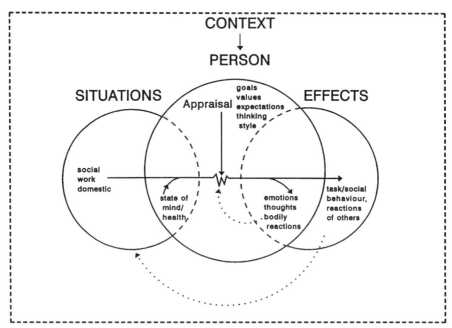

Figure 5.1: An interactional model of psychological stress.

person, and of how to respond to them. When people perceive circumstances or events as threatening the fulfilment of their goals or their values, and/or as posing difficulties for managing these threats, various effects (the right circle) follow. These include both internal changes to thoughts, emotions and bodily reactions and external changes to overt behaviour (e.g. task performance, social interaction). The dotted lines indicate that these changes feed back affecting, on a continuing basis, both the person's reactions and the situation to which the person is responding, thus modifying the person–environment relationship. (Only two of the main feedback loops are indicated for reasons of simplicity.) It is because of this mutual influence and exchange between the person and the environment that interactional models are sometimes called 'transactional' models.

The box (broken lines) surrounding the three circles depicts the fact that, when people react to situations or events, they do so in a context where particular rules, values and demands operate that help to shape their responses to those situations. A headteacher's reaction during school hours to a teenage boy who has been disruptive and rude will probably differ from the head's reaction to a boy who does not attend the school but who behaves similarly in a social or other context where different rules and demands operate for the head.

The value of a model such as that in Figure 5.1 is that it illustrates the kinds of factors and processes involved in generating distress in people. It also demonstrates a fundamental limitation of the term 'stress', namely that it is really a generic concept that embraces a variety of different appraisal processes associated with various distress reactions, but does not differentiate between the processes or reactions. Thus, stress models are generally of limited value for diagnostic purposes, providing limited insight into why and how a person becomes distressed in a particular way in a particular situation (Ostell 1988).

Anger

Anger is one emotional reaction that people often experience when confronted by, or when dealing with, situations they find stressful. (Such everyday terms as 'annoyed', 'frustrated', 'indignant', 'cross', 'furious', 'enraged', 'irritated' are frequently substitutes for 'angry'.) Thus, it is an outcome of appraisal processes and an initial distress reaction.

Emotional experience is not arbitrary. The particular emotion a person experiences in a given situation is the result of many factors operating together, such as that person's prior emotional state, physical condition, thought processes, active goals and so on. Nevertheless, thought processes have a very influential role in determining everyday emotional experience and different emotions are distinguished by the thought processes that generate them (Ingram, Kendall, Smith and Donnell 1987; Williams et al. 1988; Lazarus 1991; Ostell 1996a).

With respect to anger, the underlying thought processes have been labelled 'absolutist thinking' (Ostell 1992). This involves holding to beliefs and values in a categorical, inflexible and demanding manner. People thinking in an absolutist way see their beliefs, standards and actions as being 'right'. By definition other beliefs, standards and actions are wrong (c.f. De Rivera 1977). Such people also demand that other people and situations conform to their standards (c.f. Ellis 1989). This demanding aspect of thinking is usually expressed by imperatives and moralistic judgements such as 'He should not have done that . . .', 'They have no right to . . .', 'It's wrong to treat me that way'. When anger generated by such thought processes is not expressed publicly, people frequently ruminate privately about events. Other thought patterns generally diagnostic of absolutist thinking include: demands for justice or fairness; perfectionist demands, usually of oneself but also sometimes of others; feeling victimised or persecuted; unwillingness or inability to change views; and critical and blaming views (Ostell 1992).

Absolutist thinking: trait and state

Absolutist thinking is not concerned with what people believe but with how they articulate their beliefs (i.e. in an all-or-none demanding manner). It is a characteristic of some people to react in an absolutist way to a wide variety of situations and events. When their demands are not fulfilled, anger or its variants ensue, although that anger might not be expressed in expected ways. For example, social norms might result in the person becoming aloof and behaving coldly to the offending party rather than engaging in a blazing row. People who react in an absolutist way across a wide range of situations can be called trait absolutist (c.f. Spielberger, Jacobs, Russell and Crane 1983) and, whereas it might be thought that they represent only a tiny minority, evidence suggests they are a substantial minority of the population (Ellis 1989; Oakland 1991).

It is important to identify two other expressions of absolutist thinking. First, it is a generic style of thinking that underpins aspects of other personality traits or syndromes such as 'desire for control' (Burger 1992), 'conscientiousness' (Costa and McCrae 1992), 'perfectionism' (Frost, Marten, Lahart and Rosenblate 1990) and 'competitive achievement strivings' of the Type A syndrome (Friedman and Rosenman 1974). The behaviour patterns of each of these traits is driven by views of the kind 'I must complete this work to the best of my ability', 'This has to be re-done, I can improve it', 'I will win at all costs' – that is, by imperatives and absolute goals. Anger at the self (c.f. perfectionism and conscientiousness) or at others follows when these imperatives are not met. Absolutist thinking is less evident in such people, however, because it only applies to certain goals or values and is therefore brought into play only in particular kinds of situations. Thus, although such people are designated Type A, perfectionists, and so on, the generic thinking style underlying these particular behaviour patterns is still trait absolutist, but in a more narrow sense than above.

Second, there are many people who are not trait absolutist in the broad or narrow sense who evidence absolutist reactions in certain situations. For example, when people are excessively tired and yet are required to achieve an important goal, or are faced with critical problems that have to be dealt with almost instantly, they sometimes revert to a more categorical way of construing and reacting than is normally true of them. These responses, which are not characteristic of the person but are a reaction to particular, difficult and problematic situations, can be called state absolutist (c.f. Spielberger et al. 1983).

Demands, preferences and functional thinking

In absolutist thinking a person demands, or insists, that certain values, goals and wants are achieved or satisfied. This way of thinking largely precludes debate about the appropriateness or legitimacy of such goals and wants, they are simply held, and often asserted publicly, as unchallengeable facts. Absolutist thinking can be contrasted with preferential thinking where a person has a desire or want (not a demand) for something that can be desired and pursued in a mild way or with great intensity. A desire does not imply the legitimacy, necessity or rightness of what is desired over all other alternatives, so when a desire is not fulfilled the emotion experienced is disappointment, which can vary from mild to intense, but not anger (c.f. Ortney, Clore and Collins 1988). Disappointment usually dissipates fairly quickly, anger often lasts.

Demands and preferences differ in terms of the ways ideas are articulated, in terms of the emotions they generate and also in terms of the ways people behave. Absolutist people often drive themselves relentlessly to achieve goals, acting self-punitively if they do not achieve them. They insist that others meet specified standards, requiring them to 'put right' what has not been done, often refusing to help, as it is the others who are 'in the wrong'. By way of contrast, those adopting a preferential style of thinking typically adopt more of a problem solving orientation to such situations. They will forego those goals that cannot be achieved in a sensible, realistic manner and, where conflicts arise with others, the inclination is to be pragmatic and reach a negotiated solution, or look for an alternative means of achieving the preference.

Preferential thinking is easy to understand when applied to many social, interpersonal and domestic issues where formal rules and regulations do not apply. Most organisations, however, have well-defined rules and regulations about numerous conditions of service that a manager (or a headteacher) has to abide by. In such instances we use the term functional thinking for the non-absolutist style of thinking. Thus, a headteacher will formally apply certain rules and regulations, without debate or variation, when it seems appropriate. Their application, however, is not a moralistic and indignant enforcing of these rules, but a reflection of an essentially functional and often fairly dispassionate approach – 'You know the agreed procedure, but have chosen to deviate, in this instance the penalty will be . . . avoid a repeat'. 'We cannot accept such behaviour, you need to abide by the rules otherwise I will be required to . . .' On the surface such comments might seem absolutist. They are not, because they are applied from a pragmatic basis ('this is needed in this situation') and flexibly if possible. Anger is usually absent; instead there is rather disappointment, or perhaps a feeling of sobriety or disbelief about the behaviour that has occurred.

A study of headteacher stress, coping and health

The design of this study into headteacher stress has been reported in full elsewhere (Oakland 1991; Ostell and Oakland 1995); thus the aim now is to use the model in Figure 5.1 as a framework for exploring the main findings. One purpose of the study was to establish whether the association between absolutist thinking and poor psychological and physical health found in a therapeutic context (Ostell 1992) would be replicated in a field study.

Design

Two variables were used for grouping the headteachers: gender and type of school – first school (3–8 years) or middle school (9–13 years). Heads were chosen more-or-less randomly from the local authority lists, the proviso being that roughly equal numbers of males and females, and first and middle school heads were recruited. Eighty (80) heads agreed to participate from 87 who were approached, seven declining because of 'lack of time' (see Table 5.1). Each headteacher was interviewed for up to two hours about two stressful work situations they had coped with recently, one with a successful outcome and the other with an unsuccessful outcome.

The heads were also asked to complete a questionnaire assessing how they perceived certain aspects of their role, their personal beliefs, psychological health and physical symptoms. Seventy-eight heads returned useable questionnaires after the interview.

The classification of headteachers as absolutist (AB) or non-absolutist (NAB)

The interview protocols were analysed independently by two judges to determine whether individual headteachers had handled the two work situations in an absolutist manner or not (a dichotomous judgement). The criteria used for classifying the headteachers were evidence of: demands for perfection or infallibility; a strong sense of injustice or unfairness; feeling victimised or persecuted; unwillingness to change views and behaviour; the emphatic use of imperatives such as 'ought', 'should' or 'must'; and critical and blaming tone. Forty-nine (62%) of the heads were classified as absolutist (ABs) and 31 (38%) as non-absolutist (NABs) in the ways that they handled the two work problems. The AB group would include heads who were trait absolutist and some who were state absolutist, as the classificatory system used in this study could not distinguish between the two in a reliable way. Of the 78 heads who returned the post-interview questionnaire 48 were ABs and 30 were NABs.

In terms of the stress model, absolutist thinking represents a key appraisal variable (see Table 5.1), influencing both how the headteachers viewed the work situations they described and how they attempted to manage them.

The perception of role demands

One section of the post-interview questionnaire asked headteachers about how they perceived various demands of their role. The 17-item scale (see Table 5.2) touched upon narrowly focused operational responsibilities (such as supervising the work of others) to broader

Table 5.1: Design of the study – number of males and female heads from first and middle schools

	First school	Middle school	Total
Male	15	28	(43)
Female	28	9	(37)
Total	(43)	(37)	(80)

Table 5.2: Means (M) for all heads (GP) and for absolutist (ABs) and non-absolutist (NABs) headteachers for items of the role demands scale

Item	GP (n = 78) M	ABs (n = 48) M	NABs (n = 30) M	p[a]
1 Supervising work of others[b]	2.56	2.70[c]	2.31	0.063
2 Dealing with governors, etc.	3.36	3.50	3.14	0.134
3 Dealing with staff-related issues	2.86	2.96	2.70	0.224
4 Wide variety of tasks	1.94	2.13	1.63	0.029
5 Inappropriate training	4.09	4.13	4.03	0.207
6 Making decisions that affect others	2.83	30.2	2.52	0.011
7 No influence over decisions that affect you	4.95	5.08	4.72	0.090
8 Choosing own method of working	1.73	1.89	1.45	0.042
9 Exercising independent thought and action	1.56	1.65	1.43	0.166
10 Keeping up with technological change	2.62	2.50	2.80	0.257
11 Influence over school management methods	1.96	2.08	1.77	0.107
12 Authority to delegate	2.08	2.30	1.83	0.026
13 Responsibility for goal setting	1.90	2.02	1.69	0.092
14 Equating objectives with external demands	3.73	3.90	3.45	0.065
15 Preparing for financial responsibilities	3.74	4.08	3.20	0.005
16 Managing/adapting to changes	3.13	3.35	2.76	0.013
17 Planning ahead amidst changes	3.60	3.92	3.07	0.003

[a] p = statistical significance of the difference between the means for ABs and NABs using a t-test; all significances are two-tailed
[b] Abbreviated versions of the item used
[c] Score of 1 = extremely pleasant, 6 = extremely unpleasant

strategic ones (such as managing/adapting to educational changes). Headteachers rated each item on a six-point scale where

1 = extremely pleasant to
6 = extremely unpleasant.

The average score for the headteachers for the entire scale (i.e. the 17 items summated) was 48.62 indicating that they saw the demands of their role, taken together, as pleasant rather than unpleasant. (A neutral score, neither pleasant nor unpleasant, would be 60.) However, the NABs viewed these role demands as more pleasant than the ABs (means = 44.5 and 51.1 respectively). The difference between the means was highly significant statistically using a two-tailed t-test (t = 3.03, p = 0.002). (For readers interested in more advanced analyses of the data hierarchical regression analyses and multivariate analyses of variance are reported in Ostell and Oakland 1995 and Ostell and Oakland in press).

Comparing the mean scores for the individual items, NABs have 'more pleasant' scores than ABs for 16 items. For nine of the items (1, 4, 6, 8, 12, 14, 15, 16 and 17) the differences were statistically significant. In particular, NABs experienced coping with the impact of change as much less unpleasant than ABs (items 15, 16 and 17) and also found delegating and decision making affecting others (items 6 and 12) more pleasant.

Items in this scale (such as 2, 4, 10, 11, 13–17) can be thought of as crude measures of the educational context (see Figure 5.1) in which headteachers work. Non-absolutist heads were obviously more comfortable with their working context than absolutist heads.

Problem solving

Nature of the stressful situations

The 160 'stressful' situations described by the heads during the interviews covered a wide range of organisational and interpersonal problems. They were grouped into different categories for descriptive purposes. The six major categories were:

* Organisational (n = 30): organisational/management problems relating to the school building or organising school functions, to the changing of school procedures and policies including preparations for local management of schools (LMS) and national curriculum changes.
* External conflicts/complaints (n = 30): problems arising from complaints or conflicts involving parents, governors, outside agencies and so forth.
* Behavioural/special needs (n = 28): behavioural problems and matters concerning special needs children, including disabled children and abuse-related problems.
* Internal conflicts/complaints (n = 24): problems involving staff opposition, complaints and conflicts.
* Personnel performance (n = 17): issues relating to the heads' dissatisfaction with the standards of performance of teaching or non-teaching staff.
* Recruitment (n = 11): problems concerning recruitment of staff or resignations.

These problem groupings are interesting. They demonstrate the significance of a headteacher's managerial role and the importance of the interface between the school and the wider educational and social world for headteachers. They also illustrate the changing nature of the educational context. A decade prior to the study the head's managerial role would have been narrower; today it is likely that the personnel performance category would be larger with the increasing demands from government for improvements in teaching standards.

The effectiveness of problem-solving behaviours

There were no evident differences between ABs and NABs in the kinds of stressful situations they described but there were differences in their effectiveness as problem solvers. NABs rated the outcomes of their problem-solving efforts with the 'successful' problem as significantly more successful than ABs did (t = 3.65, p = 0.001) and felt that they handled the problem in a more effective way (t = 2.36, p = 0.020). These differences existed even though there were no differences between NABs and ABs in their perceptions of prior familiarity with their problems, the extent of other existing problems and the adequacy of advice, emotional support, financial resources, information, their personal skills and the help available to them. The following brief extracts from interviews indicate differences in the way an AB and a NAB head handled their problems:

> I've always prided myself on my discipline but over several months I've tried everything to no avail. These boys . . . laugh in my face which makes me furious – I could knock their heads off . . . I feel they're deliberately aggravating me. (AB head)

> I feel I've set things up and they haven't taken advantage of it. It's difficult because you can take a horse to water but you can't make it drink and there's little point in getting worked up about things over which I have very little control. (NAB head)

Additional analyses indicated that the availability of adequate resources (in the form of emotional support, practical assistance from other people, financial resources, relevant information) was the most powerful predictor of successful problem solving (Ostell and Oakland 1995). Thus, as there were no differences between ABs and NABs in their perceptions of the adequacy of the resources available to them, it is possible that NABs might utilise the resources they have in a more flexible and pragmatic manner when problem solving than ABs (see above and Ostell 1992).

There were no significant differences between ABs and NABs in their handling of the 'unsuccessful' problem. However, examination of these problems revealed that many were beyond the ability of the heads to solve because other parties (such as local education authority, parents, unions or police) had a crucial role to play. In an earlier study Pearlin and Schooler (1978) demonstrated that in highly structured situations, such as at work, where there were many constraints upon action, individuals often could not bring about change. Both AB and NAB headteachers also echoed this point in their descriptions of the problems with which they had to deal.

Emotion management

Emotional reactions to the problem situations

Heads were asked how they felt in relation to the problem situations. Their open-ended responses were clustered into groups of conceptually similar emotions and the results are summarised in Table 5.3. It is clear that negative emotions dominated over positive. ABs experienced anger states in response to both problems more frequently than NABs (successful problem = 65% versus 55%; unsuccessful problem = 76% versus 68%). More ABs than NABs also reported experiencing guilt and self-blame in response to the unsuccessful problem (20.4% versus 9.6%).

Two independent judges, blind to the AB/NAB identity of the headteachers, read the transcripts of their interviews and rated their effectiveness at emotion handling for the two problems. Criteria used as evidence of effective emotion management by the headteachers

Table 5.3: Frequencies of emotional reactions of headteachers to the problem situations

Emotions	No. of times reported	% total responses
Anger: hostile-type reactions such as angry, furious, frustrated, annoyed, cross	145	43.5
Anxiety: reactions such as anxious, worried, concerned, panicky, frightened	98	29.3
Depression: responses such as sadness, dejected, fed-up, depressed	52	15.5
Guilt: reactions such as guilty, remorseful, ashamed and embarrassed	28	0.08
Happiness: positive reactions such as happy, pleased, delighted and relieved	11	0.03

included: objective appraisal or reappraisal of the problem situation and their role in it; remaining focused upon problem solving while it was a feasible option rather than becoming preoccupied with emotional reactions to the problem situation; reporting lack of, or minimal, emotional distress; engaging in overt behaviours which reduced their emotional distress; self-preservation whereby they were not prepared to sacrifice personal health and well-being in the course of problem solving (Oakland 1991; Ostell and Oakland 1995). NABs were judged significantly more successful at emotion management while handling both the successful problem (t = 7.55, p = 0.0001) and the unsuccessful problem (t = 8.16, p = 0.0001). The difference in effectiveness between NABs and ABs was greater for the unsuccessful problem.

These trends of higher anger, guilt and self-blame, and the differences in emotion handling, are consistent with what would be expected for absolutist thinkers. Emotion arises as an initial distress reaction, often consequent upon appraising situations as 'unjust' or 'immoral' (anger). It interferes with the ability to solve problems effectively and leads to further distress (guilt, self-blame). Consider the following statements by two absolutist heads:

> I'm aware of the need to offer children varied activities but my expenditure is very limited so I have to try and raise the money elsewhere. It makes me resent those in ivory towers dictating policy to heads and setting the parameters within which we have to work – it's ludicrous. It makes me very angry and causes me so much work I haven't enough time for my family and they resent it. I'm at the end of my tether. I run out of patience at home and then feel guilty.

> I was annoyed with a capital 'A' when I found out she hadn't really been sick but had been to London . . . When she did return to school, I should have asked for more information and tried to 'nail' her, but I was so angry inside, I couldn't think clearly. It's water under the bridge now but I still feel angry when I think of it.

The statements can be contrasted with two made by non-absolutist heads to situations with unsuccessful outcomes:

> In a way the outcome is disappointing because it emanated from a group decision. But these things happen in management and I'll just have to go back to the drawing board and try again.

> Issues crop up all the time that don't always work first time. You can't envisage eradicating these sorts of problems, they are bound to happen with people.

Psychological and physical health

Psychological health

Longer term effects of disturbed emotion and thinking are likely to be more generalised than poor work performance and disturbances in health (see 'Effects' Figure 5.1). The headteachers' psychological health was assessed using the 12-item version of Goldberg's (1978) General Health Questionnaire (GHQ) included in the post-interview question-naire. People scoring at or below the cut-off score of 2 are considered to reflect normal functioning whereas higher scores indicate disturbance in psychological health and the highest scores, 9 to 12, severe psycholog-ical distress. Such disturbed functioning might only be transient, or may dispose a person to more enduring, poor psychological health.

The mean score of the headteachers was 3.60; 50% scored above the cut-off point; 27.5% scored more than 5; 13% scored 9 or more and 5% scored 12. These scores are not only high but are comparable with those of unemployed managers (Ostell and Divers 1987). In earlier studies with other occupational groups considerably lower mean GHQ scores were obtained. For example, Banks, Clegg, Jackson et al. (1980) obtained a mean of 0.97 (s.d. = 1.87) and Wall and Clegg (1981) a mean of 0.82 (s.d. = 1.28) in their studies of large occupational samples.

The GHQ scores for AB and NAB heads differed significantly. The former had significantly poorer psychological health (mean for ABs = 5.35, NABs = 0.87, t = 7.08, p = 0.0001). Further, only 7% (n = 2) of NABs had scores exceeding the cut-off (i.e. both had scores of 3), whereas 77% of ABs had scores greater than 2, 42% of them had scores greater than 5, 21% had scores of 9 or more and 8% had the maximum score of 12. The high mean score for the sample is due to the high scores of ABs who evidence poor psychological health.

As mentioned above, only seven headteachers, all ABs, viewed their role demands, taken together, as 'unpleasant' (i.e. role demands score >60), their mean GHQ score was 8.6. However, 32 headteachers had role demands scores less than 60 (i.e. 'pleasant' in varying degrees) but GHQ scores that exceeded 2 (i.e. evidence of psychological distress). Of these, 30 were classified as ABs.

Physical health

Physical health was assessed in two ways. First, a 17-item, self-report instrument (SYMP) in the post-interview questionnaire required headteachers to rate their experience of various stress-related and somatic symptoms over the past few weeks (e.g. acid stomach, nausea or indigestion; chest pains; faintness or dizziness – see Oakland 1991; Ostell and Oakland 1995). A six-point rating scale was used where 1 =

'never' and 6 = 'very frequently'. Second, heads were asked to indicate whether they had visited their doctor recently in relation to these symptoms.

The findings for physical health parallel closely those for psychological health and the correlation between GHQ and SYMP scores is highly significant statistically ($r = 0.72$, $p <0.001$). SYMP scores could, in theory, range from 17 to 102. The mean score for the sample was 38.8. As the scale was developed specifically for this study this mean cannot be related to pre-existing norms. The mean scores for ABs (45.94) and NABs (27.47) were significantly different ($t = 7.66$, $p = 0.0001$). Those headteachers scoring above 6 on the GHQ had a mean SYMP score of 54.2; those scoring 9 to 12 on the GHQ had a mean SYMP score of 61.1, whereas the four headteachers with GHQ scores of 12 had a mean SYMP score of 70.5.

Visits to the doctor

A greater number of AB than NAB headteachers had visited a doctor in relation to their symptoms within the previous six weeks (35.4% versus 6.7%, $\phi = 0.33$, $\chi^2 = 6.79$, $p < 0.01$). It is not possible to say that all these visits were a result of physical symptoms occasioned by having to cope with the demands of the headteachers' jobs. Some obviously arose from short-term or chronic conditions unrelated to work. Nevertheless, many heads indicated directly the linkage between their job demands and their physical health. It seems reasonable to conjecture that the large and highly significant differences between ABs and NABs in visits to their doctor could be a behavioural index of the different levels of physical distress these groups experienced through their jobs.

Headteachers, absolutist thinking and stress

Anger and absolutist thinking

Anger is an emotion all people experience at times and they usually feel it is an appropriate and effective reaction to a situation. When well managed, it can be. Short-lived, moderate anger that has a clearly understood reason and is constructive in its intent (i.e. not to demean or humiliate) can be very effective. It can clarify for children the inappropriateness of their behaviour in the eyes of their parents; colleagues or friends appreciate the seriousness of a situation as far as their manager, peers or friends are concerned; and so on.

Nevertheless, anger can be destructive both for the angered person and others involved. There are those who are readily angered by all kinds of situations that do not conform to their demands (broadly trait absolutist). There are others who tend to be angered by fewer, specific matters. They include: the perfectionist, the egocentric, the competitive type A and people high on desire for control (narrowly trait absolutist), all of whom become angered in some way (annoyed, furious, indignant, resentful) when they cannot achieve their demands (such as exceptional performance, being the focus of attention, winning, or being in charge). Both these groups of people are vulnerable because of their anger reactions. They often alienate others and, although they might argue that they were 'in the right', they usually admit such conflicts are not enjoyable and often lack any effective outcome. Some of these people suppress their anger and 'smoulder' with resentment, or simply ruminate endlessly on the issues, thus potentially damaging their own health (c.f. Chesney and Rosenman 1985).

Many of the above points were illustrated in the study with headteachers. Both absolutist and non-absolutist heads reported experiencing anger when attempting to deal with the two stressful situations that they described. In the former group, however, more of them experienced anger. This anger was frequently felt for weeks after the events concerned, it damaged their relationships not only with pupils and teaching staff but with parents, the LEA, school advisors and, importantly, with their families and friends. The strain of dealing with these situations was also seen as damaging their physical and psychological health (which was poor relative to other occupational groups), and their ability to perform their jobs effectively. Many of the AB heads attributed their disturbed emotions, health and relationships, to the problems they had dealt with and the other people who were involved, rather than to their values and ways of handling situations. Others were very self-punitive, blaming and criticising themselves for failing to handle situations as they felt they ought to have done.

By way of contrast the NAB heads had a more positive view of their role demands; they were more effective problem solvers, possibly because they better utilised the resources available to them; they evidenced more successful emotion management; and had much better scores for psychological and physical health. These heads employed a functional style of thinking. They did not lack high standards or clearly defined values but chose to hold to and pursue them in a more pragmatic and flexible way than ABs. This allowed them to accept difficult and unsatisfactory situations more easily without becoming disturbed by them and to adopt a problem-solving orientation to their work problems.

The headteacher role and absolutist thinking

It is sometimes suggested that headteachers are prone to having an absolutist style of thinking because of the nature of their role. Headteachers are adults among children, or young people; they help define the rules and standards to which pupils are expected to conform and are responsible for gaining a satisfactory level of conformity to these rules and standards; when pupils fail to conform heads often mete out 'punishments' of various forms. They also have some responsibility for the moral education of their pupils, and so on. These facets of a headteacher's role tend to distinguish it from managerial roles in most other public or private sector organisations.

On a superficial level it might seem that absolutist people would 'fit' these facets of the headteacher role well. But, today, the role of a headteacher, particularly in large middle/secondary schools, is as complex and demanding as many managerial roles in commercial and industrial organisations. The role not only entails overseeing the educational process within the school but such diverse matters as the management of teaching and support staff, responsibility for the physical estate and the financial solvency of the school. A crucial aspect of a headteacher's role also involves dealing effectively with people and organisations (such as parents, governors, police, education authorities, unions) external to the school.

The evidence from the headteacher study indicates that absolutist heads were less effective at managing these different aspects of their role and were more vulnerable to poorer psychological and physical health. If AB people are attracted to this role for various reasons they will find that they are not as well equipped as NAB heads at performing it.

Absolutist thinking and other possible explanatory variables

A number of other variables that it might be thought could account for the differences between ABs and NABs in problem solving, emotion management and health, were included in the main analyses (see Ostell and Oakland 1995) and rejected as explanatory variables. For example, there were no obvious differences between the two groups in the kinds of problems they had had to deal with. Nor was there a relationship between absolutist thinking and the age, gender, and number of years of headship of the teachers. Headteachers tended to be more absolutist in first rather than middle schools, but not in disadvantaged schools. Further, the variables age, gender, years of headship and type of school did not predict differences in headteachers' physical and psychological health but absolutist thinking did. One variable that did predict differences in psychological and physical health between headteachers was negative emotionality (Watson and Clark 1984). This variable was also correlated positively with absolutist thinking. Nevertheless, when the effects of negative emotionality were partialed out, absolutist thinking was still a highly significant predictor of differences in health scores (all differences <0.001; Ostell and Oakland 1995).

A causal role for absolutist thinking?

The implication throughout this chapter has been that differences in absolutist thinking caused the observed differences in problem-solving behaviour, emotion management and psychological health. As the headteacher study was cross-sectional in design it is not possible to infer this causal relationship with certainty – in fact the reverse could be true. For example, it could be argued that headteachers who had poorer psychological health would, as a consequence, react in absolutist ways when dealing with problem situations and be less effective in managing their emotions or solving their problems. This view is consistent with the stress model in Figure 5.1 in which thoughts, emotions and bodily reactions can affect the appraisal processes, as can a person's existing state of mind and health. It is most likely that a mutually reinforcing circle exists between thinking styles/dysfunctional appraisals and poorer psychological health.

It is important to recognise, however, that poor psychological health is not an inevitable consequence of absolutist thinking. When absolutist individuals live and work with like-minded people who accommodate their demands, when they perceive themselves to be relatively successful in achieving their demands and when they have learned not to ruminate endlessly about violated demands, poor psychological health is unlikely to ensue. When these supportive factors are removed from absolutists and they are confronted, perhaps for extended periods, by situations they cannot manage successfully, the likelihood of them experiencing reduced psychological health is greatly increased (Ostell 1992). This is what appears to have happened with many of the headteachers classified as absolutist in the above study.

The future

The teaching profession has had to cope with numerous changes over the past 15 years, which have taxed the coping resources of individuals, resulting in many staff evidencing reduced effectiveness in their jobs and poor health, and also resulting in large numbers of staff resigning from their posts (Earley and Baker 1989). Although the time at which the above study was conducted was one of considerable change, particularly for headteachers, there is no reason to suppose that significant changes will not continue to occur in the future. It is important, as in many other professions, that existing staff, as well as new recruits, are able to cope effectively with change, conflict and more general, problematic situations.

To enable (head)teachers to cope with these conditions and situations they need support at two levels: organisational and personal. Organisational, or structural, support involves providing the necessary resources (money, facilities, time, advisors, ancillary staff and so forth) so that (head)teachers can perform their roles effectively. Data from the headteacher study indicates that many of the 'unsuccessful' situations could not be solved because the heads needed help from others, which was apparently not forthcoming, or was inadequate. It was also the availability of adequate resources that permitted heads to handle the situation with a 'successful' outcome successfully. Support through the provision of appropriate resources is an important issue, but one that is beyond the scope of this chapter.

Data from the headteacher study also suggest that NABs were probably more successful at problem solving than ABs because of the ways they utilised the available resources. This is a matter of individual skills and the provision of support on the personal level is relevant here. For instance, many of the AB headteachers showed little insight into how important their appraisal and coping styles were in determining the outcome of their problem-solving and emotion management activities. This lack of awareness reflects ignorance in the broader population of the link between absolutist thinking and anger, and the role anger seems to play in mediating certain health problems.

Two forms of personal training are important – particularly for all headteachers. First, general training in managerial problem solving, which would include at least an introduction to various content areas of management (such as finance and accounting, human resource management, marketing) as well as to the techniques of technical, personal and interpersonal problem solving. Second, training in self-management skills — particularly stress-management skills. As has already been suggested, a general understanding of stress is of limited value; an understanding of how different emotions are generated and can be managed is more important. Such training should benefit all teachers considerably, and particularly absolutist ones.

References

Banks MH, Clegg CW, Jackson PR, Kemp NJ, Stafford EM, Wall TD (1980).The use of the GHQ as an indicator of mental health in occupational studies. Journal of Occupational Psychology 53: 187-94.

Burger JM (1992) Desire for Control. New York: Plenum Press.

Chesney MA, Rosenman RH (eds) (1985) Anger and Hostility in Cardiovascular and Behavioral Disorders. Washington DC: Hemisphere.

Cooper CL, Kelly M (1993) Ocupational stress in headteachers: a national UK study. British Journal of Educational Psychology 63: 130-43.

Costa PT Jr, McCrae RR (1992) Revised NEO Personality Inventory (NEO-PI-R) and NEO Five-Factor Inventory (NEO-FFI) Professional Manual. Odessa FL: Psychological Assessment Resources.

Cox T (1978) Stress. London: Macmillan.

De Rivera J (1977) A Structural Theory of Emotions. New York: International Universities Press.

Earley P, Baker L (1989) The recruitment and retention of headteachers: the LEA survey. Windsor: NFER-Nelson.

Ellis A (1989) Rational-emotive therapy. In Corsini RJ and Wedding D (eds), Current Psychotherapies (4 edn). Itasca IL: Peacock Publishers, pp. 197-238.

Friedman M, Rosenman RH (1974) Type A Behavior and Your Heart. New York: Knopf.

Frost RO, Marten P, Lahart C, Rosenblate R (1990) The dimensions of perfectionism. Cognitive Therapy and Research 14: 449-68.

Goldberg D (1978) Manual of the General Health Questionnaire. Windsor: National Foundation for Educational Research.

Ingram RE, Kendall PC, Smith TW, Donnell C (1987) Cognitive specificity in emotional distress. Journal of Personality and Social Psychology 53: 734-42.

Keenan A, Newton TJ (1985) Stressful events, stressors and psychological strains in young professional engineers. Journal of Occupational Behaviour 6: 151-6.

Lazarus RS (1991) Emotion and Adaptation. New York: Oxford University Press.

Oakland S (1991) Headteacher Stress, Coping and Health. Unpublished doctoral thesis, University of Bradford.

Ortny A, Clore GL, Collins A (1988) The Cognitive Structure of Emotions. Cambridge: Cambridge University Press.

Ostell A (1988) The development of a diagnostic framework of problem solving and stress. Counselling Psychology Quarterly 1: 189-209.

Ostell A (1992) Absolutist thinking and emotional problems. Counselling Psychology Quarterly 5: 161-76.

Ostell A (1996a) Managing dysfunctional emotions in organizations. Journal of Management Studies 33: 526-57.

Ostell A (1996b) Managing stress at work. In Molander C (ed.) Human Resources at Work. London: Chartwell-Bratt, pp. 373-423.

Ostell A, Divers P (1987) Attribution style, unemployment and mental health. Journal of Occupational Psychology 60: 333-7.

Ostell A, Oakland S (1995) Headteacher Stress, Coping and Health. Aldershot: Avebury.

Ostell A, Oakland S (in press) Absolutist thinking and health. Under review.

Pearlin LI, Schooler C (1978) The structure of coping. Journal of Health and Social Behavior 19: 2-21.

Sihera E (1989) Heads Under Pressure. Berkshire: Impact Connections.

Spielberger CD, Jacobs G, Russell S, Crane R (1983) Assessment of anger: the state-trait anger scale. In Butcher JN and Spielberger CD (eds) Advances in Personality Assessment 2: 161-89. Hillsdale NJ: Lawrence Earlbaum Associates.

Wall TD, Clegg CW (1981) A longitudinal study of group work redesign. Journal of Occupational Behaviour 2: 31-49.

Watson D, Clark LA (1984) Negative affectivity: the disposition to experience aversive emotional states. Psychological Bulletin 96: 465-90.

Williams JMG, Watts FN, MacLeod C, Mathews A (1988) Cognitive Psychology and Emotional Disorders. Chichester: Wiley.

Williams RB, Barefoot JC, Shekelle RB (1985) The health consequences of hostility. In Chesney MA and Rosenman RH (eds) Anger and Hostility in Cardiovascular and Behavioral Disorders. Washington DC: Hemisphere, pp. 173-85.

Chapter 6
The Psychophysiology of Stress in Teachers

JOHN W HINTON AND ELKE ROTHEILER

Introduction

This chapter presents a brief review of published research on physiological stress reactions relating to work stress in teaching. Physiology is an extremely important aspect of work stress yet very little research has been published on recordings of the physiological state of work stressed teachers. Research on self-reported physiological symptoms will therefore also be reviewed. Finally we focus on relevant psychophysiological research carried out by the Stress Research Unit of Glasgow University between 1983 and 1998. We refer to the development of a bio-psychological theoretical model at Glasgow and its validation through laboratory experiments and field studies, with some of the latter examining teachers.

Psychophysiological indications of acute stress reactions in the process of lecturing/teaching and the psychophysiology of chronic work-stress state in the teaching job are considered. An inexperienced or ill-prepared teacher may experience various physical symptoms before a class, such as rapid or pounding heartbeat, dry mouth, shaking and sweaty hands. These are acute, short-term responses to both anxiety (anticipatory fear before the talk) and to psychological stress during the presentation. The reactions generally indicate a state of active coping (as opposed to passive coping with a noxious situation). Ongoing perceived problems in coping with the teaching job result in chronic long-term work stress indicated by physical exhaustion, poor sleep, muscle tensions/pains and digestive disturbances and increased susceptibility to infection.

Stress responses can actually impair one's ability to teach. Acute stress responses can disrupt teaching by direct interference (such as trembling hands affecting drawing ability, sweaty hands smearing overhead projection transparencies) and by indirect interference (for example, distraction through awareness of pounding heart). Acute physiological stress responses can disrupt ability to focus on the teaching material by causing 'over-arousal' of the brain, while chronic stress responses of tiredness/exhaustion reduce the ability to concentrate on a teaching task.

Ill health is an obvious cause for concern but it would be sensible to monitor work stress physiologically before teachers become ill. Even apparently harmless symptoms can be of interest to the researcher if they can provide objective evidence of work stress, and the practitioner could be interested if the techniques are simple and cheap. The use of saliva as a convenient source of psychophysiological 'stress'-related data is advocated for the objective evaluation of the effects of changes in the demands of the teaching job.

Not all responses of the body are obvious, and many require special techniques for their measurement. A dry mouth (low saliva flow) may be obvious (indeed failure to moisten a pebble placed in the mouth was being used as evidence of guilt by Zulus a century ago). However there are less obvious changes in saliva that can be demonstrated by chemical analysis (for example, 'stress'-related hormones and immune system agents that protect against infection).

So far we have mentioned two kinds of 'stress' – acute and chronic (which occur while trying to cope with a situation). We have also referred to 'anxiety', which it must be emphasised is neither of these (it being a state of anticipatory fear before trying to cope with a situation). The word 'stress' calls for special comment. The word is generally applied in three distinct ways: (1) as a 'demand' in the environment, (2) as a set of responses/symptoms and (3) a psychological/mental state that links (1) to (2). To avoid conceptual confusion in the use of the word 'stress' we refer to (3) as 'psystress' (Hinton and Burton 1992a).

It seems reasonable to argue that a daily state of excitement by a challenging job, like teaching, is better for you than being demotivated by a boring job. Frequently people say they are stressed at work, when they really mean they are very busy with a task that they perceive as highly challenging (Gaillard 1993). Teaching is clearly a challenging job, where active coping is essential and this activation in the nervous system causes increased adrenaline, which is not due to work stress.

The potentially stressing nature of teaching today

The effect of bureaucratic reorganisation

Giving a lecture can be acutely stressing when there is insufficient prior experience, training, preparation time, materials, technical backup or social support. This is illustrated by the physiological stress responses produced in the Trier Social Stress Test (TSST) (Kirschbaum, Pirke and Hellhammer 1993) and in Houtman and Bakker's (1991a) study on inexperienced student teachers. Such deficiencies appear to be increasing in a teacher's job in Britain today, where financial cutbacks (with their associated lack of support and materials) are coupled with curricular changes and increased red tape.

Increases in teachers' chronic (ongoing) work stress have occurred at all levels (from primary to university). Teachers have experienced the 'Thatcher revolution', which considerably changed the nature of the teaching job in Britain. The new bureaucratic demands are regarded by many teachers as at best time-wasting and at worst professionally insulting. New curriculum and examination demands reduce the teachers 'scope for control', which is known to be a potent factor in work stress production (Karasek 1979). The changes in the last decade, affecting all teachers from primary school to university, are those that would increase both 'perceived non-satisfaction of needs' (PERNOS) and 'perceived coping incapacity'(perceived inability to cope) (PCI) – two factors critical to development of psychological stress ('psystress' as defined below). Hence we would expect increases in physiological stress responses and illness.

The effect of increased workload and longer working hours

In general it appears that long working hours tend to cause ill health (Sparks, Cooper, Yitzak, Shirom 1997), depending, *inter alia,* on the degree of job satisfaction and freedom allowed in work. It is also a well-known fact that in Britain today teachers have to work much longer hours than 10 years ago to meet the new teaching and bureaucratic demands. Sugisawa, Nakijima, Kikkawa, Sugisawa (1996) investigated the relationship between actual working hours and self-reported physio-logical symptoms and health status in over 3000 teachers in Japanese elementary and lower secondary schools. The objective index of workload and self-rated level of 'perceived work stress' were both found to be correlated significantly with self-rated physical ill health (after controlling for social support, teaching experience, kind of school, family responsibilities, age and sex).

Due to the reasons mentioned above, league tables of job-stress indicators and life expectancy, which have generally indicated teaching to be a relatively low work stress profession, may now be obsolete. We await new studies that investigate whether the increased job demands and longer working hours are associated with increased physiological stress responses and ill health in teachers.

A theoretical model of psychological stress ('psystress')

The practical utility of a theoretical model of psychological stress depends fundamentally on its scientific validity. The demonstration of validity depends on the development of valid and reliable assessment methods/tests to measure the factors causing psychological stress and the responses resulting from it. Regarding the responses, objective physiological 'anchor' variables are required, with test methods that are applicable in the field (Hinton and Burton 1992b, 1997). Such methods must not interfere with a job, for example teachers cannot easily stop work for blood sampling. Hinton and Burton (1992a), following on from the proposals of Cox (1978), detailed a theoretical model of psychological stress in which the concept of 'psystress' was proposed as a means of avoiding ambiguity in the use of the term 'stress'. Psystress refers to a mental state that is increased as a direct function of perceived coping incapacity (PCI) and perceived non-satisfaction of important needs (PERNOS). Whether or not we experience psystress depends on our perception of the demands made on us (for example whether the job demands are relevant to our needs and whether we can cope). A 'demand' is not a 'stressor' unless it is perceived as such, yet the two are often confused. Ideally our work should provide motivating 'challenges' (Gaillard 1993) and not 'stressors'. The stress responses in the model include changes in motivation to take action, overt behaviour, 'negative emotion' (a general state of 'upset'), and physiological responses (Hinton and Burton 1997). These responses are interlinked and feed back in various defined ways to the factors affecting psystress generation. Hinton and Burton (1997) have attempted to detail how the theoretical model can be applied in the workplace and how a multidisciplinary battery of tests could be used to measure objective job-demand factors, subjective appraisal factors and physiological and psychological response factors to obtain a comprehensive assessment of work stress (see also Hinton and Hodapp 1997).

The case for psychophysiological assessment of work stress in teachers

It may be argued that work stress can be assessed at several levels of stress causation and response (Hinton and Hodapp 1997), which consist of a number of measurable factors – but how objectively can these be measured?

Job characteristics

Initially, the 'objective' demands of a job can be measured in terms of speed, complexity and variety – easier in a factory production line than in teaching. It may be possible to define job characteristics that are stressing in general – but only after they have been confirmed with reference to stress-response outcomes. Also, organisational/management factors are important aspects of job demand. Problems arise in that people have differing skills, personalities, needs etc., so that the perception of a demand as a stressor or not depends on many personal factors that affect subjective appraisal of capability and need satisfaction: one person's stressor may be another person's pleasure! Physiological stress-response indices (including physical illness) can provide the necessary objective criteria for the degree of psystress generated.

Subjective self-appraisal factors: the psystress generation factors

Perceptual factors are critical in psystress generation as clearly outlined by Cox (1978, Ch.1). Organisational/management factors can determine the degree and type of support, which in turn influence an employee's general level of PCI. Subjective appraisal of PCI in meeting perceived job demands, in combination with perceived importance of needs and the degree to which these needs are satisfied in the job (PERNOS) determine the level of psystress (Hinton and Burton 1992a). The measurement problem is due to the necessarily subjective nature of self-assessment. Spurious validation of such measures might occur through the confounding variables of dissimulation and neuroticism: both could affect both psystress causation factors and self-reported stress responses such as psychosomatic ailments (Dohrenwend, Dohrenwend, Dodson and Shrout 1984). We have shown in clerical workers that statistically removing the effects of neuroticism and 'social desirability' reporting still leaves self-reported PCI and PERNOS as significant predictors of stress responses, including physiological symptoms (Hinton and Fotheringham 1991). We have also shown that changes in job demands correlate with changes in stress-related ailments (Hinton, Bell and Rotheiler 1990). Nevertheless, the only valid and objective criteria for validating psystress generation measures are objective physiological stress responses.

Psychological stress responses

Measures of self-reported stress response include the general emotional response to the 'stress' test (ERST; Burton, Hinton, Neilson and Beastall 1996) and the Stress scale of the Stress Arousal Check List (SACL) (Mackay, Cox, Burrows and Lazzarini 1978), which is biased towards anxiety (Hinton, Rotheiler and Howard 1991). 'Stress'-related psychosomatic symptoms/ailments can also be self-assessed (for examples the psychomatic symptom questionnaire, PSYSOM; Hinton 1991; Burton et al. 1996) and self-reports of stress-related inefficient work behaviours can be obtained. In theory, job performance criteria can provide useful and relevant information as a behavioural index of work-stress response, although it is difficult to quantify a teacher's performance. Again, physiological measures offer the only objectively measurable indices of stress response, providing the potential anchor variables for research into work stress (Hinton and Burton 1992b).

Physiological stress responses: an overview

Clearly, physiological indices can only be considered valid as measures of stress responses if they have been shown empirically to occur with psystress induction. Heart rate is often considered as a measure of 'stress' or 'mental load', but this is invalid. Heart rate rises in any situation where excitement occurs and active coping occurs. Psystress involves a state of 'negative emotion', and it is not easy to find psychophysiological indices of the nature of emotion. Measurement of activity in muscles by means of electrodes on the face (Dimberg 1988) is hardly practical for teachers in front of a class! Sampling body fluids offers a more realistic approach. Some hormones, (such as cortisol) rise in states of psystress and anxiety (Harris, Coleshaw, Mackenzie and Whiting 1994) and can be monitored from saliva and urine as discussed below. Saliva sampling is simple and cheap. Fortunately, salivary levels of the hormones relevant to psystress reflect those in blood (Vining, McGinley, Maksvytis and Ho 1983). Concentrations of cortisol increase during the phase of 'resistance' to a stressor in Selye's 'General Adaptation Syndrome' (Selye 1956). Also, levels of sex hormones (such as testosterone) reduce when stressed (Davidson, Smith and Levine 1978; Theorell, Karasek and Eneroth 1990). Most physiological studies on work psystress have used measures of cortisol. Sympathetic nervous activity, monitored by adrenaline and noradrenaline levels in the blood and urine, also increases with stressors and challenges. As with heart rate increases, it is often erroneously thought that increased adrenaline indicates 'stress'. However adrenaline rises with arousal, whether it is pleasurable excitement (such as a job challenge) or emotional upset (such as coping with a job stressor). Adrenaline increases heart rate, but heart rate decreases where only passive coping is possible. The heart rate drop in passive coping is due to 'overcompensation' by a massive increase in parasympathetic nervous activity (Carruthers and Taggart 1973). Such a response would not be expected in the teaching situation where active coping is necessary: in fact there is evidence of the opposite nervous reaction (a drop in parasympathetic activity in control of the heart) when faced with an audience (De Meersman, Reisman, Daum and Zorowitz 1996). Extended periods of overtime are experienced by many teachers today through increased bureaucratic job demands, and this can cause abnormally raised levels of adrenaline (Rissler 1977). High levels of adrenaline maintained after work can indicate inability to 'unwind', which is an important indicator of work stress (Melin and Lundberg 1997).

The body's immune system is strongly affected by psystress. Defences, such as defences against respiratory infection, include immunoglobulins. These are present in saliva – notably secretory immunoglobulin A (sIgA). The measured concentration of sIgA in saliva has been found to increase with short-term/acute challenges and stressors where active coping is involved – with either an acute psychological stressor or challenge. By contrast, chronic (long-lasting) psystress is associated with depleted sIgA and increased proneness to infection. The evidence for these stress-induced changes in immune function is reviewed by Evans, Clow and Hucklebridge (1997) and Hinton and Burton (1997). There is evidence that levels of hormones can control the immune system (Munck, Guyre and Holbrook 1984).

In research on the psychophysiology of work stress it is important to take account of the large individual differences in ability to respond in any specific physiological measure, for example in cortisol output. This individual response specificity means that large samples of subjects are needed in order to compare work groups on any particular physiological measure, and one should look at changes that occur within an individual when shifted from a non-stressing 'baseline' (totally relaxed situation) to the work situation of interest (Hinton and Burton 1992b). But how can a valid baseline be obtained when a person is in a chronically stressed condition that produces long-lasting tonic changes (for example in 'stress hormone levels')? The effect of job changes can be evaluated by looking at within-subject physiological changes over time to assess changes in psystress (Hinton and Burton 1992b). Measures taken during work should ideally be expressed as a function of a baseline resting level and within-subject changes should be monitored over time, because physiological parameters vary in a daily rhythm.

Psychophysiological monitoring of factors relating to psystress have been reviewed by Hinton (1988) and Hinton and Burton (1997) have reviewed the practical use of psychophysiological measures in the workplace.

Psychophysiological evidence of psystress in public speaking

Giving a lecture at short notice is generally very stressful. This is borne out by the finding of a significant increase in salivary cortisol (Kirschbaum, Pirke and Hellhammer 1993). Most lecturers recall feeling anxious before their first lectures as well as experiencing physiological stress reactions (such as heart pounding or racing; sweating, dry mouth) during the lecture. Giving a talk requires active coping as one cannot run away from the lectern! The physiological reactions are indications of autonomic activation in an active coping situation – as opposed to passive (avoidant) coping with a stressor (Carruthers and Taggart 1973; Obrist 1975; Fowles 1980; Sosnowski, Nurzynska and Polec 1991). Clearly the teaching process in general involves active coping, so very high cardiovascular activity would indicate not just high physiological 'arousal' but also high psystress.

The Trier Centre for Psychobiological and Psychosomatic Research has published a standardised procedure for inducing psystress that relates to the potential 'ego-threat' aspect of lecturing with little time to prepare. The Trier Social Stress Test (TSST), as it is called, comprises a period of anticipation and a test period when a speech is delivered and mental arithmetic performed in front of an audience. A description of this test, together with the resulting physiological responses of psystress and arousal, from six studies, is given by Kirschbaum, Pirke and Hellhammer (1993). Psystress induction was indicated by increases in cortisol of 2 to 4 times the baseline level, whereas heart rate increases showed the active coping/arousal aspect of the public speaking. Gender, genetic factors and nicotine intake also influenced physiological stress responsivity to the TSST.

The need to distinguish between teaching work 'stressors' and work 'challenges'

Short-term activation of the autonomic nervous system occurs with many exciting events in our lives, whether it is the perceived challenge of a task (involving active approach behaviour), or anxiety (involving active avoidance). The response of increased heart rate is due to activation of the sympathetic branch of the autonomic nervous system, while the opposing parasympathetic nervous control is inhibited. Sympathetic activity also raises adrenaline, which stimulates the heart. It is a common misconception that during the working day it is 'bad for you' to be in such a state of 'sympathetic dominance'. Teaching is challenging and exciting and should therefore involve raised adrenaline levels (though not excessively so). We need to distinguish between 'stressors' and 'challenges' in the workplace as mentioned in the introduction to this chapter (Gaillard 1993).

Physiological symptoms of teachers' work stress

Relatively little research has been reported on physiological stress responses in teaching. There are however more studies that involve self-report of physiological symptoms and these will be reviewed first here.

Kyriacou and Sutcliffe (1978) surveyed 'stress' symptoms in secondary school teachers. They found that the teachers reported a number of significant physiological symptoms including exhaustion, headaches, heart palpitations, loss of voice, raised blood pressure, indigestion and cold sweats. None the less, in 1980, Kyriacou reported that the physical health of teachers was no worse than that of workers in comparable professions. Since then, however, teachers have suffered the 'Thatcher revolution' with its potentially stressful changes. Nevertheless, it could be instructive to see what physiological stress reactions teachers have reported over the past 20 years.

Dunham (1980) administered a checklist of stress reactions (based on a survey of the literature and staff interviews) to teachers in English and West German secondary schools. The physiological stress reactions reported (average percentage incidence) were: tension headaches (32.5%); insomnia (16.5%); back pain (10.0%); ulcers (8.5%); skin rash (7.0%); migraine (7.0%); inability to eat (3.5%). The PCI factor found to be critical to development of psystress (Hinton and Burton 1992a, 1997), namely inability to concentrate, was reported by 36% of teachers together with frequent forgetfulness (29%), whereas dominant emotional/behavioural stress responses were irritability (54.5%) and depression (41%). Dunham (1984, p. 95) presented further studies of three English comprehensive schools. The averages of percentage incidence of symptoms among these schools were: exhaustion (41%); tension headaches (15.7%); sleep loss (14.3%); overeating (14.3%); back pain (7.3%); skin rash (2.7%). Other reported symptoms not on the checklist included palpitations, asthma, loss of sex drive, shoulder muscle pains, indigestion, shaky hands and high blood pressure. Dunham (1984, p. 98) gave physiological symptoms reported by work-stressed deputy heads: these included fatigue, exhaustion, tremendous tiredness, headaches, high blood pressure, tension, stiffness, backache, chest tightness and breathing difficulty. The physiological symptoms of work stress reported by Dunham are all included in the list compiled by Scheuch (in Hinton 1991), which was based on an extensive study of teachers in the German Democratic Republic who were incapacitated through work stress.

In the early 1980s, Klaus Scheuch, Director of the Institute of Work-Medicine in Dresden, carried out a nationwide symptom survey on over 1000 teachers who had been forced to stop work due to work stress. The reported symptoms included physical exhaustion, complaints related to the cardiovascular system, skeleto-muscular system, breathing, skin, sensory systems and sleep quality (see Hinton 1991). In 1987, over 40 000 German Democratic Republic teachers in all age groups were assessed in an occupational health screening programme, and compared with over 800 000 other workers (Scheuch and Vogel 1993). Musculoskeletal and cardiovascular symptoms were generally the most prevalent and at the same level as in other occupations. However, teachers of all ages had a higher risk of diseases of the nervous system (neuroses), kidney and bladder. Female teachers also had more respiratory diseases than other workers (Vogel, Koch, Haufe and Silbernagel 1994). 'Diseases of the nervous system' became comparatively more frequent in teachers with increasing age. Scheuch, Knothe and Misterek (1992) reported that, compared to non-neurotic teachers, neurotic ones did not differ in heart rate or blood pressure during work; however, the neurotic teachers were less able to recover from work, as shown by the maintenance of raised catecholamine excretion in urine at night, which is an indication of raised chronic work stress (Melin and Lundberg 1997). In a detailed symptom study on Dresden male and female teachers, Scheuch (1995) reported that the most frequent symptoms were fatigue/exhaustion, sensitivity to noise and sleep disturbance.

Temml (1995) compared Austrian male and female teachers and found that females were higher on all psychosomatic complaints investigated except blood pressure. Females had more blood circulatory complaints, infections, muscle tension complaints, digestive disorders and greater loss of libido.

Teacher 'burnout' implies a state of mental, emotional and attitudinal exhaustion resulting from a prolonged experience of stress (Kyriacou 1987). Burke, Greenglass and Schwarzer (1996) reported on job factors that predicted the occurrence of burnout and stress-related symptoms in teachers of both sexes in elementary, junior and secondary schools. They found that the prime predictors of burnout (especially emotional exhaustion) one year later were bureaucratic red tape, lack of supervisor support and disruptive students (particularly for female teachers). The main physical outcome was 'heart symptoms' including heart pounding, chest pains and breathlessness. Depressive mood was the other outcome that could be predicted.

To summarise the research findings, the descending order of prevalence of stress-related symptoms appears to be:

- physical exhaustion/fatigue and tiredness;
- skeleto-muscular tension/pains;
- heart symptoms and high blood pressure;
- headaches;
- digestive disorders;
- respiratory difficulties and complaints;
- sleep disturbances;
- voice loss.

'Short-term' psystress induction by the teaching process *per se*

As mentioned above, Kirschbaum, Pirke and Hellhammer (1993) have shown the physiological effects of acute psystress caused by having to give a public talk with little preparation time. Heart rate rises very rapidly, and cortisol levels increase during the talk.

Houtman and Bakker (1991a) reported a study on student teachers. They assessed the psystress of lecturing to an audience in a standardised situation and how this was affected by three months of lecturing practice. Lecturing without practice caused very significant increases in heart rate and anxiety (especially at the start of the lecture). The rise in cortisol concentration was found to diminish significantly with teaching practice, but did not do so in students who had no practice during the three months. The reduced rise in cortisol due to practice indicates a reduction in acute psystress reaction – consistent with decreased PCI. No relationship was found between the changes in heart rate, anxiety or cortisol. This is not surprising, since cortisol indicates psystress, whereas heart rate indicates activation of the autonomic nervous system (arousal) and anxiety is anticipatory fear, and not 'stress' (Hinton, Howard and Rotheiler 1991) – this is why the anxiety measure peaks at the start of the lecture in the Houtman and Bakker experiment.

Psychophysiological field studies on 'long-term' work stress in teachers

Travers and Cooper (1994) examined physiological changes in secondary and primary teachers over a three-month period in the school year when work stress is thought to develop strongly, namely the autumn term. Compared to population norms, the cortisol concentrations (both at start and end of term) were abnormally low, with 45% below the normal range, and the range was extremely high. The authors quote Potelliakhoff and Carruthers (1981) to suggest that the extremely low cortisol levels could indicate a state of exhaustion/fatigue. Of relevance here is Selye's model of 'stress' phases – his 'general adaptation syndrome' (GAS) – in which after an initial physiological 'alarm reaction' to a 'stress'-inducing situation, the experience of a prolonged stressor leads to an extended 'resistance' phase involving raised cortisol and 'mobilisation of reserves' and finally a phase of 'collapse', when 'stress hormones' reduce (finally to zero with death!). We could speculate that in the study by Travers and Cooper a high proportion of the teachers were in various stages of Selye's collapse phase, with a drop in disease resistance; consistent with this explanation is their finding that four teachers who were absent through illness for the second testing were in the abnormally low cortisol group. This explanation fits with the parallel finding of Pruessner, Schulz, Hellhammer and Buske-Kirschbaum (1997) that burnout in teachers relates to low cortisol levels and more body complaints. Also, if the GAS explanation is correct, this could explain why no correlation was found between cortisol and factors causing work stress in school, as for some teachers increasing work stress would elevate cortisol as the phase of 'resistance' was reached, whereas for others it would cause decrease in cortisol as the 'collapse' condition was approached.

There are many problems in evaluating this research because of the fact that only one blood sample was taken (during the morning) although cortisol levels are subject to marked diurnal change, and because biological data were obtained via blood sampling (which can be stressing for people who fear the needle). It is also difficult to evaluate whether results reported as significant are indeed so because of the multiple statistical tests on the relationships between the many variables. It is nevertheless an example of the type of multi-measure psychophysiological research that should be undertaken to try to relate job organisational factors to work stress in teaching.

Individual differences in physiological stress response and coping with lecturing

Different personalities suit different jobs. Physiological responses to work stress should indicate when there is a mis-match between personality and job demands. This is illustrated by recent research on Royal Mail letter coders doing repetitive monotonous sorting of letters using computer screens. As predicted, extroverted and neurotic personalities gave chronic indications of work stress via salivary ion concentrations in the workplace (Hinton, Burton, King and Murdoch 1996; Hinton, King, Burton and Murdoch 1996). Neurotic extroverted showed greatest physiological indications of high work stress, (reduced tonic salivary sodium ion concentration [Na$^+$]) and raised emotional stress responses and fatigue (reduced salivary potassium levels [K$^+$]) (Burton, Hinton, Neilson and Beastall 1996). By contrast, in teaching, one might predict that the introverted neurotic (anxious personality) should be the most prone to work stress. Schlenker and Leary (1982) report that social anxiety leads to exaggerated stress reactions under conditions of ego threat such as exist in lecturing. (Social anxiety may be regarded as a compound of neuroticism and extroversion.) Kaiser, Hinton, Krohne, Stewart and Burton (1995) demonstrated that introverts, and emotionally inhibited people, had the slowest recovery from raised muscle tension (neck muscle tension: EMG) after preparing to give an unexpected speech but being stopped from delivering it; this clearly indicated a deficit in ability to unwind after the lecture preparation. Neuroticism has been found to predict future reported health problems and burnout, with extroversion being related to effective coping and feelings of well-being at work (Parkes 1986; McCrae and Costa 1986).

In a study on student teachers, Houtman and Bakker (1991b) investigated the effect of three months of teaching practice on physiological reactions to, and recovery from, a 30-minute lecture that was given before colleagues and teachers. Heart rate was monitored by an ambulatory recorder. Cortisol was measured from saliva samples. There were notable differences between the sexes but the personality factors predicting physiological reactivity and long-term coping were extroversion, neuroticism and social anxiety. Cortisol increase in women student teachers, was found to be greatest in those with high social anxiety and low 'type A' (Apples 1985), which suggests that timid, non-competitive teachers with low 'drive' and high anticipatory fear are the most prone to perceived coping incapacity. In general, heart rate increase tends to indicate a positive active coping strategy (Carruthers and Taggart 1973; Fowles 1980). Thus, it is interesting to note that non-neurotic (stable) introverted women exhibited the greatest heart rate increase as a reaction to lecturing. Conversely, neurotic extroverts had the smallest heart-rate increase, which could indicate that neurotic extroverts show a parasympathetic dominance in cardiac control, consistent with an inappropriate passive-avoidant coping strategy (Fowles 1980, 1983). From the cortisol results, it may be concluded that neurotic, socially inhibited teachers are more 'at risk' of acute psychophysiological teaching stress reactions than teachers who are emotionally stable and sociable.

A person with high chronic life stress might be expected to respond to an additional stressor with a greater physiological stress response than someone who is not suffering from ongoing life stress. In fact, in our laboratory we have shown that students who have high study stress give marked salivary ion stress responses when faced with an examination paper, whereas students who are coping well do not (Hinton, Burton and Hardman 1996, 1997). Findings from a study on teachers by Brosschot et al. (1994) concord with these results. They found that the degree of ongoing life stress (ongoing daily hassles) determined the immunological response to a 30-minute interpersonal stressor involving learning and teaching a confederate to solve a 'puzzle'. (The 'puzzle' was impossible, but the subjects did not know it.) Teachers who were the most chronically stressed had acute stress responses of reduced T cells and natural killer (NK) cells in their blood, showing a sudden reduction in defence to infection. The implication is that teachers who are chronically work stressed may be more likely to react to stressing short-duration job demands, with increased proneness to infection.

Developing psystress causation scales and the PSYSOM symptom scale

Hinton (1991) reported the development of PSYSOM starting with symptoms of work-stressed teachers (Scheuch 1995). The PSYSOM was cross-validated against a questionnaire measuring PCI (the Cognitive Appraisal 'Stress' Test, CAST): a concept central to the model of Cox and Mackay (Cox 1978). PSYSOM is unique in taking into account the frequency, severity and duration of each symptom. Highly significant correlations were found between CAST and PSYSOM, especially with symptoms of muscle tension and exhaustion (Hinton, Bell and Rotheiler 1990; Hinton 1991). PSYSOM now consists of 12 items: those correlating most highly with PCI. It includes physiological symptoms of exhaustion, headaches, muscle tension, cardiovascular symptoms, skin and gut symptoms.

Studies on 15 different work populations (including teachers) have resulted in a CAST scale measuring 'mental' PCI, with items on problems of attention/concentration and decision making (Hinton and Burton 1997). High scores on these items relate maximally to reduced motivation and poor marks on university examinations (Hinton, Bell and Rotheiler 1990) and to other work-stress responses – motivational, behavioural, emotional and physiological symptoms (PSYSOM). Work populations studied included shipyard engineers (Morgan 1991), tourist office clerks (Hinton and Fotheringham 1991), nurses (Hogg 1994; Hogg, Hinton and Burton 1995), Post Office letter sorters (Hinton, Burton, King and Murdoch 1996; Hinton, King, Burton and Murdoch 1996), electronics company workers (Burton et al. 1996) and teachers (Reid 1997).

As explained above (Hinton and Burton 1992a 1997) production of psystress necessitates a state of PERNOS. A flexible PERNOS questionnaire was designed with items on basic needs plus items specific to the job situation: each is assessed for (a) 'degree of non-satisfaction' and weighted for (b) 'degree of importance', with the sum of the products [(a) × (b)] giving the PERNOS score. Combining PERNOS and PCI scores gives increased correlation with stress responses (Hinton et al. 1996a.). Our unit has now carried out a number of work-stress studies on teachers in Scotland which have provided validation of the PSYSOM as an index of physiological stress response in teachers (Reid 1997).

Development and testing of salivary ion measures of psystress for use in the workplace

Scientific evidence on the physiological controls of salivary ion concentrations ($[Na^+]$ and $[K^+]$) indicates the potential usefulness of these measures for assessing psystress, anxiety and 'arousal' (Venables 1970, p. 118; Hinton et al. 1992). In contrast to electrophysiological methods for monitoring work stress, sampling of saliva without gustatory stimulation is simple and unobtrusive. Ion concentration determination by flame photometry is easy and standardised (Willard, Merritt and Dean 1974; Hinton and Burton 1996).

Psychophysiological research on salivary ions has been conducted over 10 years by our research unit in collaboration with the Technischen Universitaet (TU) Dresden. We have demonstrated the practical usefulness of salivary ions in the assessment of both acute and chronic (longterm) psystress and state of 'arousal'/challenge (Hinton and Burton 1996, 1997). These salivary indices have also been used to further validate the psystress model and the scales for assessment of PCI and

PERNOS (Hogg 1994; Hogg, Hinton and Burton 1995; Hinton, Burton, King and Murdoch 1996; Hinton, King, Burton and Murdoch 1996). Significant relationships have been shown to exist between concentrations of ions ($[K^+]$ and $[Na^+]$) in unstimulated (non-gustatory) saliva and states of 'activation' and psystress (Hinton et al. 1992; Richter, Hinton, Meissener and Scheller 1995; Burton et al. 1996).

Salivary $[K^+]$ as an indicator of task-activation state

Salivary $[K^+]$ increases as sympathetic nervous activity increases relative to parasympathetic nervous activity. Our laboratory and field studies show that salivary $[K^+]$ relates directly to the extent to which a person is activated by a task, rather than to psystress *per se* (McLean 1988; Richter et al. 1995; Hinton and Burton 1997). We found that low tonic salivary $[K^+]$ related to work fatigue/exhaustion in an electronics manufacturing company (Burton et al. 1996) and it was related to job dissatisfaction, high PCI, perceived lack of support and inability to unwind after work in academics (Wells, Hinton and Burton 1997).

Salivary $[Na^+]$ as an indicator of chronic psystress at work

Control of $[Na^+]$ is to a large extent via the hormone, aldosterone – a mineralocorticoid released in psystress states and which induces $[Na^+]$ reabsorption in the lumen of gland ducts, thus lowering the concentration of sodium ions in saliva. The derived hypothesis is that work stress relates to lowered salivary $[Na^+]$. This has been tested and confirmed in a number of studies. Davidson (1989) sampled saliva and obtained self-ratings from children who had just entered secondary school. She found that children with high self-reported PCI (attention/concentration and decision problems in doing schoolwork) had significantly lower salivary $[Na^+]$ and that low $[Na^+]$ predicted the extent of self-reported stress-related ailments occurring two months later (Davidson 1989). Burton et al. (1996), studying factory workers, showed that reduced tonic $[Na^+]$ in unstimulated saliva was related to high PCI and emotional upset at work. This was confirmed by Hinton, Burton, King and Murdoch 1996 on Post Office letter coders, when PCI was combined with PERNOS to give a work-psystress index that was significantly negatively correlated with reduced sodium ion concentrations at work. An investigation on nurses showed that early morning $[Na^+]$ is reduced in those chronically stressed by work – that is, with the highest mental PCI (Hogg, Hinton and Burton 1995). This could be related to the finding by Pruessner et al. (1997) that a fast increase in early morning cortisol occurs in people experiencing most 'chronic stress'.

Hinton, Burton, King and Murdoch 1996 and Hinton, King, Burton and Murdoch 1996 showed the importance of incorporating personality factors (as moderating variables) with perceptual/appraisal factors in work-stress research. When an extroversion and neuroticism index was combined with the perceptual psystress factors, the correlation with the physiological tonic work-stress indicator, salivary [Na$^+$] was maximised.

Acute psystress and salivary ions

Our recent studies on acute stress induction, have shown that rapid [Na$^+$] reductions occur as a response to acute task demands, but only when these demands are highly relevant to an ongoing (long-term) stress state – as with important examinations for which a student is poorly prepared (Hinton, Burton and Hardman 1996, 1997). In other words, acute stress reactions (i.e. rapid salivary [Na$^+$] reductions) depend on high chronic psystress. Therefore, it cannot be assumed that a test demand is a stressor simply because the task is extremely difficult – perceived relevance (personal need to perform the task) is critical. Thus, a teacher who is desperate to keep his/her job and who has a high need to achieve successful teaching results, but who has a class with several behaviourally disordered pupils, can experience extremely strong acute physiological stress reactions when disruptions occur during lessons. This being a situation involving unavoidable active coping, salivary [K$^+$] would also rise (with increased sympathetic nervous activity relative to parasympathetic activity). Repeated daily acute stressors would lead to bursts of high adrenaline, which could lead to the cardiac symptoms which have high reported incidence in teachers (see above).

Physiological unwinding: a measure of psystress

In our early work on salivary ions and psystress and activation, only the ratio of ion concentrations ([K$^+$]/[Na$^+$]) was measured (Hinton et al. 1992). This confused the different physiological controls (described above). Nevertheless, Hinton et al. (1992) found that having to give an unexpected speech caused the [K$^+$]/[Na$^+$] ratio to increase considerably and to continue to be raised for some time after the task (slow unwinding). Wall (Institute of Work-Medicine, Berlin, GDR 1988, unpublished), in consultation with our unit, conducted a study on teachers with severe classroom coping problems. The data were obtained from a role play therapy session. It was found that the [K$^+$]/[Na$^+$] ratio continued to rise after role play teaching, in spite of a special relaxation session. These findings are consistent with a stress hormonal effect, as with the cortisol findings of Kirschbaum, Pirke and Hellhammer (1993).

Personality factors can be relevant to recovery from a speech stressor as shown by Kaiser et al. (1995). They found that 'physiological' recovery after preparing to give an unexpected speech (stopped before delivery) was slower in introverts and emotionally inhibited subjects, as shown by lack of relaxation in the neck trapezious muscle (the best single index of overall muscle tension).

Stockholm University has been leading research to show how 'unwinding' after work is determined by work stress and compounded with non-work stress factors (such as domestic demands after work). Frankenhaeuser (1991) showed that high work stress was related to inability to relax after work – both psychologically and physiologically. The indicated how unpaid work demands combined with paid job demands, producing excessive overall life demands, and hence contributing to total work stress and inability to unwind after paid work: a problem particularly for women who still do most of the domestic chores and childcare work on top of their paid work. Wells (1997) followed up this work and combined it with salivary ion measures in the context of psystress theory (Hinton and Burton 1992a, 1997). She conducted a psychophysiological study on university lecturers (Wells, Hinton and Burton 1997).

A psychophysiological study of psystress in university lecturers

In a psychophysiological study of psystress in university lecturers' work and non-work life and of unwinding after work (Wells, Hinton and Burton 1997), Wells obtained the cooperation of 36 lecturers and senior lecturers chosen from university departments to give a wide spread of work loadings. This was done from knowledge of student/staff ratios and levels of administrative support, both of which varied considerably. (There were only three refusals, these being due to reported excessive work pressure!) Three sets of questionnaires were administered to sample unpaid work aspects, unwinding after work, work-stress causation and response factors, and physiological work-stress symptoms. The self-testing and sampling was carried out in mid-afternoon at work (approximately 3.00 p.m.), approx. 9.00 p.m. at home, and after rising in the morning (approximately 7.30 a.m.). Standardised saliva sampling procedures were followed (Hinton and Burton 1996). One of the three sets of questionnaires was completed and finally saliva was sampled in a tube. The study was carried out with anonymity.

Relationship between self-reported teaching work-stress causation factors and stress responses

As in our previous studies, factors generating psystress at work, namely PCI and PERNOS (individually, but especially in combination), correlated highly with the work-stress responses of psychosomatic symptoms (PSYSOM), self-medication (SELFMED), emotional stress response (ERST) and negative work behaviours (WORST). The inclusion of social support (SOCSUP) (which affects overall PCI) with PCI and PERNOS maximised these correlations, and this 'combined work-psystress causation index' gave the following product–moment correlations with:

general emotional response to stress (ERST):	$r = 0.70$; $p < 0.001$
stress-related physiological symptoms (PSYSOM):	$r = 0.65$; $p < 0.001$
self-medication (SELFMED)	$r = 0.28$; $p < 0.1$
negative behavioural work stress responses (WORST):	$r = 0.30$; $p < 0.1$
combined stress responses (standard scores $1 + 2 + 3 + 4$):	$r = 0.76$; $p < 0.001$

Teaching work stress and unwinding after work

Of particular interest is the highly significant correlation between the academic work-psystress causation index and measure of level of difficulty in unwinding at home after work. To measure unwinding we used a scale that combined self-reported problems in unwinding behaviourally, physiologically and emotionally (UNWIND), and this was found to correlate 0.57 ($p < 0.002$) with the combined index of work-psystress causation. The work-stress causation measure relating most significantly with inability to unwind after work (UNWIND) was PERNOS, ($r = 0.50$; $p < 0.01$). The work-stress response that related maximally with UNWIND was PSYSOM ($r = 0.80$; $p<0.0001$) and, not surprisingly, fatigue/exhaustion at work correlated with UNWIND to the greatest degree ($r = 0.81$).

The importance of perceived unpaid demands in affecting ability to unwind

It is interesting to note that measures of non-work, domestic/social stressors, derived from Lundberg (1996, personal communication) were rather less significantly correlated with slow unwinding than were the factors causing work-stress. A combined measure of these after-work 'excessive demands' correlated with UNWIND ($r = 0.51$, $p < 0.002$).

The effect on unwinding of combined job and non-paid work stress

Difficulty in unwinding after work was predicted to a highly significant degree by combining the work-stress causation index and the total domestic/social stress factors: (Multiple $r = 0.65$; $p < 0.0001$). The combination accounted for 10% more of the variance of unwinding than work-stress causation factors alone and 17% more than the perceived non-job stressor factors alone.

Physiological state at work relating to self-reported work stress and to unwinding after work

In line with our earlier findings, work-stressed lecturers, and those showing slow unwinding after work, had lowered salivary [K$^+$], but only in saliva sampled in the workplace. This indicates a lowered autonomic arousal state due to the work (depression of sympathetic activity relative to parasympathetic) consistent with a state of lowered behavioural activation. There is evidence that phasic increase in autonomic activation by a challenging task, and short-term stressors, relates to a 'boost' in the immune system as indicated by salivary sIgA changes (Evans, Clow and Hucklebridge 1997). Of relevance here is a new finding – on a very large sample of air-traffic controllers – that salivary sIgA is very highly correlated with salivary [K$^+$] (Vogt, personal communication 1997). The conclusion from these findings is that the academics with low [K$^+$] at work would have increased disease proneness – and indeed, self-reported physical ailments (PSYSOM) and self-medication (SELFMED) were both significantly related to low [K$^+$] at work.

Early morning physiological indication of chronic life stress in university lecturers

Much research has shown that cortisol level relates to psystress. Pruessner (in press) has shown that salivary cortisol taken at a controlled time shortly after awakening is a stable measure for any person and raised early-morning cortisol concentration in saliva relates to high life-stress (Pruessner et al. 1997). (Many events during the day effect acute psychological changes and it is difficult to control for effects of diurnal rhythm on tonic levels of steroid hormones. Self-sampling of saliva, 30 minutes after getting up in the morning, helps to control for these factors.) Consistent with findings on nurses (Hogg, Hinton and Burton 1995), high university work psystress (assessed by a combined work-psystress causation index) related to reduced early-morning [Na$^+$]. Lack of unwinding after work also related to low early-morning [Na$^+$]. However, the most interesting correlation pattern occurred between a 'total life stress' index (which included perceived excessive domestic demands) and early-morning [Na$^+$]: [Na$^+$] correlated with this life-stress index in a V-shaped distribution! Half of the academics showed reducing [Na$^+$] with increasing life-stress up to a certain life-stress level (p = –0.71; p < 0.01), as expected, whereas the other half demonstrated increasing [Na$^+$] with increases in life-stress above the mean life-stress level (p = 0.66; p < 0.02). From these dramatic (and statistically significant) results, it is tempting to draw a parallel with Selye's GAS in which cortisol levels increase during the resistance phase (while the organism is struggling to maintain control), and then, with persisting stressors, comes a stage of collapse in resistance, when cortisol is depleted and the body's defences against infection are lost. In view of the depletion of salivary [Na^+] by 'stress'-related hormones – notably aldosterone (Venables 1970) – and applying the GAS parallel, one could speculate that half of our academics were 'over the top' in life stress (i.e. in various stages of loss of resistance to work stress.)

If this analysis is correct, it would be consistent with the results of a British university study by Abouserie (1996), who reported high levels of work stress in lecturers at university, with 85% in the moderate-serious 'life stress' category. This high level of 'life stress' was due primarily to work and was especially related to conducting research. Time for lecturers to research has been vastly reduced through the introduction of new bureaucratic demands from the 'teaching quality assessment', the 'research assessment exercise', the 'internal market', appraisal procedures, lack of facilities, doubled teaching and class-administration demands, withdrawal of secretarial assistance and the need to master new technology. Professional dissatisfaction (PERNOS) is raised by lowering the academic standard of teaching due to the doubling of the student intake over the last 10 years and the need to keep the 'clients' happy (to get good ratings from the students). At the same time there is constant pressure to publish and to obtain research grants from impecunious research councils. High PCI must result. It would be very surprising if these new factors did not lead to increased psystress, and therefore to more physiological stress responses and illness in university teachers in Britain today. Many of these demands on academics also apply to school teachers, who also have to cope with new detailed report writing (generally regarded as a time-wasting bureaucratic exercise), and reduction in support for children with special learning difficulties. It would be instructive to assess physiological unwinding during the holiday periods and to compare teachers with other professionals in this respect.

Concluding comments

Assessment of work stress in teachers requires the use of simple and validated psychophysiological measures. In making such assessments, other factors must be taken into account such as domestic stressors and personality. Unwinding after work should be assessed in order to obtain a complete picture of life stress, and psychophysiological measures relating to psystress should be sampled at home (early morning) and during work. Only when objective baseline measures of work stress are obtained can ongoing effects of organisational changes in the teaching job be validly assessed. A cross-disciplinary psychophysiological approach is advocated (Hinton and Hodapp 1997; Hinton and Burton 1997) with physiological indices of work stress taken from saliva samples. In this way teaching stress can be compared to work stress in other jobs, and the effects of organisational changes in teaching can be evaluated objectively.

Acknowledgements

The authors express their appreciation to the British Council for supporting an essential research link with the Department of Work and Organizational Psychology of the University of Dresden. They are indebted to the DAAD, which in conjunction with the British Council now supports an extended collaboration (ARC) with Dresden University. Thanks are due also to Professor Malcolm MacLennan and his EC Programmes Office staff at the University of Glasgow, for assistance in regard to the ARC. The first author also thanks the Wellcome Trust and the Carnegie Foundation for the Universities of Scotland, for financial assistance in aiding the European research collaborations that stimulated much of the research reported in this chapter. Finally, many thanks to Dr Richard Burton for helpful comments on the text.

References

Abouserie R (1996) Stress, coping strategies and job satisfaction in university academic staff. Educational Psychology 16: 49-56.

Apples A (1985) Jenkins Activity Survey (Manual for the Dutch version of the JAS). Lisse: Swets & Zeitlinger.

Brosschot JF, Benschop RJ, Godaert GLR, Olff M, De Smet M, Heinjnen CJ, Bailleux RE (1994) Influence of life stress on immunological activity to mild psychological stress. Psychosomatic Medicine 56(3): 216-24.

Burke RJ, Greenglass ER, Schwarzer R (1996) Predicting teacher burnout over time: effects of work stress, social support, and self-doubts on burnout and its consequences. Anxiety, Stress and Coping 9: 261-75.

Burton RF, Hinton JW, Neilson E, Beastall G (1996) Concentrations of sodium, potassium, and cortisol in saliva, and self-reported chronic work stress factors. Biological Psychology 42: 425-38.

Carruthers M, Taggart P (1973) Vagotonicity of violence: biochemical and cardiac responses to violent films and television programmes. British Medical Journal 3: 384-9.

Cox T (1978) Stress. London: Macmillan.

Davidson JM, Smith EA, Levine S (1978) Testosterone. In Ursin H, Baade E and Levine S (eds) Psychobiology of Stress: A Study of Coping Men. London: Academic Press, pp. 57-62.

Davidson M (1989) The relationship of PCI, motivation and anxiety with psychosomatic illness and salivary [K$^+$] and [Na$^+$] in new secondary school entrants and the potential of 'intermediate group work' as a stress reducer. M.Ed. Psychology thesis, University of Glasgow.

De Meersman R, Reisman S, Daum M, Zorowitz R (1996) Vagal withdrawal as a function of audience. The American Physiological Society 1363-6135/96, H1381-H1383

Dimberg U (1988) Facial electromyography and emotional reactions. Psychophysiology 27: 481-94.

Dohrenwend BS, Dohrenwend BP, Dodson M, Shrout, PE (1984) Symptoms, hassles, social supports, and life events: problem of confounded measures. Journal of Abnormal Psychology 93(2): 222-30.

Dunham J (1980) An exploratory comparative study of staff stress in English and German comprehensive schools. Educational Review 32: 11-20.

Dunham J (1984) Stress in Teaching. Sydney: Croom Helm.

Evans P, Clow A, Hucklebridge F (1997) Stress and the immune system. The Psychologist 10(7): 303-7.

Fowles DC (1980) The three arousal model: implications of Gray's two-factor learning theory for heart-rate, electrodermal activity, and psychopathy. Psychophysiology 17: 87-104.

Fowles DC (1983) Motivational effects on heart rate and electrodermal activity: implications for research on personality and psychopathy. Journal of Research in Personality 17: 48-71.

Frankenhaeuser M (1991) In Frankenhaeuser M, Lundberg U and Chesney M (eds) Women, Work and Stress. New York: Plenum.

Gaillard AW (1993) Comparing the concepts of mental load and stress. Ergonomics 36(9): 991-1005.

Harris RA, Coleshaw SRK, Mackenzie IG, Whiting PH (1994) Human cortisol and anxiety changes in response to emergency training. Journal of Physiology 53P: 481.

Hinton JW (1988) The psychophysiology of stress and personal coping styles. In Wagner HL (ed.), Social Psychophysiology and Emotion:Theory and Clinical Applications. Chichester: Wiley, pp. 175-95.

Hinton JW (1991) Stress model development and testing by group psychometrics and one-subject psychophysiology. In Spielberger CD, Sarason IG, Strelau J and Brebner JMT (eds) Stress and Anxiety 13. New York: Hemisphere, pp. 53-70.

Hinton JW, Burton RF (1992a) Clarification of the concept of psychological stress ('psystress'). International Journal of Psychosomatics 39: 42-3.

Hinton JW, Burton RF (1992b) How can stress be taken seriously? A reply to Richard Graveling. Work and Stress 6(2): 103-6.

Hinton JW, Burton RF (1996) Assessment of psystress via salivary ions. In Stamm BH (ed.) Measurement of Stress Trauma and Adaptation. Lutherville MD: Sidran Press, pp 73-5.

Hinton JW, Burton RF (1997) A psychophysiological model of psystress causation and response applied to the workplace. Journal of Psychophysiology 11: 200-17.

Hinton JW, Fotheringham E (1991) Further validation of a model of psychological stress (Psystress) and self-rating tools: the removal of neuroticism and social desirability response set from correlations between Psystress causation and Psystress outcome measures. International Congress on Stress, Anxiety and Emotional Disorders, Braga, Portugal.

Hinton JW, Rotheiler E (1990) Stress, Gesundheit und Leistung von Universitaetsstudenten. Z. Gesamte Hygiena 36: 642-3.

Hinton JW, Hodapp V (1997) The psychophysiology of work stress. Journal of Psychophysiology 11: 195-9.

Hinton JW, Bell N, Rotheiler E (1990) The development and consequences of work stress: testing a theoretical model. In Richter P and Hacker W (eds) Mental Work and Automation: Section C: Work, Mental Health and Personality. Dresden: Dresden University Press, pp. 143-53.

Hinton JW, Howard AJ, Rotheiler E (1991) Can stress be measured with an anxiety questionnaire? International Journal of Psychosomatics 38: 81-3.

Hinton JW, Rotheiler E, Howard AJ (1991) Confusion between stress and anxiety state in a much-used self-report 'stress' inventory. Personality and Individual Differences 12: 91-4.

Hinton JW, Burton RF, Farmer JG, Rotheiler E, Shewan D, Gemmell M, Berry J, Gibson R (1992) Relative changes in salivary Na$^+$ and K$^+$ relating to stress induction. Biological Psychology 33, 63-71.

Hinton JW, Burton RF, Hardman P (1996) The influence of perceived coping incapacity and perceived importance on salivary ion concentrations in students with examination simulation. The Society for Stress and Anxiety Research (STAR) International Conference, Graz, Austria, July 4-8.

Hinton JW, Burton RF, King AC, Murdoch RM (1996) Perceived coping incapacity, non-satisfaction of needs and personality traits – influence on salivary ion concentrations in VDU postal letter coders. Psychophysiology in Ergonomics 1: 35-6.

Hinton JW, King AC, Burton RF, Murdoch RM (1996) Personality factors related to salivary sodium and potassium ion concentrations in workers doing repetitive VDU letter coding. Journal of Psychophysiology 10: 85.

§Hinton JW, Burton RF, Hardman P (1997) Psychophysiological indicators of examination-stress. An invited paper for the symposium: 'Emotional and Physiological Processes in Examination and Test Situations'. The Society for Stress and Anxiety Research (STAR) International Conference, Dusseldorf, July 14-16.

Hogg KJ (1994) The Effect of Different Degrees of Clinical Training on the Stress Levels of Nurses. Honours Psychology/Physiology BSc thesis, University of Glasgow.

Hogg KJ, Hinton JW, Burton RF (1995) Changes in salivary potassium and sodium in auxiliary, student and staff nurses when recalling the deaths of patients. Journal of Psychophysiology 9(2): 178.

Houtman ILD, Bakker FC (1991a) Stress and coping in lecturing, and the stability of responses across practice. Journal of Psychosomatic Research 35: 323-33.

Houtman ILD, Bakker FC (1991b) Individual differences in reactivity to, and coping with, the stress of lecturing. Journal of Psychosomatic Research 35: 11-24.

Kaiser J, Hinton JW, Krohne HW, Stewart R, Burton R (1995) Coping dispositions and physiological recovery from a speech preparation stressor. Personality and Individual Differences 19(1): 1-11.

Karasek RA (1979) Job demands, job decision latitude and mental strain: implications for job redesign. Administrative Science Quarterly 24: 285-308.

Kirschbaum C, Pirke KP, Hellhammer DK (1993) The 'Trier Social Stress Test': a tool for investigating psychobiological stress responses in a laboratory setting. Neuropsychobiology 28: 76-81.

Kyriacou C (1980) Stress, health and schoolteachers: a comparison with other professions. Cambridge Journal of Education 10: 154-9.

Kyriacou C (1987) Teacher stress and burnout. An international review. Educational Research 29(2): 146-52.

Kyriacou C, Sutcliffe J (1978) A model of teacher stress. Education Studies 4: 1-6.

Mackay C, Cox T, Burrows G, Lazzarini A (1978) An inventory for the measurement of self-reported stress and arousal. British Journal of Social and Clinical Psychology 17: 283-4.

McCrae RR, Costa PT (1986) Personality, coping and coping effectiveness in an adult sample. Journal of Personality 54: 385-406.

McLean A (1988) Salivary Potassium, Sodium and Cortisol Relating to Mental Test-Stress. Honours Psychology thesis, University of Glasgow.

Melin B, Lundberg U (1997) A biopsychosocial approach to musculoskeletal disorders. Journal of Psychophysiology 11: 238-47.

Morgan G (1991) Psystress – The Result of Perceived Coping Incapacity: An Investigation in a Clyde Shipyard. Honours Psychology thesis, University of Glasgow.

Munck A, Guyre PM, Holbrook NJ (1984) Physiological functions of glucocorticoids in stress and their relation to pharmacological actions. Endocrine Reviews 5: 25-44.

Obrist PA (1975) The cardiovascular–behavioral interaction – as it appears today. Psychophysiology 13: 95-107.

Parkes KR (1986) Coping in stressful episodes: the role of individual differences, environmental factors and situational characteristics. Journal of Personality and Social Psychology 51: 1277-92.

Poteliakhoff A, Carruthers M (1981) Real Health: The Ill Effects of Stress and Their Prevention. London: Davis-Poynter.

Pruessner JC, Schulz P, Hellhammer DH, Kirschbaum C (1997) Chronic stress, burnout and early morning free cortisol levels. 3rd European Congress of Psychophysiology, Konstanz, Germany, May 28-31.

Pruessner JC, Wolf OT, Hellhammer DH, Buske-Kirschbaum A, Von Auer K, Jobst S, Kaspers F, Kirschbaum C (in press) Free cortisol levels after awakening: a reliable biological marker for the assessment of adrenocortical activity.

Reid G (1997) School Organisation, Teachers' Work-stress and the Effect of an Intervention Programme. PhD thesis, University of Glasgow.

Richter P, Hinton JW, Meissener D, Scheller P (1995) Changes in salivary [K$^+$], [Na$^+$] and [K$^+$]/[Na$^+$] with varied test demands. Biological Psychology 39: 131-42.

Rissler A (1977) Stress reactions at work and after work during a period of quantitative overload. Ergonomics 20: 13.

Scheuch K (1995) Psychosoziale Einflussfaktoren auf die Entwicklung auf die Entwicklung und Leistungsfaehigkeit von Berufsgruppen im sozialen Bereich – theoretische und empirische Grundlagen der Untersuchungen. In Scheuch K, Vogel H, Haufe E (eds) Entwicklung der Gesundheit von Lehrern und Erziehern in Ostdeutschland. Dresden: Selbstverlag der Technischen Universitaet Dresden, pp. 1-21.

Scheuch K, Vogel H (1993) Praevelenz von Befunden in ausgewaehlten Diagnosegruppen bei Lehrern. Soziale Praeventivmedizin 38: 20-5.

Scheuch K, Knothe M, Misterek M (1992) Personen mit neurotischen Stoerungen in der Arbeitstaetigkeit: Beanspruchung und deren Bewaeltigung. In Proceedings of International Symposium, Arbeitsbedingte Erkrankungen – Praevention und Gesundheitsfoerderung, October, Linz. Vienna: Allgemeine Unfallversicherungsanstalt, pp. 120-3.

Schlenker BR and Leary MR (1982) Social anxiety and self-presentation: a conceptualisation and model. Psychological Bulletin 92: 641-69.

Selye H (1956) Stress. Montreal: Acta Inc.

Sosnowski T, Nurzynska M, Polec M (1991) Active-passive coping and skin conductance and heart rate changes. Psychophysiology 28: 675-82.

Sparks K, Cooper C, Yitzak F, Shirom A (1997) The effects of hours of work on health: a meta-analytic review. Journal of Occupational and Organisational Psychology 70: 391-404.

Sugisawa A, Nakijima K, Kikkawa T, Sugisawa H (1996) Factors related to health status of teachers working at public schools located in the metropolitan area. Bulletin of the Physical Fitness Research Institute. 90: 167-72.

Temml C (1995) Stress im Lehrberuf (eine oesterreichische Studie 1993). In Scheuch K, Vogel H, Haufe E (eds) Entwicklung der Gesundheit von Lehrern und Erziehern in Ostdeutschland. Dresden: Selbstverlag der Technischen Universitaet Dresden, pp. 115-24.

Theorell T, Karasek RA, Eneroth P (1990) Job strain variations in relation to plasma testosterone fluctuations in working men – a longitudinal study. Journal of Internal Medicine 227: 31-6.

Travers CJ, Cooper CL (1994) Psychophysiological responses to teacher stress: a move toward more objective methodologies. European Review of Applied Psychology 44: 137-46.

Venables P (1970) Electrolytes and Behaviour in Man. In Porten R and Birch J (eds) Chemical Influences on Behaviour. London: Churchill.

Vining RF, McGinley RA, Maksvytis JJ, Ho KY (1983) Salivary cortisol: a better measure of adrenal cortical function than serum cortisol. Annals of Clinical Biochemistry 20: 329-33.

Vogel H, Koch R, Haufe E, Silbernagel B (1994) Zur Geschlechtsspezifik im Erleben und Bewaeltigen beruflicher Belastungen – Ergebnisse der Dresdner Lehrerstudien. In Kunath H, Lochmann U, Straube R, Joeckel KH and Koehler CO (eds) Medizin und Information. Munich: MMV Medizin Verlag, pp. 683-5.

Wells AS (1997) Total Work-stress from Paid and Unpaid Work, and its Impact on Physiological and Psychological Unwinding. MA Honours Research thesis, Psychology Department, University of Glasgow.

Wells A, Hinton JW, Burton RF (1997) Psychophysiology of academics' work stress and 'unwinding' after work. The 25th Scientific Meeting of the British Psychophysiology Society, Glasgow, 1-3 September.

Willard HH, Merritt LL, Dean SA (1974) Instrumental Methods of Analysis (5 edn). New York: Van Nostrand.

Chapter 7
Teacher Support Teams

HARRY DANIELS, ANGELA CREESE AND BRAHM NORWICH

Introduction

In this chapter we will discuss one way in which schools may make it possible for teachers to cope with the stresses that they may experience when working with children with special educational needs in mainstream schools. We have based our discussion on our previous contribution to this topic (Daniels and Norwich 1996) The approach with which we are concerned does not focus directly on teacher stress, but rather it makes it possible for teachers to seek and obtain support for their own problem solving in school. In our evaluation studies we have obtained evidence that teacher stress may be reduced as a consequence of this form of support (Daniels and Norwich 1992, 1994; Creese, Daniels, and Norwich 1996; Creese, Norwich and Daniels, forthcoming a and b). This chapter is therefore not about therapeutic services for teachers. It is about support for teachers that may have some therapeutic effects. It attempts to deal with some aspects of what Clandinin and Connelly (1987) refer to as the emotional quality of personal knowledge in teaching.

Part of what makes an effective school is increasingly considered to be open and collaborative organisational structures. These should permeate the school's systems and allow participants to actively engage in shaping their changing circumstances (Nias 1987, 1989, 1993; Rosenholtz 1989; Fullan and Hargreaves 1992). The organisation of large secondary schools makes this difficult. The pastoral/academic divide, the subject specialisations of different curriculum departments, advisory and support departments with their particular expertise and the general culture of professional individualism that goes with teaching mean that it is difficult to develop these desired forms of collaboration.

The reasons for this professional individualism, as Nias (1993, p. 141) points out, 'are also profoundly cultural'. Both the training that teachers receive and the organisational structure of schools seem to discourage cultures that develop professional interaction and shared knowledge with other fellow teachers.

Collaboration and communication is even more important in times of change. Many classroom teachers feel that they do not have sufficient training and support to meet many of the challenges presented by children with special educational needs (SEN) in their classes. There are, of course, informal and formal support structures available in the school for teachers to discuss such issues with colleagues. However, as time becomes more and more of an issue for teachers (MacBeath, Boyd, Rand and Bell 1997) even informal talk in the staff room at breaktimes is becoming an increasingly scarce resource. In such a climate there is a need for quality time in which teachers can talk about their professional concerns regarding their classrooms, and through this, indirectly support their students in the learning process.

Many teachers find themselves working in school situations where they regularly teach large classes with little or no internal special needs support and where external resources are rarely available. Facing the task of meeting a wide range of needs in isolation can lead to acute stress or disaffection. This can happen to capable teachers working in unfavourable circumstances.

Changes to schooling over the last decade have increased demands on school teachers' time. The demands have arisen from heightened expectations on teachers to teach and assess the national curriculum in locally managed schools under a more stringent inspection system. National policy has been to engender greater competition between schools to raise attainment standards within the context of national and, now, school-level attainment targets. This drive has led to a reduced capability to cope with pupils who are difficult to teach and challenging to manage from within schools' own teaching resources. For example, there has been a significant increase in the exclusion of children from schools and record levels of statements for pupils with SEN. The introduction of the SEN Code of Practice (1993) has clarified schools' responsibilities towards pupils with SEN in the context of a general legislative commitment towards greater inclusion in the mainstream school. The Green Paper 'Excellence for all Children: Meeting Special Educational Needs' promotes concepts of inclusion and practices of collaboration.

Teacher support teams (TSTs) act as school-based problem-solving groups of teachers that function to support pupils indirectly through teacher collaboration. They are novel in that they are an example of a school-based development designed to give support and assistance to individual teachers. They may be seen to complement existing forms of SEN work within schools and existing patterns of informal mutual peer support as and when they exist. Staff approach their peers for support in understanding problems and designing appropriate forms of intervention related to learning and behaviour difficulties. These teams aim to enable staff to develop their confidence and competence in making provision for children with SEN in mainstream classes.

The TST development should be seen in the context of recent moves towards teaching more children with SEN in ordinary schools and the recognition of whole-school approaches to SEN (ILEA 1985; Galloway 1985; DES 1989; NCC 1989). In this respect, TSTs represent a practical embodiment of a school's commitment and policy for SEN. They have special relevance to schools now with the requirement in the Education Act 1993 and its associated Code of Practice that schools specify and publish their SEN policies and practices. This is in the context of the increasing difficulties faced by schools following the Education Reform Act 1988 to provide for SEN (Daniels and Ware 1990; Evans and Lunt 1992; OFSTED 1993; Visser and Upton 1993).

How do TSTs work?

The TST is a system of support from a team of peers for class teachers experiencing teaching difficulties in relation to special educational needs. Individual teachers request support on a voluntary basis from a team.

- Typically three teachers (the SEN co-ordinator, a senior teacher and another class teacher) serve as the core team, who call on outside support and advisory staff and parents when needed.
- Teams meet weekly or fortnightly with the teacher making a request for support – meetings last about 30 minutes each (usually during lunchtime or after school). A team member usually collects relevant information about the teacher's concern before the meeting.
- Typically one case is dealt with per meeting – either a new request or a follow-up. Unless a case is closed, a follow-up date is always agreed when the situation will be reviewed.
- Teams keep confidential notes about cases to enable follow-up work and a log of meetings.
- Teachers involved in meetings need to have some time release from other responsibilities.
- The principle and practical aspects of TSTs need staff and headteacher support.

For TSTs to operate successfully it would seem that there needs to be a clear specification of the kinds of teaching problems that could be referred by teachers to the teams. It is also vital that responsibility for referral is with class teachers, not the headteacher or TST teachers. One teacher needs to co-ordinate the work of the team using clear procedures for referral, conduct of meetings, analysis of the problems and design of interventions, implementation, records and follow-up of interventions. In practice referrals are often concerned with behaviour problems, although many are also about learning difficulties. Not all referrals may be about individuals; some may be about groups or classes.

Peer support in schools

TSTs differ from much of the informal peer support that is to be found in many schools in that they develop structured approaches to collaborative problem solving with an emphasis on follow-up and review. Teachers may often ask each other for advice. However these exchanges typically take place in the context of busy staff rooms in a very short space of time and rarely with any possibility of reviewing the effects of the advice. TSTs allocate a dedicated amount of time to a referring teacher, in a calm and peaceful setting in which issues may be discussed without interruption and in confidence. Crucially they embody the problem-solving cycle in that teachers are offered the opportunity to monitor and review the situation through follow-up meetings.

Peer support teams have been discussed in a variety of professional contexts. Quality circles (Karp 1983) are used in industry and have been developed in professional educational psychology (Fox, Pratt and Roberts 1990). In the area of mental health consultation, the work of Caplan (1970) has been influential and has been extensively applied, adapted and even mandated in some states of the US (Graden, Casey and Christenson 1985 a and b; Chalfant and Pysh 1989; Ritter 1978). In the US, a Department of Education task force (Will 1986) recommended that schools establish support systems for teachers as a way of responding to concerns about referral rates, misclassification of students, rising costs and the need to maximise opportunities for all students in the least restrictive environment (Chalfant and Pysh 1989). In England there has been much work on in-class support that focuses on the work of individual support teachers and SEN co-ordinators (Hart 1986; Garnett 1988; Dyson 1990), but little on support teams. The work of Hanko (1989, 1990) is the best-known example of a school consultation and group support approach. In her approach, school consultation is led by outside professionals in a way that mirrors some of the American work. She has offered this as an approach to meet the recommendations for teacher peer support systems that were made in the Elton Report (DES 1989, recommendation 6). Whereas Hanko acted as a group facilitator, Mead (1991) advocated task-oriented peer support groups (PSG) to increase the reflective nature of work in schools and thereby reduce teacher stress and increase teacher effectiveness. PSGs were seen to provide forms of organisational structure that reinforced informal social support and to result in greater feelings of ownership and personal competence. Chisholm (1994) also reports an evaluation of peer support approaches that were 'directed by teachers themselves within their schools and subsequently self-evaluated, according to their own criteria'. The Newcastle educational psychology service has also been involved in training teachers to act in a support capacity to their colleagues (Stringer, Stow, Hibbert, Powell and Louw 1992).

Teacher tolerance and active engagement

There is much prescription about managing schools that is relevant to SEN as well as much prescription about teaching pupils with SEN, but few specific theories about the conditions that affect the tolerance, capability and engagement of class teachers and schools in doing so. Gerber and Semmel (1985) and Gerber (1988) have developed a theoretical position on the costs to class teachers of extending their range of tolerance, which takes account of the purpose of class teaching, structural constraints and teaching resources. They suggest that in the context of limited resources that tolerance conditions the relation between equity and excellence. In using the concept of teacher tolerance we propose a number of theoretical assumptions. First, we suggest that pupils come to be seen by teachers as varying in their difficulty to teach and manage and that teachers have a range of teaching tolerance for variations in attainment and social behaviour. Beyond the limits of tolerance pupils come to be seen as unresponsive to teaching and can come to lower the teacher's perception of her/his teaching competence and therefore her/his professional self-evaluation. This can lead to feelings of insecurity and anxiety that, in turn, can result in less appropriate teaching and even further unresponsiveness from pupils. By this process teachers come to see certain pupils as beyond her/his teaching tolerance.

The range of tolerance is not a generic characteristic, but specific to each class and teacher, being influenced by pupil, teacher and school factors, including teaching materials and equipment, and teachers' teaching competence and confidence. Structural aspects – that is, the class size – and the purpose of class teaching, also influence tolerance. Underlying the concept of tolerance is the dynamic that class teaching involves a dilemma over aims for teachers. Specifically, the dilemma concerns whether:

- to seek an increase in the average attainment of the class (to seek excellence);
- to decrease the variation in class attainment (to seek equity).

The first aim involves a strategy of concentrating teaching time on the average to above average, because this is most likely to increase average class attainments. The second aim involves the contrary strategy of concentrating teaching time on the below average, as this is most likely to reduce variation of class attainment. This dilemma arises because of pupil differences in learning abilities and is significant because teaching resources, including time available for class teaching, are relatively fixed and scarce. It is assumed that teachers respond to this dilemma by achieving a balance between:

* bidding for and seeking more teaching resources;
* opting for ability setting / grouping;
* trying to transfer responsibility for difficult to teach pupils to others, such as support teachers, inside or outside their classes or referring for statutory assessment and statementing.

Part of the current integrationist climate is the expectation that teachers increase their range of teaching tolerance for pupils with SEN. By making increased tolerance legitimate it is often assumed that the range of tolerance can be readily increased. However, this has not been easy to achieve, particularly now in the context of a national educational policy to increase average school attainment levels without major increases in resources for schools (Daniels and Ware 1990). The effect is to weight the trade off even more towards increasing average class attainment.

Ironically those teachers with the most effective teaching strategies for low-achieving students might be those who report that they tolerate less maladaptive behaviour in their classrooms and that they may actively resist placement of handicapped students in their classrooms (Gersten, Walker and Darch 1988, p. 433)

Studies undertaken in the US suggest that there is a dilemma concerning quality of instruction and access to the mainstream class-room.

> The 'effective' teachers – those with high standards and low toler-ance for deviant behaviour – are those most likely to seek help in dealing with these problems. Moreover, the most successful teachers are those who efficiently use their instructional time. Therefore, one reason for the type of resistance identified in this study may be the effective teacher's attempt to guard against ineffi-cient use of academic instructional time, which could result in an overall decreased level of student performance. If the necessary technical assistance could be provided to implement teaching models that are effective for all students, it is likely that these skilled teachers with high standards would be the first to accept handicapped students into their classrooms. (Gersten, Walker, Darch 1988, p. 437)

What is needed to increase teaching tolerance, given the social psycholog-ical, structural, functional and resource conditions, is an organisational strategy to extend and make good use of existing teaching resources. TSTs, by enabling teachers to support each other and share their teaching competence, can provide one way to increase the range of teaching tolerance and enhance active engagement in providing quality teaching for pupils with SEN.

We have proposed the following dimensions to contrast TSTs with other kinds of school-based teacher groups and teams, such as staff and department administrative meetings, in-service training groups, curriculum and general planning groups, statement review groups, outside consultant groups and whole-staff case discussions. These dimensions do not represent absolute differences, but are a matter of degree and emphasis.

• Quick response with follow-up versus delayed response with less follow-up.
• Analysis of particular concerns/cases versus general planning for groups.
• Non-directed/voluntary versus directed/involuntary.
• Teacher/teaching focus versus learner/learning focus.

Using the first pole of each dimension, TSTs can be characterised and contrasted with the above-mentioned school groups and support approaches as involving a quick response with follow-up based on the analysis of particular teaching concerns where the focus is on the teacher who participates on a voluntary basis.

The way in which schools, both primary and secondary, approach pupils with SEN can be understood in terms of the processes of tolerance and active engagement at institutional and teacher levels. Active engagement and tolerance can be seen as complementary and interrelated processes with active engagement referring to the ways in which teachers and schools include and provide for the diversity of pupils, and tolerance referring to the limits of the challenges within which schools and teachers can operate. Active engagement involves planned attempts to provide quality learning opportunities for children with SEN, to include them in the general planning and teaching of all children. It is expressed in both curriculum and behaviour management at a school level, the level and quality of internal and external support for SEN and the differentiation of teaching and class management at teacher level. Tolerance, by contrast, involves enduring the challenges and unresponsiveness of pupils with SEN. At a school level, it is expressed through requests for external support, advice or exclusions, willingness to accept pupils with SEN, satisfaction with SEN policy and practices and complaints to parents and LEAs. At a teacher level, it is expressed by attitudes to integration and inclusion, by views about the feasibility and desirability of making classroom and teaching adaptations and by personal teaching priorities. It is indicated by teachers' perceptions of: (1) how well they can cope with the range of teaching challenges; and (2) the teaching demands made by children in their class.

Theoretical framework of active engagement and tolerance

The potential advantages of TSTs may be described as follows:

- as a school resource for collegial assistance and support;
- as a forum for teachers to share expertise and understanding;
- as a way of enabling teachers to develop their approaches to children with special educational needs;
- as a support for the implementation of stages 1 to 3 of the Code of Practice;
- as a system for schools to offer more effective provision for children with special educational needs in the context of local management of schools.

In the context of devolved and perhaps dwindling resources for meeting SEN, questions of cost-effectiveness spur the need for the development of services which make the best use of what is available. Teacher support teams offer the possibility of intervention that is distinctive by dint of the focus on teachers rather than children or school policy. They utilise the sadly under used resource of the potential support that consultation and collective problem solving can offer teachers. They also provide a way in which a school may structure and organise its response to the Code of Practice. In so doing they may well enhance and refine the role and effectiveness of the SEN co-ordinator. TSTs may support the formulation and review of Individual Education Plans (IEPs) as part of the practice of offering more general support to teachers. They may help schools to

	Active engagement	Tolerance
School level	• curriculum management • behaviour management • internal support activity • external links	• referral activity • willingness to accept pupils with SEN • support for SEN policy/practice • policy and practice for sanctions
Teacher level	• class organisation/pedagogy • class management • links with support	• concepts/reasons for support • attitudes to pupils with SEN • personal teaching priorities

Figure 7.1: Theoretical framework of active engagement and tolerance.

establish priorities in their negotiation for external support services. Issues raised in TSTs may also feed back into the institutional and SEN policy development planning process.

Responses to TSTs in action

Eight primary schools in the south-east of England undertook to set up and run TSTs. The Economic and Social Research Council (ESRC) funded a study that aimed to evaluate the processes of setting up and maintaining TSTs in addition to their short-term effects and perceptions of their usefulness. Baseline assessments were compared with follow-up assessments in order to assess any changes that might have resulted from TSTs. The evaluation used a mixture of quantitative and qualitative methods that focused on several dimensions relevant to schools' approaches to SEN. This included aspects of the schools' curriculum, behaviour and support systems; the teachers' approaches to teaching, behaviour management and work with outside support systems; the training of TST members and the setting-up process; the actual working of the TSTs; and the case outcomes and perceptions of TST usefulness.

The evaluation showed that TSTs were set up and run in six of the eight schools. In one of the other two schools a TST was set up but no referrals were received. This could be attributed to the way in which the senior teacher member of the team communicated the TST principle to colleagues as about personal counselling rather than work-related support. Staff in this school felt that they were already well supported and so they questioned the value of a TST for them. The other school set up a TST but had difficulties in running meetings. The teachers were in favour of the system but there were management and organisational difficulties in carrying through their commitment. This school was coping with a high degree of social disadvantage.

Most of the teachers in the other six schools were supportive of the TST arrangement. Referring teachers felt encouraged to request support, whereas only a minority of non-referring teachers felt unencouraged. The most common reason given by non-referring teachers for not requesting support was that they already had support from colleagues. Some reported that they did not have any teaching difficulties and others mentioned not being willing to consult particular colleagues who were in the TST.

TST meetings were between 30-45 minutes, usually during lunchtime or after school. In a few schools they were during the last period of the timetable in the afternoon, with some teaching cover arranged. Typically one case was dealt with per meeting, either a new request or a follow-up. There were between six and seven TST meetings on average per term across the six schools. Teams kept confidential notes about the cases to enable follow-up work, and a log of meetings. Most of the referrals were about behaviour problems, though many were about learning difficulties. Not all referrals were about individuals; some were about groups or classes. Support included providing emotional support and encouragement, specific approaches to managing behaviour, teaching strategies and consulting others, such as the headteacher, the educational psychologist and involving parents.

Teachers appear to be supportive of the TST concept and its practice. Teachers who have used TSTs state that it leads to increased confidence and that the strategies and approaches offered by the teams were workable and useful. All but one of the referring teachers reported that they would be happy to request support again. Most teachers (95%) felt that strategies and approaches offered by the TST were fairly or very workable. All were able to use them and all felt that they had been fairly or very useful. The majority (78%) had also used them with other children. This was true despite the fact that the approaches, strategies or materials suggested were already familiar to the teachers. 'Nothing new but of real value nevertheless' summarised a common attitude. Teacher support teams were seen to help teachers access relevant aspects of their own teaching competence. They saw the TST as giving them the chance to air problems in a sympathetic setting and that this enabled them to distance themselves from the problems and to re-examine what they were doing. One experienced class teacher commented:

> The teacher support team were really good and they reflected back and they said 'Look for goodness sake, you've actually been wonderful with this child'. I got some pats on the back and also some practical suggestions of help which didn't mean extra work for me it just gave me some support with dealing with it.

When teachers refer to a TST they are helped to cope with a difficult situation. Their increased confidence may lead to a situation appearing more tolerable. This is particularly the case when they find a way of engaging with a problem that had previously seemed intractable. In the words of an experienced class teacher:

> I think we have actually become more tolerant and we are developing our skills as a staff in dealing with that. We are getting together more and seeing that it's not just one person's problem but it is a problem that we share with the child and if we want our lives to be OK then we all have to have some input as well and help the child to make a valuable input as well.

An inexperienced teacher said:

> I've used it twice and I've found it very useful. Perhaps because I am an inexperienced teacher, I have only been teaching for a year,

I don't have strategies to cope with things and I do feel that there is a great sense of . . . I don't know when you go there it's not as if it's a major thing they just make you feel at ease about it really. The confidentiality as well, I know that it's not going to go any further and I do feel very relaxed about going in there. I do think it's working very well in the school because everyone is using it, everyone's booked up and they are all eager to get in there. It's working very well.

Referring teachers report significant benefits from finding that their perceptions of difficulty were validated and that the utility of their own intervention strategies were reaffirmed by TST teams. This was a significant source of encouragement.

I felt that I was 'allowed' to feel as frustrated as I was feeling, that it was quite understandable.

It was OK to have the feelings I did – and still is.

Although some of the suggested TST strategies were unfamiliar, most were not. The high level of satisfaction with advice indicates that TSTs acted to stimulate teachers to access a pedagogic competence that had already been acquired but was not available in their particular contexts. Non-referring teachers had distinct attitudes to TST. They either felt that it was not relevant to them or that, although it was not of immediate value, it might be of use in future. The following comments are from non-referring class teachers:

No, no I haven't had any contact at all with the TST in the time that it's been running. I think because I did feel that I was keeping on top of the class last year, I mean it drained me but I did feel able to cope and because of my network of contacts here I felt I was already receiving a lot of suggestions that I could put into practice.

I don't really mean to imply that it's a paper tiger, but I do think it could be just a sop. If they had hours allocated for support if you went to them or something, then I think it would be much more powerful and I might go along.

Headteachers became supportive of the TST in action. The confidential nature of TST activities made it difficult for them to comment on their usefulness. However, headteachers perceived no negatives in having a TST in the school. Where benefits were cited it was felt that TSTs led to a smoother running school with a happier staff. Some headteacher comments were:

> I don't know what problems I would have had to deal with myself if the TST hadn't been there because I am sure that it has diffused some situations that could have been worse had it not been there.

> I've so far been wrong because I didn't want it, I voted against it, I was very sceptical about it for, I thought, very sound reasons. My colleagues on the whole were very much in favour of giving it a go and without doubt they've been proved right.

TST members believe that they gain much from the TST experience; for example, the importance of listening, learning new teaching strategies and gaining confidence themselves. There was also a widespread view that TSTs positively affected the work of the SEN co-ordinators in that they increased awareness of SEN across the school.

Setting up TSTs in schools

Evaluations show that setting up TSTs depends on clear and detailed initial communications and negotiations between the schools and those with the development ideas and training resources. This involves the heads and the whole staff in understanding what is involved, considering what the TST arrangement has to offer the school and then deciding to commit the school and the resources to enable TSTs to work. In addition to these factors, evaluation indicates the importance of the whole staff and headteacher needing to support the principle of TSTs. School staff would therefore be given the choice to adopt the TST approach and to design it to fit the school's particular circumstances and needs.

Preparing a school for a TST should involve enabling participating teachers to:

- be familiar with the concepts and principles of school-based TSTs as providing peer support and meeting special educational needs;
- understand the function, risks, constraints of designing and running TSTs;
- have, through consultation with colleagues, designed an appropriate TST for their schools;
- be aware of and sensitive to the needs and feelings of the teacher making requests for support;
- be proficient in
  - receiving requests for support
  - conducting meetings
  - liaising with parents and support services
  - making sense of teaching problems

- devising appropriate forms of advice
- assessing outcomes in the classroom
- reviewing and evaluating the overall TST arrangement
- adapting team procedures.

Above all, team members need to be involved in simulations of the processes of analysing and conceptualising problems, deciding on intervention goals, planning and evaluating interventions. This involves consideration of issues common to many consultation settings such as active listening. If they are to function successfully, TSTs need to be designed to fit the perceived needs of the schools by the TST team and their colleagues.

How do arrangements work?

When a TST is being planned in a school there are a number of issues that need to be resolved. The following list may serve as an *aide-mémoire:*

- Who is the target population?
- Who can refer to the team?
- Some schools may wish to extend the TST principle to all staff including classroom assistants.
- Who serves on the team and how are they to be identified?
- Who co-ordinates the team?
- Receiving referrals
  - how many referrals may be handled at one meeting?
- Conducting meetings.
- Timing of meetings.
- How to make use of others
  - parents, psychologists, advisors, teacher
  - support services.
- How to co-ordinate and overlap with other support systems.
- How to make recommendations and gain access to resources.
- How to minimise the amount of recording in the design of recording sheets.
- How to follow-up recommendations.
- How to support and encourage team use.
- How to review and evaluate the team process.

TST members value the mutual support given by the regular meetings of networks of other schools running TSTs. The guidance given in the recent circular on the organisation of special provision provides strong support for the notion of such cross-school collaboration.

National survey

Although there is a widespread view that collaborative approaches play a crucial role in effective provision for pupils with special educational needs, there is little detailed knowledge about the nature and extent of collaborative teacher groups on a national scale. The aim of our study (Creese, Norwich and Daniels, forthcoming a) was to address this issue with a national survey. The results reinforce the point that collaborative opportunities in schools can serve to deal with the problem of isolation experienced by many teachers. The usefulness of collaborative teacher groups to special educational needs co-ordinators (SENCOs) and their work was clearly indicated in the data. A large majority of SENCOs indicated the usefulness of all the kinds of groups through their ratings and written comments. SENCOs also commented that collaborative teacher groups assisted in easing the implementation of the Code of Practice (CoP), led to more successful IEPs, increased the SEN's profile in the school, increased teacher confidence, helped in the pooling of resources and expertise, and created cohesion and consistency in schools' policies and practice.

Although all groups were found to be useful to the SENCOs, schools found it easier to run some types of teacher group than others. It is perhaps not surprising that, given the many comments on pressures of time and lack of other resources for running all the groups, it should be the teacher support group that was the most-used form of support run in schools. This group is an *ad hoc* gathering of teachers experiencing problems with a child or class. Its *ad hoc* nature suggests that the arrangements were less formal than many of the other groups, requiring less forward planning, document preparation and follow-up work. The least-used form of support was the TST for individual teachers. The reasons for this are not clear. Perhaps this was less likely in schools because this form of support starts with an individual teacher referring a problem for the group to discuss together. Providing such intensive support for one teacher may seem too costly for schools. Interestingly, cross-school collaborative groups also proved to be well used in our sample. Again, perhaps this is related to the savings that can be gained in terms of costs. Groups that met to review and plan IEPs were also popular. Comments indicate that such groups were often part of a school's SEN policy.

Smaller schools tended to find it easier to set up and run more forms of teacher support than the larger ones. Both the quantitative and qualitative data support this. It could be that a good flow of communication is difficult to achieve in large secondary schools, which can result in the professional isolation mentioned at the beginning of this chapter. Ironically, it is these schools – the ones that are likely to find it difficult to set up collaborative teacher groups – which have a greater need for these groups. In this chapter we have focused on the usefulness of collaborative teacher groups to SENCO's work. However, these groups are clearly important at many different levels, most obviously in sustaining and increasing teacher morale and confidence and thereby contributing to a positive ethos in the school.

The rate of return was low – 25%, n = 246 (all percentages have been rounded up to the nearest whole number) – this was interesting in itself. Of those who did reply, 89% (n = 218) reported running some form of teacher group involving support, whereas only 11% (n = 28) reported not running any form of teacher support. We think it possible that those schools not having any form of teacher support did not return the questionnaire, whereas those schools that did were eager to let us know what they were doing. This means that at least 25% of schools reported having some form of teacher group involving support. This is a low estimate and could even be higher. The highest percentage of schools ran three teacher groups but we were impressed by the high proportion running at least five groups – that is five, six or seven groups, some 22% of all schools running any groups. Yet, none of our surveyed school variables, the kind of school, SENCOs on the management team or the proportion of pupils with different degrees of SEN, differentiated between schools with more or less teacher groups. Further study is needed to examine other factors related to the degree of use of teacher groups. Relatively little is also known about the relationships between collaborative working, provision for the diversity of pupils, including those with SEN, and the currently popular school outcomes of public exams, test results, attendance and exclusions. This opens up important links between schools' improvement and provision for SEN and raises questions about the extent of formal and informal collaborative working in schools, what conditions support this kind of working and how this relates to provision for pupils with SEN.

Teacher groups and collaborative problem solving can play a central part in enhancing provision for SEN. As SENCOs, the key teachers in the sample schools that use such schemes, found them useful, we would venture to suggest that their wider use should be considered as a further way to improve whole-school approaches to SEN. Such schemes could become a key part of a school's SEN policy and practice. Schools could pursue this by engaging in a review of their formal and informal collaborative practices as the basis for deciding on their development needs in this area.

Conclusions

Our findings illustrated the pressing demands on schools and teachers of teaching the range of children in mainstream schools, and the extent to which schools organised their own internal support systems. Schools and teachers were dissatisfied overall with the level of internal support and wanted more external support services.

The secondary school Department for Education and Employment (DfEE) funded project (Creese, Daniels and Norwich, 1997) showed that teachers appreciate the value of collaboration as a principle and practice and its contribution to implementing the SEN Code of Practice. This means that governors and senior managers need to recognise teacher collaboration and support as an issue and ensure that it has a prominent place in school life. That is, they need to develop a common under-standing of how support systems relate to the needs of teachers and their pupils. Senior managers need to understand the implications of this in terms of time, money and management backing. Both informal and formal methods of teacher support and collaboration need therefore to be included in reviews as part of school development planning. The aims of support need to be clarified and the experience of teachers to be drawn upon. One way of gauging teachers' opinions about setting up and running of various forms of support, is to use a questionnaire to staff (for an example, see Creese, Daniels and Norwich 1997, p. 10). Our findings also suggested that SEN policy and practice were improved when based on collaborative problem solving. In schools where the staged system of the CoP and the writing of IEPs is overly bureaucratic, the TST can provide opportunities to discuss problems. It is best that TSTs be promoted as complementing existing schemes, not replacing them. If a school wishes to set up and run a TST, careful planning is needed. Consideration should be given to the membership of the team, publi-cising the team, the role of team members and the nature of referrals, amongst other factors (see Creese, Daniels and Norwich 1997, p. 14 for further details). In secondary schools, perhaps even more so than in primary schools, the complex nature of inter-departmental relationships, pastoral and academic systems and special systems means that TSTs depend on the commitment of time and resourcing from the SMT if the team is to fulfil its potential contribution to the school.

Setting up TSTs depends on clear and detailed initial communica-tions and negotiations between the schools and those with the develop-ment ideas and training resources. This involves the headteachers and the whole staff in understanding what is involved, considering what the TST arrangement has to offer the school and then deciding to commit the school and the resources to enable TSTs to work. Despite initial reservations about finding time for TSTs to meet with referring teachers, this did not turn out to be a problem once the time was committed. Our study also showed the importance of the training approach, which not only enabled TST members to simulate giving and receiving support, but to plan the process of setting up their TSTs with their school colleagues. Support teams were designed to fit the perceived needs of the schools by the TST team and their colleagues.

When teachers refer to a TST they are helped to cope with a difficult situation. Their increased confidence may lead to a situation appearing more tolerable. This is particularly the case when they find a way of engaging with a problem that had previously seemed intractable. Referring teachers found that their perceptions of difficulty were validated and enhanced and that the utility of their own intervention strategies were reaffirmed. This was a significant source of encouragement. Structured follow-up that permitted extended systematic discussion was also highly valued. This form of follow-up distinguishes TST from informal peer support, which TST was seen to complement.

Given appropriate conditions within the school, TSTs can make a significant difference to the quality of teaching and learning. Schools may become more actively engaged as organisations by not treating support as provided mainly by individual co-ordinators and support teachers to individual teachers. Difficulties may be dealt with more collectively and collaboratively. TSTs can also be seen to enable individual teachers to become more actively engaged with SENs in their class teaching through the systematic approach used by TSTs in analysing difficulties, making positive action suggestions and following-up referrals. TSTs may make it possible for schools to be more actively engaged with SEN in that better use may be made of staff resources and individual teachers may have opportunities to both rediscover and develop their own teaching knowledge and approaches. As such, the operation of TSTs has some contribution to make in alleviating some of the stresses of teaching.

Acknowledgements

We wish to acknowledge the support of the Economic and Social Research Council and the DfEE in funding the projects on which this chapter is based. For the primary school study: Evaluating Teacher Support Teams: A Strategy for Special Needs in Ordinary Schools. Award Number R-000-23-3859. For the secondary school study: Provision of a Teacher Centred Strategy for Implementing the SEN Code of Practice DfEE Contract Number: D/0254/112030.

References

Caplan G (1970) Theory and Practice of Mental Health Consultation. New York: Basic Books

Chalfant JC, Pysh M (1989) Teacher assistance teams: five descriptive studies on 96 teams. Remedial and Special Education 10(6): 49-58.

Chisholm B (1994) Promoting peer support among teachers in Gray P, Miller A and Noakes J (eds) Challenging Behaviour in Schools. London: Routledge.

Clandinin DJ, Connelly FM (1987) Teachers' personal knowledge: what counts as personal in studies of the personal. Journal of Curriculum Studies 19(6): 487-500.

Creese A, Daniels H, Norwich B (1997) Provision of a Teacher Centred Strategy for Implementing the SEN Code of Practice. Project Contract Number: D/0254/112030 Report to the DfEE.

Creese A, Norwich B, Daniels H (forthcoming a) Evaluating teacher support teams in secondary schools: supporting teachers for SEN and other needs.

Creese A, Norwich B, Daniels H (forthcoming b) The prevalence and usefulness of collaborative teacher groups for SEN: results of a national survey.

Daniels H, Norwich B (1992) Teacher support teams: an interim evaluation report. London: Institute of Education, London University.

Daniels H, Norwich B (1994) Evaluating Teacher Support Teams: A Strategy for Special Needs in Ordinary Schools. Final report to ESRC— award number R-000-23-3859.

Daniels H, Norwich B (1996) Supporting teachers of children with special needs in ordinary schools. In Upton G and Varma V (eds) Stresses in Special Educational Needs Teachers. Aldershot: Arena.

Daniels H, Ware J (1990) Special Educational Needs and the National Curriculum, the Impact of the Education Reform Act. Bedford Way Series. London: Kogan Page.

DES (1978) Special Educational Needs (Warnock Report). Cmnd 7212 . London: HMSO

DES (1989) Discipline in Schools (Elton Report). London: HMSO.

DfEE (1997) Excellence for All: Meeting Special Educational Needs Green Paper. London: HMSO.

Dyson A (1990) Effective learning consultancy: a future role for special needs co-ordinators. Support for Learning 5(3): 116-27.

Evans J, Lunt I (1992) Developments in special education under LMS. London: Institute of Education, London University.

Fox M, Pratt G, Roberts S (1990) Developing the educational psychologists work in the secondary school: a process model for change. Educational Psychology in Practice 6(3): 163-9.

Fullan M, Hargreaves A (1992b) What's Worth Fighting for in Your School? Buckingham: Open University Press/OPSTF Buckingham.

Galloway D (1985) Schools, Pupils and Special Educational Needs. London: Croom Helm.

Garnett J (1988) Support teaching : taking a closer look. British Journal of Special Education 15(1): 15-18.

Gerber MM (1988) Tolerance and technology of instruction: implication for special education reform. Exceptional Children 54(4): 309-14.

Gerber MM, Semmel MI (1985) The micro-economics of referral and re-integration: a paradigm for evaluation of special education. Studies in Educational Evaluation 11: 13-29.

Gersten R, Walker H, Darch C (1988) Relationship between teacher's effectiveness and their tolerance for handicapped students. Exceptional Children 54(5): 433-8.

Graden JL, Casey A, Christenson SL (1985a) Implementing a pre-referral intervention system. Part 1: The model. Exceptional Children 51: 377-84.

Graden JL, Casey A, Christenson SL (1985b) Implementing a pre-referral intervention system. Part 2: The data. Exceptional Children 51: 487-96.

Hanko G (1989) After Elton – how to manage disruption. British Journal of Special Education 16(4): 140-3.

Hanko G (1990) Special Needs in Ordinary Classrooms, Supporting Teachers. Oxford: Blackwell.

Hart S (1986) Evaluating support teaching. Gnosis 9: 26-32.

ILEA (1985) Equal opportunities for all? (Fish Report). London: Inner London Education Authority.

Karp HB (1983) A Look at Quality Circles – 1983 Annual for Facilitators, Trainers and Consultants. Baltimore MD: University Associates

MacBeath J, Boyd B, Rand J, Bell S (1996) Schools Speak for Themselves: Towards a Framework for Self-Evaluation. London: National Union of Teachers.

Mead C (1991) A City-Wide Evaluation of PSG Training. Birmingham: Birmingham Local Education Authority.

National Curriculum Council (1989) Circular Number 5. London: National Curriculum Council.

Nias J (1987) Seeing Anew: Teachers' Theories of Action. Deakin: Deakin University Press.

Nias J (1989) Primary Teachers Talking. London: Routledge.

Nias J (1993) Changing Times, Changing Identities: Grieving for a Lost Self. In Burgess R (ed.) Educational Research and Evaluation for Policy and Practice. London: Falmer Press.

OFSTED (1993) Education for disaffected pupils 1990-92. London: Department of Education.

Ritter DR (1978) Effects of school consultation program on referal patterns of teachers. Psychology in the Schools15(2): 239-43.

Rosenholtz S (1989) Teachers' Workplace: The Social Organization of Schools. White Plains, NY: Longman.

Stringer P, Stow L, Hibbert K, Powell J, Louw E (1992) Establishing staff consultation groups in schools. Educational Psychology in Practice 8(2): 87-96.

Visser J, Upton G (1993) Special Education in Britain after Warnock. London: Fulton.

Will M (1986) Educating Students with Learning Problems: a Shared Responsibility. Washington: US Department of Education, Office of Special Education and Rehabilitative Services.

Chapter 8
The Benefits of Whole-school Stress Management

JACK DUNHAM AND VIVIEN BATH

There are good reasons for recommending the benefits of whole-school approaches to stress management for staff. The first of these is the very strong evidence that one of the major causes of work stress is the school organisation. This evidence is clearly presented in the chapters in this book by Kyriacou, Brown and Ralph, and Travers and Cooper.

The significance of organisational factors in understanding staff stress can be seen in the following summary of Dunham's consultation with a primary school teacher who wrote to him in November 1996:

> I have recently read your book 'Stress in Teaching' and noted with interest that you are a freelance stress management consultant. I am in my second year of infant school teaching and much as I enjoy the work, I am also finding it very stressful. I would be interested in having a consultation with you regarding this – either on a one-to-one basis or within the context of a workshop/group situation.

Dunham visited her in her flat in December 1996 and after the consultation he prepared a stress review and action plan and sent it to her. These are the details:

The stress review and action plan (1)

Pressures at school and at home

- Working with colleague suffering from myalgic encephalitis, in very difficult and frustrating planning meetings, who makes me angry and anxious.
- So many things to do at work – e.g. record-keeping, filing, planning, displays, working with emotionally disturbed children and 'difficult' parents.

139

- Derogatory statements about me made to me by my colleague.
- I have derogatory thoughts – poor self-image sometimes – 'I will be sacked if . . .' (I do or I don't do).
- Health hassles.
- Financial worries.
- Big upheaval in move to flat.

Stress reactions

- I feel 'I'm no good'.
- Worried about being sacked.
- Angry, edgy and anxious inside but do not express my feelings in school – cannot say to colleagues 'I've had (am having) a bad day/interview with parent etc. . . .' because school climate is 'this is a cheerful school'.
- 'I feel very inadequate'.
- 'Feeling overwhelmed by work, cannot think clearly'.
- Sometimes tearful.
- Exhausted.
- Perhaps colitis and colds.

Positive actions/resources

- Swimming.
- Boyfriend.
- Girl friends.
- Tutor.
- Dad.
- Cognitive therapy.
- Supportive head.
- Usually well organised.

More positives for action as soon as possible:

- Vitamin B complex tablets.
- Relaxation tapes.
- More assertiveness learning/practice.
- Learning to work more comfortably and confidently with my mentor.
- Positive thoughts.
- No work for school on Sundays.
- Ask headteacher for appraisal.

At the end of this first consultation a second was agreed and Dunham visited her again in February 1997. After this discussion he sent her a follow-up stress review and action plan. These are the details of the second one.

The stress review and action plan (2)

Pressures

- Things are better with my colleague but she still tells me what to do.
- The frustration of preparing lessons which I cannot teach because the assistants are absent.
- The children are difficult to control.
- A few of the children are very clever at winding me up.
- The classroom assistants are unreliable.
- What upsets me most is my colleague's attitude to education – she bullies children and will not allow them to express themselves.

Stress reactions

- Still have occasional feelings of 'going under'.
- High blood pressure.
- A lot of absence from school because of illness (not all of it stress related).
- I get really snappy with the children, which makes me feel guilty.
- I feel angry with the children and try not to show it to them but I still feel guilty.
- I have feelings of being no good at my job.

Strategies and resources added since last review

- Improved relationships with my mentor and stepmother.
- Christmas at home was good.
- Very good news about starting work as a reception teacher after summer holiday.
- Yoga, aerobics and massage.
- Approached headteacher a lot more and am more able to express my feelings about the work and my reactions to it.
- I have not felt so threatened in the Wednesday meetings with my colleague and my mentor.

More positives for action plan as soon as possible

- Listen to the relaxation tape in convenient parts.
- Be firm about no school work on Sundays.
- Be firm about appraisal with headteacher in summer term.
- Learn and practise when possible the skills of being assertive with children to prevent the build-up of suppressed anger.
- To continue being assertive with my colleague – it works!
- Explore the countryside around where we live with boyfriend.

A further consultation was arranged for March should she feel that it was necessary. Shortly before the date of the proposed consultation she rang to say that she did not now think it was necessary as things had improved so much at school.

There were no stress-management policies, programmes or plans in her school. Her approach to understanding and reducing her work stress was individual and outside school. In our experience this approach is still used by many teachers. The reason for it has been clearly stated by two of the contributors to this book in their report of a recent research project:

> What we found most strongly expressed in the many self-reports and interviews was that in Britain at least there appears to be a major stigma attached to the idea that individual teachers suffer from stress and often our respondents were afraid to discuss this for fear that it might indicate to colleagues and superiors that they were not up to the job. (Brown and Ralph 1997, p. 17)

The need to remove this isolating and inhibiting stigma is the second reason for advocating a whole-school stress-management programme. The removal of stigma is a major goal in Dunham's approach to stress management in schools, which he developed in an attempt to help teachers on his courses achieve a number of objectives related to organisational stress. These included:

* how to avoid stress;
* coping strategies;
* how to help people smile and stay sane;
* how to improve the quality of life within school;
* how to reassure colleagues;
* survival skills;
* how to provide active support for colleagues.

His programme for reducing teachers' stress has six parts:

* acceptance of stress;
* learning to understand the meaning of occupational stress;
* beginning to tackle the problem by identifying the major pressures at work (Stress Audit 1);
* identifying and sharing the strategies used to cope with these pressures (Stress Audit 2);
* recognising the signs of stress (Stress Audit 3);
* developing personal and whole-school stress-management programmes and policies.

The first part, the acceptance of stress, is essential for the successful implementation of the whole programme. It can be effectively blocked by the barrier of stigma and cynicism of colleagues who associate stress with failure, incompetence and weakness. If schools arrange stress conferences without tackling this first concern, even though they have well-organised plenary and group work sessions, the result can be mainly a cosmetic exercise of lists of time management, relaxation and assertiveness skills which may not affect staff attitudes and feelings.

The second task of the programme is an understanding of the meaning of stress. Dunham has noted that teachers find it helpful and reassuring to think of stress as a significant increase of pressures beyond their coping strategies resulting in stress reactions, rather than thinking of stress as a personal problem or sign of weakness.

The third part of the programme emphasises beginning to develop a policy in school based on a stress audit. A stress audit has assumed greater significance recently because of the health and safety legislation that defines the 'duty of care' responsibilities of employers for their employees. This legislation states quite clearly that, in order to carry out the 'duty of care' responsibilities, employers must make a proper assessment of the risks to the mental and physical well-being of their employees from their working conditions. This is usually carried out by means of a stress audit, which attempts to answer a number of questions. These include:

- What levels of stress exist within our organisation?
- Are job satisfaction and physical and mental health better in some parts of our organisation than in others?
- Does it look as if we have a problem – if we do can we identify its causes: what appear to be the stressors?
- Are the stressors departmental or organisational?
- Are some of the stresses time- or site-specific – for example, in the playground, at school dinners, break or leaving school, or on a wet-weather day?

Stress audits typically take the form of a self-report questionnaire although diagnostic instruments such as the Occupational Stress Indicator (Cooper, Sloane and Williams 1988) are increasingly being used. Another alternative is to ask employees to keep a stress diary in which they record any stressful events they encounter during the course of a working day (Earnshaw and Cooper 1996, pp. 16-23). Sutherland, cited in Smith (1997), has warned against 'simply opting for a standard measure such as the OSI (Occupational Stress Indicator) rather than taking the trouble to develop something organisation specific that will yield a much more detailed picture'. (Smith 1997, p. 11)

A good example of a school developing something 'organisation specific' can be seen in the following stress audit that was prepared for Dunham's first visit to a secondary school as its consultant. He was asked to prepare a report on his analysis of stress in the school and present his recommendations to the school development committee for managing it more effectively. He interviewed teachers from each of the groups on the following list and based the interviews on the teachers' replies when they were asked for two responses to the task in Table 8.1.

Table 8.1: Task administered to each subject group
Jack Dunham – Education Consultancy

Task: State two responses from your group. What elements of school life should Jack focus upon in his research at the school?

Humanities	1 Juggling with so many demands (sense of failure through not completing tasks) 2 Balancing status against workload against responsibility against colleague's expectations
Arts	1 Managing, maximising people resources – teaching and non-teaching staff 2 Forward planning skills in the face of uncertainty and unpredictability 3 Matching staffing skills to curriculum needs in a time of contraction
PE	1 Role conflict by staff in the PE area – pastoral commitment as year heads 2 Rooming facilities – conflicts between PE/arts needs
English	1 Volume of administrative work/documentation set against student contact 2 Uncertainty of national curriculum developments/changes 3 Class size
Science	1 Communication/decision making/prioritising within the school – senior management planning 2 Areas of stress over which we may seem to have no control
Tutorial	1 Problems associated with the duality of roles set alongside and parallel to the evolution of role away from original job description 2 The conflict experienced due to the immediacy of certain tasks. What is 'now' becomes most important
Languages	1 Wanting to do our job effectively, given a finite time and an increasing work load 2 Looking at the work load over the school year
Mathematics	
Technology	1 Identifying things that cause stress (a) that we can do something about; (b) that we may not be able to control 2 Working with senior management to support them in managing priorities

Table 8.1: cont.

Marketing	1 The structures of school – responding to changes in the environment, using the technology we have, or care to devise 2 Establishing more points of contact with the environment, collegial structure in the school
Non-teaching	1 Clear liaison between management and non-teaching staff 2 Being valued within the school 3 Having a voice in school affairs; not being involved in decisions 4 Meetings provision for non-teaching staff

A stress audit, whatever form it takes, can yield helpful information not only about stressors but also about two other parts of Dunham's six-part framework. These are the fourth and fifth parts – identifying and sharing coping strategies and recognising the signs of stress. He also uses the audit method to prepare for stress management workshops. A brief questionnaire is sent to the participants in good time before each workshop giving them adequate time to complete it and return it to him. When he recently conducted workshops for the members of teams in a service for special educational needs he used the following questionnaire and received the following replies to the questions from the 15 members of the workshop, whose roles were support teacher – special educational needs (4); early years hearing impaired teacher (4); emotional and behaviour support teacher (4); visually impaired support teacher (1); visually impaired resources co-ordinator (1); centre manager – family centre (1).

The questionnaire

(Each number identifies the reported pressures, coping strategies, stress reactions and recommended stress-management strategies of each member of the workshop.)

> **Coping with stress: skills and strategies**
> with Jack Dunham
> At: The Conference Centre
> On: Tuesday 15th January 1996, 9.15 am – 4.30 pm.

In preparation for this workshop Jack Dunham has asked if members would please complete this questionnaire. It is anonymous.

What are your major pressures at work?

1. Getting from school to school on time; difficult SENCOS (special educational needs co-ordinators in ordinary schools); extra unplanned work.
2. Effective management of time; timing appointments; keeping on time; managing work effectively as I work part

time; sometimes feel under pressure to work; make phone calls from home when I am not working which leads to difficulties with my children; effective communication skills with 'difficult' families.

3. Completing the necessary documentation and report writing for the caseload in the time allocated.
4. Overload – too little time; working with young people in crisis; working with organisations in crisis (schools/social services); admin.
5. No one to delegate to generally; very distracting work environment – difficult to concentrate.
6. Paperwork – meeting deadlines; staff in school where I work seeing me as the 'expert' – asking my advice for resources/ideas/information.
7. Saying 'No' – I find this very hard.
8. Fear of the way things may develop in the future.
9. Organising time – peripatetic – driving involved; demands made by colleagues – prejudices of colleagues.
10. Feeling I have to prove myself in schools because I feel the staff don't know why I'm there or what I do; feeling that other staff seem to want to catch me out (my perception probably).
11. Balancing my home commitments – emotionally and in terms of house management skills with work; the major pressure at work is to provide a quality service that often involves working in my own time – I always feel I can cope but is that good enough?
12. Numbers of referrals – limited time to do the sort of work sometimes required, such as long-term counselling; follow-up visits to staff; work with parents; meetings – very often a complete waste of time.
13. Isolation – I work on my own; my intimate knowledge of the children in my caseload and their difficulties some of which are beyond my ability to solve.
14. Trying to balance the very different aspects of the role – management, teacher, advisor, counsellor; trying (unsuccessfully) not to feel constantly guilty.
15. Meeting deadlines, which involves working at home in the evenings – I'm usually too tired by the time I've put my little boy to bed to do any work.

What strategies do you use to cope with these pressures?

1. Try to plan ahead and not to feel too guilty if time-scales cannot be met due to unavoidable circumstances; use 'switch-off' mode if the problem is someone else's and they are trying to make it mine; try to use a realistic appraisal of what I can

take on and what I cannot (this doesn't always work).

2. Timing – try to cram things into the day and often don't leave enough time for travel etc.; try to be more disciplined with time but find it hard to walk out of an overrunning meeting for the next appointment; hard to draw a visit to a close when there is a need to stay longer – and thus overrun.
3. More effective planning of my time.
4. Work late regularly; supervision; make constant lists.
5. Prioritise work; have certain times when I shut myself away to concentrate.
6. Make notes in my diary warning me that the time is approaching for a report or review of a child's progress, etc.
7. Try to be more organised; drive faster.
8. Occasionally saying 'No'; coming in to catch up with work at weekends; try to put it to the back of my mind.
9. Talk things through with colleagues; avoid conflict.
10. I keep a private note of the good relationships I have with my pupils so as to prove to myself that I am worthwhile; our house is small and we are adding an extension of a study – partly for me.
11. I find sitting down at home with a glass of wine and the newspaper after a long day very relaxing. The trick is to think of things that are nothing to do with home or work – I can usually face anything after this. I find the only way to cope with pressures of work is to spend time on all the planning/reports etc. as this provides peace of mind; I need to feel satisfied with my own quality of service.
12. Gardening – totally relaxing – the plants are silent. I am a member of a martial arts group – great for getting rid of aggression and tension. Bee-keeping – far more stressful than the job!
13. Arrange to meet weekly with colleagues; peer supervision for work issues; arranging projects that require creativity.
14. I try to laugh and bring in a light-hearted approach where possible. I am trying to delegate more and take on less where appropriate.
15. Don't know – just try to be organised so as soon as my son is in bed I can work.

What are you stress reactions if your coping strategies are not effective?

1. Headaches, or I get very tired.
2. Frustration at being late for next appointment – rushed and tense at times.
3. Take it out on the family at home.
4. I get angry and tearful; I become ill.

5. I become flustered.
6. Anxiety, tiredness, outer calm but inner irritability; feeling of being swamped; loss of confidence in myself.
7. Tiredness, low self-esteem, depression.
8. Inability to think straight so less gets done; eating too much; worry, tiredness, forgetting things.
9. I become irritated by family; opt out of home 'chores'.
10. Moan; crave a drink; shut off from family and feel irritable; feel nervy and flustered.
11. If I can't unwind at some stage then I feel very resentful and cheated. I become short-tempered. If I can't do the work I feel I need to do, I worry. The irony is that one can usually cope with the next day through thinking on one's feet.
12. Intense headaches; extreme lethargy; lack of interest in food; smoking; very tetchy with my own family; feeling isolated and becoming isolationist.
13. Angry with my family; tired – too tired to prepare evening meals leading to a poor diet; too tired to think about social activities; feel I don't have time to listen to my children.
14. Waste time – half starting things until another thought or task comes along and then changing to that. Net result – nothing of importance is actually accomplished and the sense of panic as the ever-increasing tasks mount!
15. I shout at my husband; I become moody.

What recommendations do you have for helping yourself and your colleagues to cope more effectively with work pressures and stress reactions?

1. More realistic time management perhaps. Many situations of stress are triggered by others and catch me unawares! I am sending this in but I assume that you will just repeat a standard programme and therefore it will be very difficult to be specific.
2. Sometimes I need to look at day-to-day issues with a broader perspective; stand back and try to look at situations objectively; have realistic time scales for achieving set targets; also take a hold at times on the fact that 'there is more to life than work'.
3. Share problems with colleagues and inform team leaders.
4. Time management and organisation; take time out; aromatherapy; massage; exercise.
5. Keep calm; prioritise and use time management effectively.
6. An early night with a good book now and again; make time (at weekends) to relax – 'taking the night off'; aromatherapy massage; bottle of Chablis!

7. Talking to colleagues; sharing experiences to help put work in perspective; yoga; outside interests like badminton.

8. Saying 'No' more – but this is not always possible. Try to face possibilities and work out how I would cope with them if they happened.

9. More open discussion of time management; slimming down of non-essential paperwork; stable goalposts; improved communications.

10. Write lists of things to do; plan free time and shut off; make long- and short-term plans; give yourself something to look forward to; count your successes, however little (in this job there aren't enough).

11. Treat yourself to sauna/jacuzzi/work out. Set yourself more realistic goals. Don't try to be superwoman. Buy a cream cake. Make time for yourself – time spent on yourself is never time wasted. PS: any suggestions for coping with interviews gratefully received – I tend to have sleepless nights and worry excessively before one – with the new authority emerging there may be a few interviews on the horizon.

12. Humour – sharing ludicrous reactions; talking about interests other than work; being entirely honest with clients/staff/colleagues about levels of skill, times, dates and locations of type and nature of possible work; being 'real' – empathising, listening and responding as 'another colleague' rather than the so-called emotional and behaviour disorders specialist.

13. Time together to discuss work and social life; sharing work issues and difficulties; time together to solve problems.

14. Prioritise and complete top level tasks first; have clearly established work times with no phone interruptions and a DO NOT DISTURB sign on the door; keep one book for tasks, phone calls etc. and write things down; check frequently and cross off tasks; develop an effective filing system; minimise paperwork and file regularly; build in write-up time after 'teaching' times.

15. None – I'm hoping somebody is going to offer me some.

These responses of the workshop members which are typical of the other six workshops for the service for special educational needs again provide strong support for the recommendations that the European Commission has recently re-stated for creating a policy on stress.

European Commission Recommendations

Not all organisations will have a problem with stress. Problems are more likely to come to light and be dealt with early and effectively, however, if organisations adopt a clear policy on stress in consultation with their employees or their representatives, and make it part of their general management arrangements.

The key to the success of any policy is to show that it has the full support and commitment of those at the very top. It is also important to ensure that all involved:

- take action to raise awareness of the issue;
- acknowledge that work-related stress is not a personal problem nor a weakness but an issue that the organisation as a whole can address;
- encourage people to come forward when problems seem to be emerging and make stress awareness part of management systems. (European Commission 1997, p. 10)

These recommendations may be used as a very helpful framework of expectations to guide those members of senior management teams in schools who daily are attempting to solve the serious problems caused by staff stress. They can also be used by workshop leaders and consultants to evaluate their efforts, for example.

Dunham's evaluation of these special educational needs service workshops was that the director of the service was closely involved in their planning and preparation and in the actual work in the conference centre. He sent out the questionnaires to those people who had applied and forwarded them to Dunham when they had been completed and returned to him. He came to the conference centre during each workshop. Dunham made a report to him of the workshop members' problems and recommendations (with their permission) after each workshop and to the team leaders of the service at one of their regular meetings. Stress-management resources, such as a copy of Dunham's relaxation tape, were made available at each of the team's work bases. It is fair to say that the workshops raised awareness in the service that work-related stress is an issue that the organisation as a whole could and should address. The recommendations of the workshop members pointed the way for effective action plans to be introduced to strengthen personal, interpersonal, organisational and community strategies.

Inviting recommendations for the reduction of work stress from staff is the sixth and final part of Dunham's whole-school model. The significance of this part has been noted by Brown and Ralph as a:

Focus on the importance of teacher voice as a bridge between organisational and personal stress reduction policies. These voices need to be heard at the whole school level and senior management teams need to adopt a considered approach to the management of staff stress. Only an organisational approach can provide the appropriate help for all teachers (NUT 1990). What schools need is a coherent strategy that recognises the importance of stress as a crucial personnel management issue and this incorporates stress-related issues into the school strategic development plan. (Brown and Ralph 1997, p. 17)

It is important to remember that a whole-school plan, policy and programme for stress management includes non-teaching staff as well as teachers. The recommendation for support staff involvement is important because in a whole-school model of staff care they are fully integrated into the stress-management programme and in the development of support groups. They should be members of the school's stress- management committee, which should not be dominated by senior management and should include representatives from every level of responsibility and faculty.

Implementing a stress-management policy in a sixth-form college

Dunham (1992, p. 184) has given more details of how all the different members of the support staff can be included in a school's development programme and so enabled to make strong contributions to it. He has reported that, after his involvement as a consultant during a stress-management training day, decisions were taken by the senior manage-ment team to improve the management structure and practice in a sixth-form college. These were successfully implemented and in a six-month review of progress the following changes were noted:

- Office staff have access to all meetings in the college.
- A non-teaching and teaching staff support group was started. It meets weekly and it acts as a focus for the identification of new pressures on staff.
- The senior management team has tried hard to respond to the demands from the support group.
- A year plan has been placed on a wall in the staff room providing information about dates, deadlines and activities.
- Steps have been taken to reduce role conflict by improving role defin-ition. The management structure in the college has been redrafted to clarify all roles and areas of responsibility – including the kitchen staff. (Dunham 1992, p. 184)

These are good grounds for suggesting that the college is beginning to enjoy the benefits of a whole-school approach, which have been proposed as: 'working from a common understanding, addressing common issues and sharing common skills, practices and approaches' (Rogers 1996, p. 70).

Importance of middle management

Dunham also has sought to gain recognition for the key middle manage-ment roles in the implementation of whole-school approaches. He has reported the perceptive observations and recommendations of very experienced heads of year, departments and faculties (Dunham 1994, pp. 129 41). Three excerpts from their small school-based action research projects are included here to illustrate the wide range of their potential contributions. The first excerpt from a project report is an attempt to delineate the management responsibilities of middle managers:

> Middle managers have a responsibility to provide different types of support to members of their team. This might range from a weekly meeting with a probationary teacher to delegating parts of the management role to another member of the team who is interested in taking on more responsibility. Middle managers have to be sensitive to the pressures on particular people and within certain constraints give them special consideration, such as an appropriate timetable or spread of classes. It is also vital that they receive appropriate training about running meetings, appraisal, time management and good communications. They should constantly be updating their skills.

The second report is concerned with the significance of middle management roles in the effective introduction and implementation of changes in the school:

> The middle manager is often a key person when changes are being introduced. This may put them in a position where they are on the receiving end of other people's stress. Their role is also difficult because they act as an intermediary between the team and the senior management of the school . . . Stress is not just a personal matter, it can also have a domino effect, for example, one team member undergoing severe stress can put the cohesion of the whole team at risk if this is not managed sensitively.

The third brief observation is concerned with the crucial impact of middle managers' attitudes and actions on the well-being of their colleagues:

> The implications of a failure of middle managers to recognise and deal with stress in themselves and their colleagues are enormous. The build up of stressors over recent years means that without the necessary coping strategies, more teachers will suffer stress-related conditions. Effective middle managers hold the key to promoting the adoption of coping resources. They know their teams, they are aware of the limits that their teams can operate within and they are able to deal with their teams' stress because they have the ability to deal with their own.

Implementing a stress-management policy in a secondary school

Bath has recently taken early retirement from the post of Deputy Head of a comprehensive school. She has been involved in preparing and implementing the school's policy of 'caring about staff' for more than 10 years. This policy aims to promote the development of the school as a healthy community for staff and pupils. The policy is implemented through a number of strategies:

- The management of staff development is concerned with meeting the needs of all members of the teaching and non-teaching staff.
- There is a staff development working party made up of representatives from all areas of the school in order to achieve full consultation and participation in the school's aims and policies. There is a two-way feedback between the working party and the faculties and support staff.
- Individual consultation with the head of faculty in a yearly staff development review is organised during an in-service education and training (INSET) day in the spring term.
- Individual consultation is also available with any member of the senior management team if a member of staff wants to talk to about work problems.
- An important thrust of the policy is to reduce the stress of the heads of faculty through the support of the senior management team.
- The senior management team reduces its work pressure by staff review interviews, weekly meetings that have a non-business part (in which concerns about individual teachers are discussed and decisions are taken as to the appropriate action – for example, a concern about the health of a teacher leads to a decision about which member of the stress-management team should support that teacher) and off-site whole-day sessions for strategic planning and training in effective teamwork.
- The governors' personnel committee regularly reviews staff stress and the senior staff development teacher has conducted a stress audit.
- A supply teacher induction booklet has been produced (*A Guide for New and Visiting Staff 1997-98*).
- The induction programme for newly qualified staff is being reviewed and a network of local schools is planning to run its own programme in addition to the local education authority programme. A senior staff development teacher sees newly qualified teachers (NQTs) individually and in groups. A subject mentor is appointed from the faculty to monitor their progress and to observe their lessons.
- The induction programme for new experienced staff is the responsibility of the heads of faculty, whose job description includes the requirement 'to induct and support newcomers to the school'. These new experienced teachers are also invited to join the appropriate sessions of the programme for NQTs – for example, the special needs teaching in the school.
- Staff who are promoted internally have a mentor.

- One of the governors is a psychologist who advises on issues related to stress-management counselling.
- A high quality of physical care is expressed through the maintenance of high standards by the provision of a desk for each member of staff, clean and attractive toilets and the employment of a person to make coffee for staff and to keep the kitchen clean.

Recommendations for the implementation of an effective stress-management policy and programme may also be obtained from outside the school. Examples of best practice for stress management in organisations have been reported by the Industrial Society (1995) after a survey of 11 699 personnel and human resources professionals concerning how organisations in the UK manage stress. The case studies of best practice in the report include East Sussex County Council. The stress-management strategy of the County Council is to:

- issue a policy specifically addressing stress at work;
- provide training for managers enabling them to put this policy into practice;
- raise managers' awareness of how existing policies, practices and facilities contribute to reducing or addressing stress at work;
- provide employees with the support they need to deal with stress when it does occur. (Industrial Society 1995, p. 28)

The stress-management policy is circulated to all employees by means of a document that presents concise information about:

- What is stress?
- Recognising the signs of stress in the individual.
- Recognising the signs of stress in the workplace.
- Possible sources of stress in the workplace.

It also includes:

- Statement of policy – 'Stress in the Workplace' – 'the recognition and management of stress are integral to the County Council's staff care responsibilities and to the role of managers and supervisors'.
- Action points are: recruitment and selection, pre-employment screening, induction and promotion, absence management, return to work after absence, training and development and critical incident stress debriefing.
- Self -help.
- Getting help – 'If you would like to see a counsellor contact the Staff Welfare Officers on their direct line'. (Industrial Society 1995, pp. 28 and 44)

Guidelines for a successful whole-school approach

Contributions towards the development, implementation and evaluation of a whole-school stress management policy and programme may also be gained from an unexpected source: the DES Sheffield Bullying Project.

Following on from the Elton Report – 'Discipline in Schools' (HMSO 1989) funding was provided by the DES to a number of local education authorities to develop some of the recommendations made within it. The recommendations of the report in relation to bullying led to funds being made available to conduct the Sheffield Bullying Project. It started with a survey of 24 schools in the Sheffield area; 23 of them decided to take part in the project, which was carried out by staff from Sheffield University from 1991–93. Each school was asked to develop and implement a whole-school policy that would address the problems of bullying after being given information about a range of interventions and asked to select those that they were most interested in or felt most appropriate to the situation within their school.

Discussions between representatives from all the schools and the project team led to agreement on the methods to be used to introduce an effective whole-school policy on bullying. All the schools agreed to:

- Develop the policy through an extensive process of consultation, which involves teachers, lunch time supervisors, parents, governors and pupils.
- Include a clear definition of what bullying is as well as guidelines for staff, pupils and parents detailing what they should do if they become aware that bullying is taking place.
- Attempt to create a climate where children can talk about their feelings and feel able to tell someone if they are being bullied or if they are aware that another child is being bullied.
- Ensure that the policy is communicated throughout the school community to ensure consistency in practice.
- Be well motivated to ensure effectiveness over time. (Sharpe and Smith 1991, p. 50)

The two organisers of the project recommend these five points because 'This framework reflects key points highlighted in the Elton Report (1989) concerning essential features of any successful whole school policy development which aims to promote co-operative behaviour' (Sharpe and Smith 1991, p. 50). These five points can also be recommended to schools for the development of whole-school policies for stress management, which need as much consultation as possible in the school with support staff as well as teachers. A clear definition of occupational stress and guidelines for its effective management are essential. The issue of creating a school climate in which teachers can talk about their feelings of stress without being stigmatised is the necessary environment for consultation and co-operation; for listening and learning and for accepting the professional responsibilities for the 'due care' of staff. If the stress-management policy is to be effective in practice it too must be communicated throughout the school community and it must be evaluated regularly for feedback and modification when necessary. In this way it will continue to be relevant to staff needs. Sharp and Smith (1991, p. 54) also note the importance for the bullying project of each school developing its own policy: 'Recognising that all schools are complex systems which are unlikely to be the same as any other school, we aim to provide advice which will help schools decide the best course of action for them'.

Importance of a 'User-friendly' Policy

This awareness of the individuality of schools is equally true for effective implementation of stress-management policies and programmes. Dunham has found that teachers in different schools develop different rank orders of coping strategies. The teachers in four schools were invited to identify their coping strategies in a checklist prepared from teachers' questionnaire replies. Their answers identified the relative frequency that the coping strategies were used in the four schools. These are shown in Table 8.2.

Table 8.2: Rank order of use of coping strategies by staff in four secondary schools

Coping strategies	School A	School B	School C	School D
Deciding priorities	1	1	2	5
Working evenings and weekends	2	9	1	1
Planning well ahead	3	10	3	2
Talking to colleagues	4	3	6	5
Hobby to get away from school mentally	5	5	12	10
Preparing and marking less well than I would like	6	10	15	2
Becoming more philosophical: do what you can but do not worry too much	7	6	5	7
Catching up with family life in the holidays	8	3	14	4
Dropping low-priority school tasks	9	2	7	13
Exercising	10	10	13	8
Developing different styles of teaching	11	8	10	15
Working harder	12	6	4	10
Working from 9 a.m. to 5 p.m. then forgetting about the job	13	15	16	18
Relaxed breathing	14	16	17	16
Saying 'sod the school work' and going out	15	13	8	10
Making compromises	16	17	18	8
Muscle relaxation	17	18	11	17
More sporting activities	18	14	9	13

Dunham (1992, p. 116) has also reported the percentages of staff identifying coping strategies in School D. These results are given in Table 8.3.

Table 8.3: Coping action of teachers in School D

Coping action	% of staff using it
Working evenings and weekends	68
Preparing and marking less well than I would like	60
Planning well ahead	60
Catching up with family life in the holidays	56
Deciding priorities	54
Talking to colleagues	54
Becoming philosophical: doing what you can but without worrying too much	40
Exercise	34
Making compromises	34
Hobby to get away from school mentally	32
Work harder	30
'Sod the school work – go out'	30
Dropping low-priority school tasks	26
More sporting activities	26
Different styles of teaching	20
Relaxed breathing	10
Muscle relaxation	10
Working 9 a.m. to 5 p.m. – then forgetting about the job	6

The recognition of what resources are available in the school already that staff use to tackle work pressures is a good basis for a 'user-friendly' policy. The importance of this approach has been very persuasively presented by a middle manager in School C:

My perception of the school is one of a high level of mutual support between all grades of staff and this greatly reduces the potential stress from poorly motivated, less able and disruptive pupils. The school culture also gives a relatively high degree of control of the situation and hence reduces stress. Also the school does not tend to jump on bandwagons but weighs up the benefits to pupils before embarking upon change. It would seem from the survey on the stress reactions of staff that middle managers are suffering less stress than teaching or non-teaching staff.

This observation clearly indicates that staff support in times of change is an essential management skill for leaders in senior and middle management positions. The main management factors required for successfully implementing innovations in school have been identified in a project conducted by Bristol University researchers. They sent questionnaires to the teachers in 57 schools and interviewed staff in 12 of them to find which factors were identified by staff in their successful adaptation of external initiatives such as the arrival of a new headteacher. These factors included:

- The management style of the headteacher and the senior management team had encouraged the development of co-operative planning, consultation and decision making.
- The headteachers and the senior management team had helped to reduce staff stress by developing teamwork and by being sensitive to the effects of change on staff and by reassuring them that they had the skills to manage it. (Bolam, McMahon, Pockington and Weindling 1993, p. 98)

The implementation of a whole-school policy and programme of stress management is promoted by the same management skills. The management motto could be 'From audit to awareness to action!'

Conclusion

At the beginning of this chapter it was claimed that a whole-school model of stress management has important benefits and we have tried to identify them. We believe that the greatest benefit is that it helps to develop an awareness in the teaching and support staff that they are now working with the governors, parents and students in a 'sharing-learning culture' to improve the quality of life for all the members of the school community.

References

Bolam R, McMahon A, Pockington K, Weindling D (1993) Effective Management in Schools: A Report for the Department of Education via the School Management Task Force Professional Working Party. London: HMSO.

Brown M, Ralph S (1997) Change-linked Work-related Stress in British Schools. British Psychological Society (Education Section) Annual Conference, 14-16 November.

Cooper CL, Sloan SJ, Williams S (1988) Occupational Stress Indicator. Windsor: NFER-Nelson.

Dunham J (1992) Stress in Teaching (2 edn) London: Routledge.

Dunham J (1994) Developing Effective School Management. London: Routledge.

Earnshaw J, Cooper CL (1996) Stress and Employer Liability. London: Institute of Personnel and Development.

European Commission (1997) Health and Safety at Work – Report on Work-Related Stress. Luxembourg: The Advisory Committee for Safety, Hygiene and Health Protection at Work, Euroforum L2920.

HMSO (1989) Discipline in Schools. Report of a Committee of Enquiry chaired by Lord Elton. London: HMSO

Industrial Society (1995) Managing Best Practices – Managing Stress. London: The Industrial Society

NUT (1990) Teachers, Stress and Schools. London: National Union of Teachers.

Rogers WA (1996) Managing Teacher Stress. London: Pitman.

Sharp S, Smith PK (1991) Bullying in UK Schools – The DES Sheffield Bullying Project. Early Child Development and Care 77: 45-55.

Smith J (1997) Stress at work: litigation conference emphasises need for stress audits. Stress News 9(4): 11-12 October.

Chapter 9
Stress-management Training for Teachers: A Practical Guide

MARION TYLER

Introduction

In recent years the teaching profession (along with many other professions) has identified ' the rapid pace of change' as a major source of stress. Teaching is stressful – it is the nature of the job: '. . .a high level of stress is part of the job. In areas of social deprivation, where the pupils import problems into school matters are worse. However even in more normal conditions, the constant exposure to a class of demanding children, the tyranny of the timetable, and the endemic shortage of recovery time, is bound to lead to stress' (Everard 1986).

Some of the recent changes identified as stressors include changes to the school curriculum and visits from OFSTED, which have been perceived by many individuals as threatening and fearful.

Many surveys have shown that stress levels for teachers are uncomfortably high. Stress-management training programmes to reduce these levels are still not readily available to all schools and staff members. There are pockets throughout the country where training programmes on in-service education and training (INSET) days for staff members have been evaluated as being of great benefit in increasing awareness, reducing the stigma associated with reduced levels of coping, and introducing effective coping strategies. A whole INSET day is preferable, when lessons and interruptions do not distract from the main aims of the training. If a whole day is not possible then several sessions of approximately two hours each could be just as successful.

The programme subsequently described is primarily aimed at training for teachers on INSET days. The group leader/ trainer should be knowledgeable and competent on the subject of stress and its management. A suitably trained local authority advisor, senior teacher, or an outside specialist/consultant may be considered as a suitable expert.

The support of the head and the school's management team is vital. Discussion of any problem areas that are known to exist before hand will enable possible solutions to be suggested. It is also important that management and senior staff are familiar with the course content, approach, and expected outcomes.

Stress-intervention programmes should be tackled from different levels due to the complex nature of people and problems. Both the organisation (school and/or local education authority) and the individual have a responsibility to actively manage the stress in order to eliminate the stressor at source or reduce its effects.

Primary intervention

Primary and secondary intervention approaches are essentially appropriate preventative actions to try to eliminate or reduce potential problems that may cause stress. Matters that may need to be addressed at this level could include:

*   looking at staff levels;
*   job design;
*   career developments and opportunities;
*   job control to evaluate autonomy and responsibility;
*   management styles etc.

Secondary intervention

Stress management at this level means looking at improving responses to the sources of stress and developing personal skills. This training is best designed following a stress audit or a training needs analysis. The programme may include:

*   understanding the physical stress reactions;
*   assertiveness training;
*   improving coping skills;
*   cognitive behavioural training
*   exercise and positive health approaches.

Tertiary intervention

Stress management at this level is remedial action for those who may already be affected and addresses methods of treating or reducing the symptoms of stress. This is a level of support for people who have fallen through the net and become victims of exposure to stress. It normally involves training on a one-to-one basis, either through a counselling service, an employee assistance programme, a staff support service (all of which would be provided by the employer) or reliance on community-based services.

Benefits of early intervention

All interventions are important but the training programme will address issues mainly at the primary and secondary levels. Stress-management programmes mentioned in this chapter aim towards helping teachers to develop personal skills and gain a better understanding of the negative and positive effects of 'stress'.

The educational, cognitive approach provides the knowledge and skills to empower individuals to accept responsibility for recognising their personal stressors and for planning an effective programme to improve their coping strategies. Training may be offered to individuals on a one-to-one basis or through group training. The latter approach is strongly recommended. It often shows that participants gain enormous support from sharing ideas and feelings with each other as well as from the value of the programme. It is, of course, also much more cost effective.

Stress-management training

To be alive means facing 'stress' in some form or other. It is a fact of life. Without new experiences and challenges, life could become dull, boring and often depressing. The right amount of pressure can act as a spur, enabling us to meet deadlines by increasing our energy and drive. The increased alertness can improve our performance in the face of competition. These feelings of exhilaration are rewarding and improve the quality of life itself.

Stress is not a medical problem but a managerial one. The effective management of stress is an important part of a person's well-being. 'Stress' is a word that is often loosely used when people are referring to feelings or situations related to distress. There are many different definitions of 'stress'. Some have been quoted in previous chapters in this book. A recent definition offered by Dr Noel McElearney (1997), a Marks & Spencer's occupational physician, is 'a feeling that you just cannot cope with all that you face'.

The challenge in life is to balance the pressures effectively, so that life is more productive and enjoyable. The essential message is to aim for an overall balance between:

Stimulation Work Exercise Responsibilities Laughter		Relaxation Play Rest Freedom Tears

Failing to maintain a good balance may result in some of the psychological, physical or behavioural symptoms related to stress.

A one-day stress-management training programme

A lot can be achieved in a one-day training programme to increase awareness of stress and its effects. The typical programme outlined in the following paragraphs has been found to work extremely well in a variety of organisations as well as the teaching sector.

Before adopting this or any other training programme, a discussion of specific training needs should be examined carefully. The programme can then be modified or redesigned to meet particular problems and issues according to the nature of the course members.

Programme aims and objectives

The overall aim is to help individuals to understand the causes, symptoms and impact of stress at work on themselves and on their colleagues. In particular, the programme should:

- provide a clear understanding of the meaning of stress and an awareness of the difference between pressure and stress;
- provide an understanding of the causes of stress so that individuals can assess the impact of stress on both themselves and their colleagues;
- help individuals understand their own behaviour and assess whether it could be a cause of stress for other people;
- enable individuals to recognise the symptoms/manifestations of stress so that full intervention can take place to prevent the build-up of pressure resulting in distress;
- help individuals to recognise the need to control pressures or demands put upon them and to realise that to do so is their responsibility;
- help individuals to develop strategies for managing their own stress in both the short-term and the long-term;
- examine ways to reduce/prevent stress occurring whilst maintaining a high level of performance;
- indicate ways an individual can ease pressures for colleagues both above and below them in the organisational hierarchy.

Pre-course preparation

Planning and discussion with management and staff should be undertaken before finally deciding on the programme aims and objectives.

The trainer will need to ascertain the nature of the training group, i.e. the numbers on the course, the approximate ages, sex, and previous experience/training on this subject (if any). Some research into the course members' occupations and their work is essential before planning a suitable programme. It is also important to clarify what grade of staff will be attending and whether there would be a mix of staff and managers (or junior and senior teachers) from the same or different departments/schools.

A pre-course information pack should be given out to each course member to encourage participation and provide an opportunity to outline the main aims of the course. It may also contain details of the day's programme, time, venue and possibly include recommendations to wear leisure clothing if preferred.

The training centre should be warm and comfortable with privacy and excluding intrusive outside noises. A breakout room (if available) would be very useful – this is a syndicate room for group work. Seating arrangements are important to encourage all members of the group to take an active part in discussions without feeling threatened. It may be preferable to arrange chairs in a 'U' shape, with or without tables.

Checklist to prepare for running a course

The trainer will require some of the following resources to carry out the complete programme:

Training manual	Biofeedback equipment
Overhead projector and acetates	Library books and cassettes
Video/TV player and videos	Mattresses and cushions
Cassette player and tapes	Heater or a warm room
Flip chart and pens	Photocopying facilities
Handouts/leaflets	Evaluation forms
Refreshments	Guest speakers

A handout or training pack for each course participant should be prepared. This should include information on the day's training and a possible resource for future reference.

One successful style of teaching encourages the delegates to participate throughout the day's activities. This involves brainstorming activities, working in buzz groups, experiential relaxation sessions and the use of biofeedback.

Detailed programme timetable

The following programme timetable will be suitable in most cases, with minor changes if necessary to meet particular requirements.

Typical timetable for a one-day stress-management workshop

9.00 a.m.	Introduction to course.
9.15 a.m.	The difference between pressures and stress. How to recognise the negative and positive effects.
10.00 a.m.	Video – Managing Pressures (part one).
10.15 a.m.	Solving the problems. Identifying physical, psychological and behavioural symptoms of stress and some of the causes.
10.30 a.m.	Refreshments.
10.45 a.m.	'The Challenge Zone'. Recognising main 'stressors'. Suggestions to maximise performance and avoid exhaustion.
11.30 a.m.	Relaxation techniques and movements. Ways to avoid muscular strain and pain.
12.00	Signs of burnout. How to prevent the build-up of stress and maintain control of your life.
12.15 p.m.	Group questions and discussion.
12.30 p.m.	Video – Managing Pressures (part two).
1.00 p.m.	Lunch.
2.00 p.m.	Coping strategies – a look at methods that help us to cope better.
2.15 p.m.	Relaxation session.
2.30 p.m.	Counselling as a management tool. How to approach and support a member of staff.
3.00 p.m.	Refreshments.
3.15 p.m.	Organisational stress (causes and consequential effects).
4.00 p.m.	Reducing stress in the workplace.
4.20 p.m.	Developing an 'action plan' for individual needs. Building long-term resilience. Short-term coping techniques.
5.00 p.m.	Close.

The International Stress Management Association (UK) at its 1995 National Forum recommended the following subjects as the 'core content' for a professional stress-management training course and recommends the inclusion of 60% of 'core content' subjects in each course.

* Change: understanding and managing change.
* Cognitive coping strategies: to include anxiety management.
* Communication skills: to include assertion and the use and misuse of aggression.
* Control: its locus, and the perception by the individual.
* Human function curve.

Table 9.1: A typical lesson plan for the one-day stress-management training programme

Time	Content	Methods/activity	Aids
9.00 a.m.	Introduction to course	Names on cards expectations from group scribed onto flip chart Issue biodots	Training manual Biodots Cards and pens Flip chart
9.15 a.m.	Difference between pressure and stress How to recognise negative and positive effects	Brainstorming activity to highlight definitions of stress Gingerbread templates for buzz groups to identify signs	Flip chart and pens Tables for buzz group work Blue tack for graphs
9.45 a.m.	Plenary from buzz groups of signs/symptoms	Group leaders feed back	Flip chart: blue tack
10.00 a.m.	Video (part one)	Group participation	Video player/TV
10.15 a.m.	Personal programme	Handout to discuss signs and symptoms	Handout
10.30 a.m.	Refreshments		
10.45 a.m.	'The Challenge Zone' Causes of stress Recognising perceived control	Describe and demonstrate the human performance curve Buzz group work Tutor presentation/group	Tutor presentation Overhead projector and screen Flip chart and pens Biofeedback machine
11.30 a.m.	Relaxation techniques and movements	Group participation Relaxation on a chair	Extra room and volunteer
12.00	Signs of burnout	Tutor presentation	Overhead projector and screen
12.15 p.m.	Group discussion and questions	Group participation	Flip chart
12.30 p.m.	Video (part two)	Group participation	Video player/TV
1.00 p.m.	LUNCH		
2.00 p.m.	Coping strategies Methods of coping better	Buzz groups	Flip charts and pens/blue tack
2.15 p.m.	Relaxation session	Whole group activity Tutor-led session	Cassette player and tape
2.30 p.m.	Counselling as a management tool	Whole group Tutor-led session	Video player/TV
3.00 p.m.	Refreshments		
3.15 p.m.	Organisational stress. Causes and consequential effects	Tutor presentation and brainstorming activity	Flip chart and pens
4.00 p.m.	Reducing stress in the workplace	Buzz group work and plenary session	Flip chart and pens
4.20 p.m.	Developing an action plan Building long-term resilience Short-term coping techniques	Tutor-led session Buzz groups on healthy lifestyles Tutor demonstration on breathing '60 second tranquilliser'	Handout and flip chart Card with breathing technique
5.00 p.m.	Summary and close	Group questions and evaluations	Evaluation forms

- Lifestyle and health promotion with reference to nutrition, exercise and substance abuse.
- Personality and stress.
- Recognition of the causes and signs: to include endocrinology and stress-related illnesses.
- Relaxation and breathing with reference to meditation.
- Self-awareness.
- Social support: to include the significance of enjoyment and laughter.
- Values and beliefs: without critical scrutiny.
- Workplace stress: the organisation, working environment and the individual's responsibility.

A typical lesson plan for the one-day stress-management training programme is given in Table 9.1.

Trainers/tutors

The trainer should have a sound knowledge of the subject combined with teaching and communication skills. Teaching and training qualifications that are relevant and that support these skills are advantageous. Many trainers may be practitioners with no formal qualification either in teaching or stress management, however, due to the lack (until comparatively recently) of an appropriate qualification.

The RSA Examinations Board, in conjunction with Living with Stress Ltd, have developed a syllabus for a training course for trainers, leading to a formal qualification, which defines the requirements necessary to achieve their Certificate in Stress Management. These requirements are that a trainer in stress management should have the basic training, understanding, knowledge and competence to teach the following Units of Competence.

- Create, design and present information on the physiology of stress.
- Create, design and present information on the physiology of breathing.
- Design and present information on voluntary muscles and their function.
- Create and design methods to describe the main contributing factors and causes of stress-related problems.
- Identify methods and techniques to elicit the relaxation response.
- Create and design information to describe the benefits of healthy lifestyles and effective coping strategies.
- Basic communication skills.
- Basic presentation skills.
- Basic teaching skills.
- Programme planning

The RSA Examinations Board Certificate in Stress Management is an NVQ equivalent qualification that requires demonstrated knowledge/

ability/experience in the above 10 units. The aims and objectives for each of these units are judged as follows.

Unit 1: design and present information on the physiology of stress

Trainers should have the ability to:	
Present evidence on the basic under-standing of the physiology of the stress responses	(a) Give an appropriate definition of stress (b) Explain the fight/flight response (c) Describe the 'chemical co-ordination' during the alarm response and the resistance response (d) Compare the sympathetic and parasympathetic responses of the autonomic nervous system
Demonstrate understanding of the negative and positive effects of stress	(a) List the positive effects of the stress response (b) Explain the negative short-term ill-effects of stress (c) Describe the psychological, physical and behavioural symptoms of excessive amounts of stress
Give a presentation on the physiology of stress	(a) Present essential points within a limited time using several items of training equipment

Unit 2: design and present information on the physiology of breathing

Trainers should have the ability to:	
Demonstrate the skills, knowledge and expertise required to convey accurate information on the physiology of breathing	(a) Select appropriate methods and resources to describe the mechanism of breathing (b) Describe problems associated with dysfunctional breathing patterns
Present practical/experiential advice to correct poor breathing patterns	(a) Demonstrate skills to train individuals on diaphragmatic breathing using appropriate methods (b) Present methods to control breathing to reduce anxiety and panic

Unit 3: design and present information on voluntary muscles and their function – the basic programme

Trainers should have the ability to:	
Select appropriate resources to convey accurate information on the functions of muscles	(a) Identify all muscle groups and their functions (b) Describe unnecessary muscle tension and signs of fatigue in voluntary muscles (c) Demonstrate ways of testing for unnecessary muscle tension (d) Demonstrate the importance of sitting properly (e) Demonstrate and or describe the benefits of good posture in walking and standing (f) Explain the sensory homunculus

Unit 4: create and design methods to describe the main contributing factors and causes of stress-related problems – the basic programme

Trainers should have the ability to:	
Select appropriate material to convey information on the causes of undue stress	(a) Present accurate information to describe the human performance curve (b) Describe common causes of undue stress that affect individuals (c) Describe some of the main causes of stress within the workplace (d) Explain the major life change events and effects on individuals (e) Describe problems with under- and over-achieving (f) Describe stages of burnout (g) Describe signs of burnout (h) Describe causes of burnout
Explain individual performance and self-perceptions	(a) Offer evidence to describe causes of over-arousal and individual responses

Unit 5: identify methods and techniques to elicit the relaxation response – the basic programme

Trainers should have the ability to:	
Present accurate information on the benefits of relaxation	(a) Describe a variety of methods in popular use (b) Give practical instruction to learners to teach them relaxation skills
Explain the benefits of relaxation movements	(a) Describe problems associated with unnecessary muscle tension (b) Demonstrate relaxation movements to ease tension in different parts of the body

Unit 6: create and design information to describe the benefits of healthy lifestyles and effective coping strategies – the basic programme

Trainers should have the ability to:	
Select and present information on the benefits of a healthy life style	(a) Describe the main factors that contribute to good health including exercises of various types (b) Identify reasons for improving health (c) Suggest ways to improve health and well-being
Identify/describe risks to health	(a) Describe the main risks to health (b) Describe in general terms how to reduce the risks to health

Unit 7: basic communication skills

Trainers should have the ability to:	
Locate and abstract relevant information on stress management for a stated purpose to present formally or informally	(a) Select the means of communication appropriate to the learning situation and the learning group (b) Identify and minimise barriers to communication (c) Identify communication skills required by learners within the subject and communicate to them (d) Monitor learners' communication abilities, identify problems and give feedback (e) Provide appropriate action and support to assist learners to solve identified communication difficulties (f) Devise situations to provide practice for learners in the identified communication skills required
Barriers to communication	(a) Recognise barriers to opportunities for the demonstration and assessment of achievement (b) Identify and minimise barriers to access of learning opportunities

Unit 8: basic presentation skills

Trainers need the ability to:	
Organise and manage the learning group	(a) Produce a lesson plan to identify learning outcomes, structure and content (b) Produce appropriate teaching and learning resources
Demonstrate skills to present effectively to the learning group	(a) Use appropriate methods of delivery to the learning group (b) Organise the environment in a way that assists learning (c) Use language that does not discriminate against any member of the learning group (d) Use appropriate learning resources (e) Encourage feedback from learners (f) Assess learning by appropriate methods

Unit 9: basic teaching skills

Trainers need the ability to:	
Adopt appropriate teaching methods relevant to a variety of lessons	(a) Use strategies that are relevant to the specified objectives (b) Facilitate exercises and activities to provide learning in groups (c) Make effective adaptations and interventions that are likely to improve the effectiveness of the learning process (d) Use appropriate language and behaviour (e) Present appropriate visual material to demonstrate principles of visual communication in order to maximise learning (f) Employ questioning techniques and listening skills to facilitate learning

Unit 10: programme planning

Trainers should have the ability to:	
Plan and organise learning	(a) Identify learning outcomes (b) Match subject topics to outcomes in a planned activity for learners (c) Produce plans for learning sessions (d) Identify ways in which learning will be recognised
Produce	(a) Produce a lesson plan that relates to identified learning outcomes and justifies structure and content (b) Produce appropriate teaching and learning resources

Course handouts

It is recommended that course attendees are given a comprehensive handout that covers the day's subject matter to act as a future resource. Preferably, this should be in the form of a manual. The following summary of principal messages that will hopefully be remembered may be given out as a 'memory jogger'.

- **Learn to relax**

  Find a method that suits you!

- **Time management**

  Prioritise and delegate

- **Good nutrition**

  Avoid excess of alcohol, caffeine, nicotine and sugars. Eat well

- **Emotional needs**

  Laughter, crying and sharing thoughts or worries with a confidant helps

- **Exercise**

  Burns up adrenalin and restores the balance

- **Communication skills**

  Share problems and listen to others

- **Be assertive**

  Take action to modify aggressive or passive behaviour patterns

- **Avoid stressors**

  Recognise things that 'wind you up' and plan ways to reduce, avoid or eliminate them

- **Sleep well**

  Improve patterns and adopt a routine

- **Avoid negative thoughts**

  Think and 'play positive tapes' in your head

- **Socialise**

  Social contacts with friends is important

- **Leisure pursuits**

  Hobbies, holidays, time with the family

Further guidelines on communication, presentation and teaching skills

Other chapters in this book deal in detail with the subject matter of units 1–6, and it may be relatively easy therefore to research stress-management topics further, but guidance on communication skills, presentation skills, teaching skills and programme planning (units 7–10) are not included. The following guidelines may therefore be helpful.

General

The influence exerted as a presenter depends largely on the ability to communicate and project oneself and one's ideas to other people. Effective communication involves getting messages across to individuals and groups, informatively and persuasively, using both the written and spoken word.

The prospect of speaking in public and addressing a large and perhaps unfamiliar group can create feelings of apprehension and even fear in most of us. Some people appear to have a particular talent for speaking in public. They are able to communicate facts and ideas in a confident, interesting and persuasive manner.

Making a 'presentation' is as much a skill as other methods of formal business communication. By applying a few basic techniques, an approach can be developed that will increase the presenter's confidence and enhance the effectiveness of his or her presentations.

There are four questions the presenter must ask when planning and preparing oral presentations. The answers to these questions will give guidance towards making presentations that achieve the anticipated outcomes.

- Why am I saying it? The purpose.
- To whom am I saying it? The audience.
- What am I going to say? The content.
- How am I going to say it? The form.

The purpose

The types of oral presentations that presenters are required to give generally fit into three categories. Each category defines the main purpose of the presentation as follows:

- To communicate information. The content is predominantly factual and the presentation may take the form of a briefing to a group of people.
- To make a proposition. The content is ideas supported by reasoned argument and personal judgement designed to persuade and win the

support of the audience.
- To inspire and motivate. The content, whether it is ideas or facts, should reflect and reinforce the feelings of the audience and generate enthusiasm, boost morale and encourage positive attitudes.

Each of these types of presentation will place different demands on the speaker and is intended to produce a different response from the audience. It is vitally important to establish the purpose of the presentation if the desired results are to be achieved.

The audience

Before deciding the content and the form, it is essential to discover as much as possible about the audience. Considerations such as size and characteristics of the audience and their knowledge of the subject determine the content, language, structure and tone of the presentation. Presenters should ask themselves three questions as follows:

- *How large is the audience?* Size will influence the degree of formality and audience involvement that can expected or reasonably encouraged. As a guide, with a group of less than 10 people a conversational approach may be adopted and intervention may be welcomed. As the group size increases there will be a need for formality with few, if any, opportunities for audience involvement except, perhaps, at the end of the presentation.
- *How much do they know about my subject?* The audience's knowledge and understanding of the subject will determine the level at which the presentation should be pitched. Audience attention and interest will quickly decline if the presenter talks above their heads. The complexity of facts and ideas that are included must be appropriate to their knowledge and understanding.
- *Who is the audience?* The presenter should establish the significant characteristics of the audience – for example, their position and role. Their special interests and concerns can then be reflected in the presentation to help attract interest and win support.

Choosing and using visual aids

A good presentation with visual aids can be more effective than a good presentation without them. The presenter should remember that a visual aid is intended to support the verbal presentation, not to replace it.

Visual aids should be related to the audience. The words or pictures should not serve as a script for the presenter to read from, nor should the audience be required to read long, wordy passages from the screen or flip chart.

The decision about which visual aids to use must be made early in the preparation and planning, (during the identification and structuring of 'the middle'). A scientific or technical presentation is impossible without some form of visual material setting out the data, structural relationships and processes.

A tip is to remember the analogy of trying to describe a journey to someone else, without drawing a map. The most important use of visual aids is to simplify the complex into an easily recognisable form.

Visual aids can also be used to amplify and to reinforce what the presenter is saying. A key word or words can be displayed to keep these in the audience's mind during the presentation.

Another use of visual aids is to orientate the audience. It is important to create transitions (signposts) within the verbal delivery. Similarly, visual aids can be used as markers. A presentation with four key points, for example, might list all four during the introduction and each in turn at the appropriate time. The same list can be used during the summary.

The flip chart

Flip charts are essentially 'point of origination aids' – that is, they are used during the presentation, rather than being prepared beforehand, (this is not a rule – they can be prepared beforehand if complex).

The presenter should remember to:

- Make drawings bold and simple.
- Use combinations of upper and lower case lettering.
- Print, rather than write.
- Use dark colours, red, blue, green, black, etc.
- Have a plan.
- Prepare complex diagrams in light pencil beforehand

The presenter should not:

- Talk and write at the same time.
- Use light coloured pens, yellow, pink, etc.
- Put too many words on the same page.

The overhead projector

The overhead projector is probably the most versatile means of adding visual emphasis to a presentation. It will allow the presenter to:

- Project a big, bright image in normal room lighting conditions.
- Operate the equipment and change transparencies while facing the audience.

- Project prepared transparencies.
- Write on a blank transparency during the presentation.
- Add to prepared transparencies during the presentation.
- Highlight key areas during the presentation.
- Build-up information using overlays.
- Reveal information using 'reveal' or 'masking' techniques.
- Point to the transparency using a pencil or pointer.

When using the projector, the presenter should remember to:

- Keep it switched off when not in use.
- Put the transparency on the overhead projector before switching on and switch off before removing it.
- Leave the projector switched on only for as long as necessary, (but never less than 10 seconds) before switching off.
- Use a pointer on the transparency when pointing out detail and put the pointer down to avoid movement. He or she should step to one side to ensure the audience can see the screen.

When preparing transparencies the presenter should remember that 'a picture may be worth a thousand words' but nine hundred of these may be irrelevant.
The presenter should:

- Keep transparencies simple.
- Use key words – bullet points only.
- Use a layout that will allow for reveal techniques to be used.
- Use bold lettering – lettering should never be less than a quarter of an inch high (18 point).
- Explain figures using appropriate graphic techniques – bar chart, pie chart etc.
- Frame transparencies in a card frame or flip frame.
- Number transparencies on the frame to create a sequence and insert the appropriate numbers into the notes as a prompt.

35-mm slides

These slides can provide good examples of real items, situations etc. For best effect, 35-mm slides need to be projected in either a blacked-out room or subdued lighting conditions, and this can create difficulty in maintaining contact with the audience.
The presenter should remember to:

- Check that slides are clean before putting them in the magazine.
- Insert slides into the magazine upside down, right-side facing rear.

- Number each slide in sequence.
- Insert blank or black slides to break up the sequences.
- Start and end with a blank or black slide.

The presenter should remember not to:

- Mix vertical (portrait) and horizontal (landscape) slides in the same sequence.
- Use too many slides.
- Use irrelevant slides.

Video

Video tape has taken over from film as the most often-used, moving visual aid. These days video is a normal experience for the audience, they won't be overawed by it. The presenter should beware of 'in-house' video productions. If a video is to be used, it should be planned, produced and presented to the very highest standard. Video is commonplace for the audience – and for this reason audience expectation of the medium will equate to what is broadcast every day of the week.
    The presenter should:

- Preview all video tapes before using them.
- Check the equipment before the presentation begins.
- Cue up the tape to the point at which the presenter wishes to start.
- Practice with the remote control.
- Ensure the screen or screens can be seen by the audience.
- Check the volume on playback so that adjustments do not have to be made during the presentation.
- Introduce the video tape – or segment – with a few words before it starts.

The presenter should not:

- Use video for the sake of it

Presenting the material

Before the presentation, the presenter should:

- Dress appropriately.
- Arrive early.
- Get to know the organiser of the event.
- Check the layout of the room; the availability of tables, visual aids and

the location of power points, light switches etc.
- Where necessary re-organise the room to suit his or her own personal presentation style.

During the presentation, the presenter should:

- Establish rapport with the audience.
- Speak clearly to all parts of the room.
- Speak clearly and audibly, varying the pace, tone and volume.
- Extemporise.
- Use language that is appropriate to the audience and the occasion.
- Pause occasionally and use the pause for effect.
- Show enthusiasm, confidence, honesty and sincerity.
- Make moderate use of gestures but only if they help to make the point.
- Face the audience.

The presenter should not:

- Apologise for him/herself or the subject.
- Fix his/her gaze on one individual – eye contact should be varied.
- Memorise the presentation, or read from cards or script.
- Speak to the screen, television monitor or flip chart.

Evaluation of training

Evaluation of training and outcomes is essential to monitor standards and improve quality. Adequate feedback can ensure that future programmes are modified and or designed to meet specific needs. The following evaluation form shown is recommended:

Evaluation form

Course title   ....

Tutor ....   Date ....

Your feedback on the course you have just attended enables us to make future courses more effective by highlighting any possible changes that are required. We would therefore appreciate your constructive comments on aspects that are well done and any that could be improved. Please indicate below by ticking the box against the phrase that most accurately describes your feeling.

1. How much did you enjoy the course?

    4   ☐   Very enjoyable
    3   ☐   Most of the course was enjoyable
    2   ☐   Some of the course was enjoyable
    1   ☐   I did not enjoy the course

Comments:

2. How many of the course objectives were achieved?

    4   ☐   All of the stated objectives were met
    3   ☐   Most of the objectives were met
    2   ☐   Some of the objectives were met
    1   ☐   Few, if any, of the objectives were met

Comments:

3. Was the subject material and pitch appropriate to you?

    4   ☐   Was excellent
    3   ☐   Was about right
    2   ☐   Only some of it was right
    1   ☐   On the whole it was poor

Comments:

4. How effective were the exercises in helping you learn?

    4   ☐   Very effective
    3   ☐   Effective
    2   ☐   Some were effective
    1   ☐   None were effective/there weren't any

Comments:

5. How do you rate the technical expertise of the tutor?

    4   ☐   Excellent
    3   ☐   Good
    2   ☐   Satisfactory
    1   ☐   Poor

Comments:

6. How effective was the tutor at presenting the topic?

    4   ☐   Excellent
    3   ☐   Good
    2   ☐   Satisfactory
    1   ☐   Poor

Comments:

7. What was the quality of the course handouts?

    4   ☐   Excellent
    3   ☐   Good
    2   ☐   Satisfactory
    1   ☐   Poor

Comments:

8. How would you rate the course environment/facilities?

    4   ☐   Excellent
    3   ☐   Good
    2   ☐   Satisfactory
    1   ☐   Poor

Comments:

9. How appropriate was the timing of the course in terms of your job/career?

    4   ☐   Excellent
    3   ☐   Good
    2   ☐   Satisfactory
    1   ☐   Poor

Comments:

10. Confidence in applying the information given:

    4   ☐   I feel I will have no problem applying the skills/information learnt
    3   ☐   I will be able to apply most of the skills/information learnt
    2   ☐   I will only be able to apply some of the skills/information learnt
    1   ☐   I feel that I will be unable to apply any of the skills/information learnt

Comments (please state skills/information not able to apply):

Conclusion

I have had the pleasure of facilitating and leading numerous INSET training days on the subject of stress management for headteachers and teachers (secondary and junior). I have participated in a number of 'cluster' training days, in which several schools group together to share training, with a variety of topics being covered. I have also participated at many secondary and junior schools by carrying out short training sessions for the pupils. These have been extremely well received, particularly before examinations. Training teachers would therefore not only be of benefit to them but would also have extra value for the pupils in their care.

The evaluations from my training with all grades of teachers have highlighted the need for stress-management training earlier in their career. The general consensus of opinion would appear to be that this should be part of the training undertaken at college/university. Further, if subjects on life skills were part of the school curriculum, there is little doubt that the pupils would benefit enormously. Some degree of training in stress management, assertiveness, relaxation techniques, healthy lifestyles and so forth could have a positive effect on the problems of extreme shyness and bullying in our schools.

References

Everard KB (1986) Developing Management in Schools. Oxford: Blackwell.
McElearney N (1997) Pro-Active Interventions – Lessons to be Learnt from Marks & Spencer. Paper presented at Stress at Work Litigation Conference, London 15 May 1997.

Chapter 10
Case Studies in Stress Management

ADRIAN MILES

Background

Stress is increasingly cited as an issue of concern in the workplace on the basis that it is a major source of lost productivity. Indeed, the CBI (1997) suggested that stress-related illness in the United Kingdom during 1996 cost £12 billion. This figure is undoubtedly significant in macro-economic terms, however its relevance is far removed from the personal experiences of 'front-line' public service workers. For instance, of what interest are global figures of lost productivity to teachers grappling with the day-to-day realities confronting them in the classroom, or social workers struggling to make crucial decisions concerning child protection? Indeed the social consequences of stress amongst public service workers are far more compelling than those concerned with economics.

Equally important within a public service context is how stress experienced by employees impacts upon service users. Indeed this was starkly illustrated by a report produced by the London Borough of Hammersmith and Fulham (August 1984) into the death of a young child, Shirley Woodcock:

> Perhaps the greatest significance of this case lies in the way it demonstrates the need to recognise the seeds of stress at many levels . . . There is then a consequent duty to remedy the causes of that stress.

It is therefore the tangible impacts of stress at a local level upon managers, employees and service users that lead to the need for organisations to address problems such as low morale and high levels of absenteeism in a practical manner. Indeed it is reasonable to think that seeking practical solutions to such problems would lie at the very heart and purpose of stress research. Nevertheless it is a question that the vast array of stress literature has struggled to address effectively. Instead much time has been spent on cause-and-effect analyses of work environments. Keenan and Newton (1987) suggest that this approach can produce contradictory results. They suggest that this is often due to:

(i)   difficulty in holding variables constant;
(ii)   cross-sectional studies do not account for the temporal aspects of stress;
(iii) dependence on questionnaires where common language and terminology are difficult to attain.

Another major thrust within the stress research field has, of course, focused on coping mechanisms and in recent years an increasing number of public sector organisations have been prepared to introduce employee counsellors and stress-management courses. It is significant that both these strategies focus upon the individual rather than the organisation. Indeed, the danger of adopting this approach is that stress may be seen as belonging to the individual rather than something with which the organisation should have to deal.

Dunham (1984) recognised the dangers of such an approach and highlighted the organisation's responsibilities to the individual. However, 14 years further on, there have been relatively few organisational intervention strategies within the public services arena. Given the complexity of the stress process, this may not be surprising. Nevertheless, Kahn and French (1970) wrote:

Understanding the stressful characteristics of large scale organisations is certainly grand, but it is not grandiose . . . Understanding them more fully is a pre-requisite to making them more liveable.

However, although there may be common themes of occupational stress that can be addressed by a public service organisation, within each overall organisational framework there will be literally hundreds of individual workplaces with their own particular characteristics. It is only by understanding the specific context of the workplace that issues relating to occupational stress can be made sense of and real change effected.

Carroll and White (1982) suggest an 'ecological approach':

it is essential both to evaluate person and environmental variables and their interactions and to develop and implement intervention strategies that address simultaneously, both the person and their environment.

Using an essentially ecological approach I undertook a study between 1988-94 within an urban Social Services Department with the objective of implementing stress-intervention strategies within a range of workplaces. Eliciting support from the Director of the Social Services Department did not prove to be difficult. He was very keen that I meet with senior managers and work with specific teams. However, it was first necessary to:

- understand something of the stress process within a number of workplaces in the organisation;
- understand the language of stress within this particular professional context;
- test the appropriateness of a range of data gathering tools.

I therefore undertook pilot work with a range of social services teams (64 people). Three methods of data collection were used: focus groups; individual interviews; diaries. A stress and motivation checklist, which I had devised, was also tested for appropriateness of language and ease of analysis.

Three key learning points emerged:

- *Language and definitions.* Staff were not always able to distinguish between stress and motivation. 'I can't always tell the difference between stress and enjoyment.' 'I need stress to do a good job . . . the more the pressure, the better I cope.' The following, which were quoted both as sources of motivation and stress, reinforced this: 'uncertainty', 'risk', 'difficult decisions'.

- *The client.* Clients were spoken of more in terms of motivation and job satisfaction than as sources of stress.

- *Methodologies.* Focus groups produced a rapid overview of key issues in the workplace. However, the use of third person by members of the focus groups, when describing what were clearly personal experiences of stress, suggested that stress was perceived by most as being a weakness and something that should be concealed. Within individual interview situations, more complex and personal explanations of stress experiences were revealed.

Use of diaries revealed that stress can manifest itself in both the short term and the medium-term. However, their completion was inconsistent and difficult to enforce. It therefore seemed more appropriate that in the interventions the temporal dimension is captured by using the checklist, which proved easy both to administer and analyse. A small number of alterations were made to its terminology. In particular, the terms stress and motivation were removed altogether (see Table 10.1).

Table 10.1: Stress and motivation checklist

(A) Please indicate the extent to which you are currently satisfied with the following factors in your workplace.

	(5) Very satisfied	(4) Satisfied	(3) Changeable	(2) Dissatisfied	(1) Very dissatisfied
1. Workload					
2. Promotion Prospects					
3. Leadership from Line Manager					
4. Level of Autonomy					
5. Personal Level of Skill					
6. Pay					
7. Relationships with Work Peers					
8. Relationships with Senior Staff					
9. Relationships with Clients					
10. Other Departmental Services					
11. Working Hours					
12. Physical Working Conditions					
13. Clear Aims and Objectives					
14. Equal Opportunities Policy					
15. Level of Client Contact					
16. Leadership from Central Management					

(B) Do you feel that concerns about your work situation have caused you to experience any of the following?

	(4) Often	(3) Sometimes	(2) Rarely	(1) Never
1. Sleeplessness				
2. Headaches				
3. Skin Rashes				
4. Irritability with Clients				
5. Irritability with Colleagues				
6. Irritability with Family				
7. Feeling Sick				
8. Aches and Pains				
9. Forgetfulness				
10. Depression				
11. Loss of Appetite				
12. Withdrawal from Contact with Clients				
13. Withdrawal from Contact with Colleagues				
14. Withdrawal from Contact with Family				
15. Apathy				
16. Serious Illness				
17. Overeating				
18. Other Please Specify				

(C) How likely are you to engage in the following activities when you experience pressure at work?

	(5) Very likely	(4) Likely	(3) Sometimes	(2) Unlikely	(1) Most likely
1. Talk to Someone					
2. Work Hard					
3. Go Sick					
4. Increase Alcohol Consumption					
5. Engage in Recreational Activity					
6. Take Drugs					
7. Sleep					
8. Eat Excessively					
9. Increase Smoking					
10. Avoid Being in Stressful Situations					
11. Pray					
12. Think Positively About Yourself					
13. Seek Professional Help					
14. Complain to Others at Workplace					
15. Tackle Problems Directly					
16. Try to Improve Skills					
17. Relaxation Exercises					
18. Think Problems Through					

Case studies

Each intervention was to take approximately six months. The prime objectives were to:
- assist managers and their teams in understanding their workplace environments in relation to factors influencing levels of stress and motivation;
- present teams and individuals with a range of strategies to help them cope effectively with workplace pressures;
- evaluate the changes arising as a result of the interventions.

My first step was to meet with a number of area managers who rapidly identified those teams they wished to participate in the project: a children's home; an elderly persons' home; a learning disabilities community team; a day nursery; a hospital geriatric social work team and a children's area social work team. However, as became apparent only later, of the six teams, two were in serious difficulties: staff relationships with managers were on the verge of complete breakdown and one was thought by its senior manager likely to become a management problem in the near future. Consequently, the enthusiasm displayed by area managers for my assistance in interventions was not always reflected within the teams. I have detailed two of the interventions that reflect experiences at both ends of the spectrum.

Case study 1: children's home

The home catered for eight boys and girls, aged between 10 and 14 years, who presented moderate behavioural and emotional problems. The staff group consisted of two men and six women, including a manager and deputy. Five of the women were single parents. Three of the staff were African-Caribbean and one was Asian. Only one member of the staff had a formal social work qualification. Three of the staff were employed on temporary contracts.

An initial meeting with the home manager suggested there was considerable tension between some members of the team. There was also the perception that 'increasingly difficult' children were being admitted to the home. In addition, it was clear that a poor relationship existed between the home manager and the relevant Area Director; 'I sat next to him on the bus the other day and he didn't recognise me'. However, in spite of the tensions, the home manager was positive about my input and appeared eager to make the most of the opportunity that the project offered.

Checklist 1

An initial meeting was held with the team in a smoke-filled room. I explained the objectives of the project, although I was frequently interrupted by phone calls. The team completed copies of the stress checklist. The scores for each variable were aggregated on a spreadsheet in order to construct a team profile prior to any intervention. These were presented on a five-point scale where 5 = very satisfied and 1 = very dissatisfied. Profile 1 revealed that the highest levels of satisfaction with workplace factors were expressed towards: relationships with clients (3.5); relationships with work peers (3.5), physical working conditions (3.5); level of client contact (3.5). Only one clear area of dissatisfaction emerged: leadership from central management (2.7).

The most frequently occurring effects of workplace pressures, on a four-point scale were 4 = often and 1 = never, were reported to be: sleeplessness (3.3); irritability with clients (3.0); irritability with colleagues (3.0); irritability with family (3.0). In this particular workplace, therefore, there was evidence to suggest that staff stress was impacting upon others.The most frequently used responses to pressures, on a five-point scale where 5 = very likely and 1= never, were: talking to someone (4.6); thinking problems through (4.2); tackling problems directly (3.8); improving skills (3.8).

Workshop 1

Workshop 1 was held four weeks after the initial meeting. This involved a team discussion lasting one-and-a-half hours. The schedule was as follows:

- What do you understand by the term 'stress'?

- How does stress affect you: (a) as an individual; (b) as a team?
- Is stress a problem in the workplace?
- Can you give some examples of what causes you stress?
- How do you cope with stress?
- Does stress in your home life affect your levels of job stress and vice versa?
- Do you think clients are aware when you are under stress?
- Do different types of people suffer more stress than others?
- What motivates you at work?
- What can be done to help carers deal with stress?

In-depth interviews were then held over a four-week period with each team member. The interviews lasted approximately one-and-a-half hours. The interview schedule was the same as for the team discussion. An analysis of the focus groups and in-depth interviews indicated the following.

Causes of stress

Staff felt that their personalities made them more vulnerable to the pressures of the job:

> You need to be tender-hearted in this job.

> Lack of confidence in my own abilities.

However, they also recognised that personal circumstances as well as personality characteristics could add to pressures:

> One-parent family status increases the pressure of work.

The low level of training and qualifications was a source of great concern to the staff:

> . . . unfair for staff and young people to have to do this job without any training.

> People wouldn't let their children be managed by unqualified staff.

Generally, residents were only perceived as being stressful to the team when misbehaviour was coupled with poor support mechanisms. However, it was recognised that at times residents could place staff under extreme pressure.

> . . . all hell breaking loose and having to dodge the glass.

. . . trying to bring a client down wears you out.

The interviews revealed great concern about team relationships. This apparent problem did not emerge as clearly in focus groups or in the checklist. This confirmed the usefulness of interviews in eliciting sensitive data and revealed some very serious interpersonal issues that were bubbling beneath the surface. In particular, there seemed to be a lack of trust in colleagues:

Just after Christmas, all the children ran off and a member of staff said to me that I managed to lose them.

Lots of bickering, the staff group needs shaking.

Both the Home Manager and Deputy indicated a number of particular pressures with which they had to contend.

Expected to answer calls 24 hours a day.

. . . picking up the pieces after other people.

Black staff perceived that racism in their neighbourhoods had a major impact upon their lives:

Children outside often call me a black bastard . . . they see black as bad.

Last summer I was called a Paki. I laughed because he was so wrong, I'm Trinidadian!

Similarly, there was intense feeling around the Department's equal opportunities policy:

Equal opps policy is patronising.

Lots of good committed people in the Department, but unaware of what it is like to be black.

There was a strong feeling that the residential task was unsociable – for example, shift work. To a large extent this was considered as inevitable. However, there were some significant concerns raised regarding contractual conditions.

It would be nice to have a permanent contract not temporary!

I'm supernumerary and feel a bit half in and half out . . . I want to be a real person.

Senior managers came in for severe criticism, particularly around their levels of support:

You need to scream down the phone at management to make them listen.

I wouldn't know who senior managers were.

Effects of stress

Staff reported many personal reactions to pressure. Most of these effects seemed to manifest themselves as psychological rather than physical problems:

I feel as though I am falling apart at the seams.

At home, I panic when the phone rings.

The home manager was particularly disconsolate:

Very depressing seeing everything that you have worked for slipping through your fingers.

Team members reported high levels of interaction between work stress and their home lives:

My kids at home cop for it.

Are you sleeping in again mom?

Coping

A small number of positive strategies were identified by the team:

Staff meetings are very helpful.

Work through problems in a methodical way.

Many comments referred to the benefits of experience in the job. It was however, hard to distinguish whether the nature of this experience resulted in positive action or desensitisation:

> You get used to problems after a while.

> You get hardened to what the kids throw at you.

Many staff used alcohol as a means of coping:

> I go for a pint on the way home . . . go home and have another . . . then another and finally I unwind.

> Can't cope . . . drink no longer works.

A wide range of symptom management strategies was reported:

> I do evening work at the town hall, it's something completely different.

> Having a large family helps take your mind off things.

> Sometimes I hold a tree at the bottom of the garden to get strength.

Remedies

There were few positive suggestions concerning resolution of difficulties within the home. Training was the most frequently suggested remedy:

> Need assertiveness training or full-time course.

> More training.

Motivation/positives

A number of motivating factors emerged but it is interesting to note relationships with other team members were not amongst them! Residents were the most frequently reported source of satisfaction, in spite of the difficulties that they presented:

> I get a sense of achievement when young people achieve.

> At the end of the day, the kids are worth it.

The building was regarded as a significant benefit to both children and staff:

> I like the building.

This is the nearest there is to being homely.

In spite of the undercurrent referred to earlier, the management style of the home manager was seen to be positive:

The home manager is fair.

Get treated like a person not a number . . . always included in staff meetings.

Money was seen by four of the staff team to be the most significant reason for coming to work.

Workshop 2

Workshop 2 was held approximately four weeks after the completion of the interviews. The workshop lasted two hours and its purpose was to help the team understand:

- the importance of stress and motivation in the workplace;
- possible causes and effects of stress;
- specific issues within their teams in relation to stress and motivation.

I outlined the principles of stress and motivation and provided an analysis of the checklist, group discussion and individual interviews. An information pack containing this information was provided to each team member.

The workshop proved positive and discussion was lively and frank, particularly in relation to departmental managers. However, there were some areas on which team members were reluctant to focus, such as interpersonal difficulties. Nevertheless, when it came to identifying positive intervention strategies, few suggestions were forthcoming. There was a feeling that many factors that caused stress fell outside the team's control. This generated both a sense of apathy and hopelessness.

Workshop 3

Workshop 3, entitled 'Coping with Stress', was held four weeks after Workshop 2. A summarised team coping profile, was presented. The objectives were to identify:

- the most effective means of team and individual coping;
- the team coping profile of the workplace;
- possible action points to promote more effective workplace coping.

An information pack outlining personal and team coping strategies was provided to each team member. At this point in time, friction was gradually building up between the home manager and area manager and the general atmosphere of the home was tense. Nevertheless, the team identified a number of steps that could be taken to alleviate the effects of workplace pressures. In particular, the issue of temporary contracts was raised and the home manager agreed that she would contact her line manager in an attempt to resolve this issue. However, whilst the intention was to agree team coping strategies at this session, this did not happen and was put off for future discussion. I was somewhat sceptical as to whether any action would be implemented.

Checklist 2

Two months after Workshop 3, the checklist was re-administered to staff to determine whether any changes within the team profiles had taken place. The profile was as follows:

- *Satisfaction with workplace factors.* Whilst the overall change was not substantial, the most noticeable decreases were in three key areas: leadership from line manager (–0.3); relationships with senior staff (–0.4); equal opportunities (–1.0). The change in satisfaction with equal opportunities was particularly marked and reflected an overall deteriorating situation within the home. This change in the rating is consistent with the tensions that had emerged within the workplace between members of staff and senior departmental managers.
- *Effects of stress.* Two areas of slight change occurred. The incidence of feeling sick and depressed had increased slightly: feeling sick (+0.2); depression (+0.3).
- *Responses to workplace pressures.* There were significant increases in using the following strategies: seeking professional help (+0.8); engaging in recreational activity (+0.8); relaxation exercises (+1.0). There was also a slight increase in alcohol consumption (+0.3). The increase in the first three responses was perceived by team members as being largely attributable to increased awareness arising from my intervention. Equally, however, their increased usage may have been a response to increased pressures within the workplace, which may in turn have moderated the potential effects and might explain the relatively minor changes noted in the previous section.

Workshop 4

Workshop 4 was to be held within four weeks of the checklist being administered and was intended primarily as a means of providing feedback and to take any comments or points the team wished to make about the overall process. However, after the third workshop was held, the home manager left the unit and tensions continued to escalate between unit staff and departmental managers. In view of these difficulties, it was not possible to hold Workshop 4. Following a period of attempted resolution of the difficulties by the Department the home was closed.

Discussion

With the exception of Workshop 4, each stage of the proposed intervention programme was implemented. However, in spite of the fact that the team indicated that increased use of positive coping strategies was due to my involvement, the intervention was the least successful of the six. Three key factors contributed to this:

- Difficulties within the team and with departmental line managers were all-pervading and had virtually reached crisis point before my intervention, making the likelihood of achieving positive change very remote.
- Whilst the workshops and team profiles were initially well received by the unit staff, the home manager was never able to implement the steps identified to address the issues of stress.
- The influence of external variables suggested that levels of stress amongst team members could not solely be attributed to workplace factors; for example, five staff members were single parents and there were comments regarding neighbourhood racism.

In the light of the above, it is impossible to determine whether any changes within the team's stress profile were directly due to the intervention.

Case study 2: day nursery

This unit provided day-care provision for up to 20 children aged between 0–4 years of age. However, the nature of referrals meant that the unit had become a family centre by default – the staff worked with wider family problems. Indeed the unit provided a popular service and had the highest usage rates within the local authority. The unit had five full-time staff, including a manager and a deputy and two staff who job-shared. All staff were women, with only one black member of staff. Six of the seven staff were qualified. There was low staff turnover and the majority of the staff had significant experience. The home was attractively laid out and best possible use was made of limited space.

The manager was extremely enthusiastic for the team to participate in the project and an initial meeting with staff was extremely well received.

The team viewed themselves as a stable, self-contained unit, providing a service almost independently from other departmental employees, particularly social workers. Only two possible areas of stress were perceived to exist within the team: volume of work handled by the unit, and pay and conditions that were not equal to those in family centres.

Checklist 1

The checklist revealed the highest levels of satisfaction with workplace factors of any of the interventions. The three highest scoring factors were: equal opportunities (4.0), relationships with work peers (4.0) and level of client contact (3.8). Satisfaction with leadership from line manager was also reasonably high (3.5). Only pay (2.8) fell below a score of 3.0.

Similarly, scores relating to the effects of workplace pressures were the lowest of all the teams participating in the study, suggesting an environment that was not perceived by the staff as being exceptionally stressful. The most commonly reported effects were: headaches (3.0), irritability with family (2.4), forgetfulness (2.4). The most frequent responses to stress were: talk to someone (4.8), think problem through (4.2), improve skills (4.2), tackle problems directly (4.2). However, it should be noted that some strategies recognised as being less effective, or indeed maladaptive, also scored quite highly: work harder (3.4), avoid being in stressful situations (3.0), increase smoking (3.0), increase alcohol consumption (2.2).

Focus groups and in-depth interviews

Causes of stress. A great deal of self-confidence was exhibited by the team. This was probably rooted in their many years of experience and high levels of professional qualifications. Sometimes high standards caused problems:

> I get angry with myself for not getting decisions right.

Occasional references identified parents as a source of stress:

> Parents really, really annoy me! Why do they keep getting pregnant?

> I get frustrated with families making the same mistakes over and over again.

Most anxiety generated by clients occurred when dealing with cases of non-accidental injury (NAI). Concerns for the child, plus worries around media attention and lack of support from the Department, turned this into a stressful experience.

> Seeing bruising on babies is worrying. But it's when you get home and wonder if you forgot to record it correctly that is really distressing.

Little friction was evident between team members. Difficult situations were invariably talked through and resolved at an early stage. Similarly, the manager was not considered by the team to be a source of stress, although they considered that a number of management arrangements could be improved, in particular supervision. They also expressed frustration that they were not always able to utilise their skills to the best possible effect:

> Some parents gravitate to the Manager rather than key workers.

> I get frustrated at not being invited to case conferences.

The other key issue raised related to the fact that staff sometimes felt isolated. This was partly due to the physical structure of the building, which was felt to be cramped and badly designed. However, it was thought that higher levels of contact with the manager and deputy would be helpful.

The Department was frequently criticised. However, social workers were perceived to be a particular problem.

> Social workers think all we do is wipe noses and change nappies.

> We are undervalued by other professionals who think we have a tradition of non-academic day centre work!

Effects of stress

Staff reported that they rarely felt ill effects as a result of stress. Neither did they perceive any negative interaction between workplace pressures and their homes. This stood out in contrast to the other case studies.

Coping

Many comments indicated that the most effective coping measures were frequently implemented by staff, perhaps to a more marked degree than in any other case study:

> I do not take things home. I deliberately switch off.
> I talk the problem through.

Similarly, symptom management appeared to be well utilised by team members, with a wide cross-section of interesting and varied activities:

I have a vintage car that helps my stress.

In spite of the above, some maladaptive responses to stress were also in evidence:

I smoke.

I enjoy going out and getting drunk!

Suggested remedies

Unsurprisingly, the staff group identified the provision of more space as being a key step to relieving some of the internal pressures. However, every single member of staff, other than the manager, identified a need for greater consistency to be achieved through increased supervision.

Motivation/ positives

The team provided many examples of good practice and areas of motivation, which indicated to the researcher that there was a healthy work environment. Four key areas were identified:

(a) Clients

Seeing children get on is stimulating.

There is an intrinsic pleasure in working with children.

(b) Internal management style

The manager is generally supportive.

The manager has established good professional procedures

The above comments linked to the constructive criticism concerning lack of supervision seem to indicate an environment where staff were able to make rational and honest judgements concerning their manager.

(c) Colleagues. Comments towards colleagues were almost unanimously positive

I have confidence in my colleagues.

(d) Conditions of service. The two staff who job shared, both saw this as positive

Being job share is good. It allows me more time at home.

Process of team development

The enthusiasm and commitment of the team was evident from the outset. At the behest of the staff and manager, an action list to tackle a number of workplace pressures was developed. Each point raised was entered onto an action sheet and progress reviewed regularly. In addition, there was much enthusiasm to test out individual coping techniques. However, as the workshops progressed it became evident that the team was experiencing increased work pressure. This seemed focused around three main issues:

- Work overload. The team members felt that they were being asked to undertake increasingly complex family work that was outside their remit and indeed their salary scales. Team members consequently felt undervalued by the Department.
- The saga of shortage of space remained an ongoing source of irritation.
- All team members were undergoing a compulsory training course relating to the Children's Act, which meant a shortage of staff in the unit from time to time.

However, at the end of the intervention, yet a further change had taken place, with the mood of the team becoming exceptionally positive. Two key factors had significantly impacted upon the establishment: (a) a new wing was to be added to the centre; (b) the unit was to be redesignated as a Family Centre.

Checklist 2

Satisfaction with workplace factors scores represented the highest level achieved by any team in the study, with nine of the workplace factors measured showing an increase, the most marked being workload ($+0.7$) and autonomy ($+0.8$).

Surprisingly, effects of workplace pressures scores indicated an increase in frequency in 15 of the 17 variables. In only two cases was there a decrease: sleeplessness (-0.1) and headaches (-0.6). Significant increases in frequency were reported in the cases of irritability with family ($+0.8$); forgetfulness ($+0.6$); overeating ($+0.6$); apathy ($+0.6$). Two positive responses to workplace pressures appear to have increased: thinking positively about yourself (+0.5); complain to others in the workplace (+0.7). The latter may well be a result of the active promotion by the manager of discussing difficulties in the workplace in a more open manner. A large increase in sleeping (+1.3) as a coping mechanism, may be a product of the high level of pressure the team was experiencing and would possibly account for the decrease in relaxation exercises (–0.9).

Discussion

This particular intervention was, in my view, the most successful in bringing about effective change within the workplace. Feedback from all staff had been positive. In particular, a number of internal mechanisms, thought by staff to be effective responses to stress, were put in place, arising directly from the researcher's intervention and subsequent discussion with the team:

* increased supervision;
* introduction of special interest groups/quality circles;
* increased daily support from the manager;
* increased regularity of staff meetings with shared agenda setting.

It is important to note the contribution to the success of the intervention made by a number of factors outside of my control:

* the resilience of the manager throughout the study;
* the general 'healthiness' of the team, which was evident at the outset;
* the ability of the team to function in a semi-autonomous state outside of mainstream Department activities;
* the considerable experience within the team;
* the approval for a building extension;
* redesignation of the unit as a Family Centre.

The latter two changes were both perceived (erroneously) as somehow connected with my intervention.

The changes concerning individual coping behaviour of members of staff presented some apparent contradictions, in particular the relatively common usage, amongst a team that coped well under pressure, of coping responses that are usually regarded within the avoidance or maladaptive category, such as consumption of alcohol. It is not possible to provide a clear explanation, but an interesting hypothesis might be that so-called maladaptive strategies when used within a balanced range of coping responses might have little negative impact upon the individual. In spite of the apparent success of the programme, a cautious approach should be taken in drawing any substantive cause-and-effect conclusions from this intervention, since on the surface, the checklist provided contradictory results – higher satisfaction with workplace factors, but an increase in reported adverse effects of stress. There are a number of possible explanations: it is possible that the team members now had a greater sense of awareness of stress issues, as indicated by the manager, and were therefore more easily able to identify the relationship between work pressures and effects. A number of external pressures remained:

- legislative changes requiring attendance at special workshops;
- feelings of lack of Departmental support;
- changing home circumstances, such as the birth of a baby, undoubtedly impacted upon the workplace.

Parent workshops

During the course of the intervention, staff asked if I would run two stress workshops with the parents of children attending the centre. This arose out of their own increased awareness of stress and from a discussion in which parents had expressed their need for support in this area. Each workshop contained a brief discussion of causes and effects of stress from their experiences and how it might be managed. Each session lasted for two hours, with a break for coffee in the middle. Each was attended by a care worker plus seven parents (all women).

Causes of stress

Children were described in both affectionate and exasperating terms.

I could kill them sometimes.

At the end of the day, they're all I live for.

Male partners were seen as a major source of stress, in particular, by continually stereotyping women in the traditional female role as provider and carer of the home. However, women were also seen as responsible for bringing in money from part-time work whenever possible:

He expects me to do everything and more.

There was clearly resentment at the perceived inability of statutory services to deal effectively with their problems. However, the Day Centre

was much appreciated and somehow distanced from the rest of Social
Services:

> Social workers cause me stress. They never do what you want
> them to.

> Staff at the centre are really helpful. They help me sort out my stress.

Parents did not present as being resentful of their personal situations.
This contrasted sharply with professional carers who generally viewed
home as their escape from work pressures. To these parents there
seemed little escape.

> My house is terrible. It's damp and makes the children ill.

> I hate the area where I live . . . but I'll never be able to move. I just
> know it.

Coping

The participants generally felt there was no solution to their problems.

> I've tried everything. Praying . . . we've all tried that haven't we,
> but it doesn't make any difference.

> I've tried drugs. I used to use them quite regularly, but I've
> stopped now. It did make me feel better.

Some of the comments made by parents were highly amusing but also
deeply moving:

> If I'm feeling miserable, I put my wedding dress on and do the
> shopping. It makes other people laugh and it makes me laugh too.
> I've never got to use it at a wedding!

There was both interest and amusement at some of the suggestions put
forward in the popular stress-management literature. Strategies such as
holidays and going to the theatre had no relevance to these parents.

In some cases, the reactions to pressures were extremely radical and
indeed worrying:

> When I get uptight I feel like belting the kids. Not afterwards, but
> at the time I don't know what to do.

> Last time I fell out with my boyfriend, I felt so angry that I took a
> hammer to his car. I must admit I felt better afterwards.

In terms of what was most required by the participants, it seemed that some emergency coping techniques would be useful in preventing 'over-the-top' reactions. The most useful stress-management technique seemed to be emergency relaxation (Madders 1981), which was enthusiastically received by the participants.

Parents enjoyed the workshop and stated that they felt better by simply talking about their stress. Each was given a handout of simple stress-management strategies.

Discussion

Many coping strategies within the stress literature have little relevance for service users.

Parental disaffection with social workers and their perceived inability to deliver what was required of them stands out in sharp contrast to the positive way in which the centre was viewed. Therefore potential conflict between the centre staff and other departmental employees is likely to be reinforced by differing expectations of clients, social worker and centre staff, increasing the potential stress for all parties!

Evaluating the interventions

Understanding the workplace

All six interventions assisted managers and staff in understanding better the dynamics of stress and motivation within their workplaces. Some key learning points emerged.
(a) Common stressors were found across all six sites of intervention:

- the Department;
- senior managers;
- differing expectations;
- media – poor public image of social work;
- 'looking over their shoulders';
- communication difficulties associated with the Department and its policies;
- conditions of service;
- lack of appropriate training;
- organisational attitudes towards women and black staff.

Significantly, clients did not appear to be a common source of stress as much of the literature suggests. Indeed, the opposite was true: clients were identified by all groups as the key source of satisfaction.
(b) There were stressors specific to:

- Client groups. elderly – death, difficulties in discharges from hospital; children – child protection; appearances in court; learning difficulties – role of Health Service.

- Provision: Residential work: unsociable working hours; sleeping-in duties; levels of contact with clients; fewer staff qualified; less experience.
- Teams: Interpersonal relationships (staff and local managers); personality characteristics; physical conditions; home circumstances.

The range of specific stressors demonstrates the variation in dynamics that can exist between each individual workplace.

Individual/team coping strategies

The relevance and effectiveness of a wide range of individual and team coping strategies were explored with the teams. Most of the individual coping strategies used by staff were consistent with those outlined by McDerment, Dunham and Shapiro (1988) and Howard, Rechnitzer and Cunningham (1975). The majority was within the control or adaptive category, for example talking the problem through or tackling the problem directly. However, it was noticeable that experience played a crucial role in the ability to cope and that long-term employees within the organisation were more likely to implement control strategies.

Generally, levels of maladaptive strategies were reported to be low, with the exception of 'working harder', which appeared to be a not infrequent response to pressure made by all types of carers. This response may be related to recruitment policy – managers regard this attitude as positive.

Within one particular team there was a culture of excessive alcohol consumption, which had manifested itself in the same way as a psychogenic illness. However, there were a number of staff working in relatively 'healthy workplaces', who combined control strategies with increased consumption of alcohol. This did not appear to have any obvious negative effects upon the individuals concerned – indeed the opposite appeared to be true. This suggests that avoidance strategies may not always be maladaptive if used in conjunction with other strategies.

It was noticeable that coping strategies such as yoga, recreation, going on holidays, were not greatly used by staff on lower salary grades, like the Day Centre parents. Thus I would suggest that the relevance of coping strategies varies according to socio-economic status (see Figure 10.1).

This model directly parallels the medical studies of Marmot, Rose and Shipley (1984) and Marmot and McDowell (1986), who found a similar socio-economic relationship with sufferers of heart disease. Whereas the potential pressures and stressors encountered by high wage earners will differ in nature, they are not necessarily any greater or less in intensity

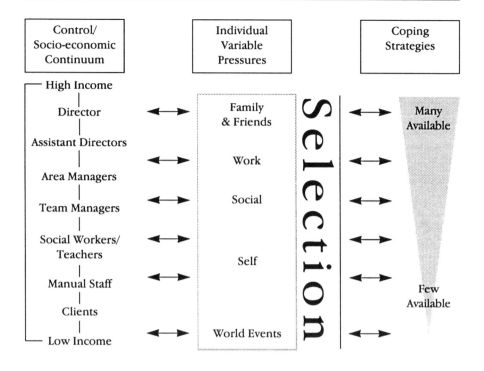

Figure 10.1: Access to coping continuum.

than those to which lower wage earners are subjected. However, the high wage earner will have a vastly greater array of coping strategies which he or she will be able to access.

The most effective team coping strategies appeared to be:

- induction;
- clarification of problem areas;
- management support;
- supervision;
- regular staff meetings – sensible agenda setting;
- quality circles;
- prioritisation of workload.

These strategies are consistent with the findings of McDerment, Shapiro and Dunham (1988). In particular, from the staff's perspective, supervision appeared to be crucial. On this point it is worth considering whether the management practice of work supervision, very much associated with the area of social work, has its equivalent in other public services such as teaching.

The work of McNeely (1988) suggests job sharing and career breaks as effective management intervention strategies. However, most staff in the studies reported that returning from career breaks or maternity leave was extremely difficult, particularly when practice and legislation had changed, and frequently described the experience as traumatic. Similarly, job sharing produced feelings of guilt and a tendency to take work home to compensate. The exception to this was in the Day Centre and this may illustrate that its effectiveness as a response to work or home stress lies in the extent to which staff are allowed to work within their contracted hours by their line managers.

Effectiveness of interventions

In three of the six case studies there was evidence to suggest that the interventions did lead to a range of positive coping mechanisms being implemented at both team and individual levels. However, the greatest impacts were achieved within the three healthiest teams, where the work environments were characterised by:

*   a high degree of consensus between front-line staff and line managers concerning their aims and objectives;
*   a committed manager who placed great emphasis on building on the positive factors that already existed;

These two factors undoubtedly contributed to the development of team cohesion.

Workplace climates in the other three case studies were, to varying degrees, less healthy and characterised by:

*   poor interpersonal relationships;
*   disagreements concerning aims and objectives;
*   managers who were negative or had been overwhelmed by workplace pressures.

Conversely, these factors contributed to low levels of team cohesion.

The severity of these difficulties in some cases was such that resolution of the problems by the interventions was not feasible. This supports the views of Fineman (1985) who suggested that some workplace pressures are part of 'organisational life' and to a large extent unchangeable. The studies suggest that when there is no attempt to cope with these pressures at an early stage, they become all-pervading and change is difficult to achieve. The checklists demonstrated changes in the profiles of the teams over the six months or so of each intervention, but they did not always demonstrate clear linkages between the interventions and the three key variables measured – satisfaction, levels of stress and coping. Most significantly, the interventions suggested that high levels of work pressure do not automatically create an unhealthy environment. Indeed the impact of these pressures upon staff varied according to both the individual's and the team's ability to cope effectively with them. This suggests that the study of coping is of greater relevance than the eradication of potential sources of stress.

The thoughts and feelings of staff and some of the scenarios painted in the studies I have outlined will be familiar to colleagues in other public service professions and the interventionist approach described is clearly transferable to other settings such as the classroom or hospital ward. However, understanding the pressures within public services does not mean that they can be eliminated. Nevertheless a thorough understanding of the stress process in the local workplace by a committed manager can provide an opportunity to change the operating conditions within specific situations. It is likely that such changes will contribute to the overall ability of the team members to cope more effectively with the range of pressures that they face on a daily basis. This can ultimately only be of benefit to individual employees, the organisation and most significantly, the users of our services.

References

Carroll JFX, White WL (1982) Theory building – integrating individual and environmental factors within an ecological framework. In Payne WS (ed.) Job Stress and Burnout: Research, Theory and Intervention Perspectives. London: Sage Publications.

CBI (1997) Stress study ordered, Guardian 9.6.97: 4.

Dunham J (1984) Stress in Teaching. London: Croom-Helm.

Fineman S (1985), Social Work Stress and Intervention. Aldershot: Gower.

Howard T, Rechnitzer PA, Cunningham DA (1975) Coping with job tension – effective and ineffective methods. Public Personnel Management (September/October): 316-26.

Kahn RL, French JRP (1970), Status and conflicts: two themes in the study of stress. In McGrath JE (ed.) Social and Psychological Factors in Stress. New York: Holt, Rinehart, Winston.

Keenan A, Newton TJ (1987) Work difficulties and stress in young professional engineers. Journal of Occupational Behaviour 6: 151-6.

London Borough of Hammersmith and Fulham (August 1984) Report on the death of Shirley Woodcock. London.

Madders J (1981) Stress and Relaxation. London: Martin Dunitz.

Marmot MG, McDowell ME (1986) Mortality decline and widening social inequalities. The Lancet (August 2).

Marmot MG, Rose G, Shipley MJ (1984) Inequalities in death – specific explanations of a general pattern. The Lancet (May).

McDerment L, Dunham J, Shapiro J (1988) Managing stress: organisational and personal strategies. In McDerment L (ed.) Stress Care. Kingston-Upon-Thames: Social Care Association.

McNeely RL (1988) Five morale enhancing innovations for human services. Social Casework: The Journal of Contemporary Social Work: 204-13.

Chapter 11
Workplace Stress and the Law

JOHN USHER

Introduction

Stress is the occupational disease with the most significant ramifications for teachers and their employers and indeed for lawyers at work, as employers and employees. In considering the legal aspects and issues we still have to ask the question 'What is workplace stress?'

The best definition could well be 'an excess of demands beyond an individual's ability to cope'. Here I will include reference to related issues such as bullying.

The week after the 'landmark case' (and to my knowledge, the only case that was tried at court successfully) of *Walker v. Northumberland County Council* in November 1994, the *Law Society Gazette* warned lawyers and law firms of the risks of injury and claims.

The *Local Government Chronicle,* 25 November 1994, said:

> The Association of Metropolitan Authorities is advising Councils to review their management of employee stress, after last week's ruling that Northumberland County Council was responsible for a social worker's nervous breakdown.

Andrea Kennedy writing in the *Independent* on 18 January 1995 in an article entitled 'Put the stress on leadership' said:

> There is a saying in the training community, 'Don't try to teach pigs to sing. It is a waste of time and it annoys the pigs'. Until now this could have been applied to teaching lawyers to be good managers. Maybe at last, however, thanks to Mr Walker, the pigs might at least learn to hum a few notes.

How many headteachers, year heads, senior management team members make good managers? What is the cost of their failure?

Being sued for damages

The cost to Northumberland County Council of their failure in the *Walker* case was over £400 000. Damages of £175 000 were eventually paid. The costs of the two-week trial alone were £150 000 and the total costs were significantly more than that.

In addition they paid sick pay and there was an ill-health pension for John Walker. Total costs in the region of £500 000 for the damage the employers caused to one man – in addition to the loss of a well-trained resource, loss of 'production' and additional pressure on those remaining.

One of the reasons for drawing attention to these facts is to encourage those involved to avoid being sued by dealing responsibly with the risk of injury and the other legal obligations to which I will refer later.

It is also worth emphasising that 'Research suggests that stress is responsible for over one third of all days lost [due to employee sickness absence] at an estimated cost of 3.5 billion pounds' (Health Education Authority 1995).

The total annual cost to the UK of work-related accidents and ill health is estimated by the Health and Safety Executive (HSE) to be between £11 billion and £16 billion. Of this total, £7 billion can be accounted for by workforce stress (HSE 1995).

The 1996 TUC survey of 7000 union health and safety specialists found overwork and stress as the number one workplace hazard, affecting workers in large and small companies and in all occupational groups. In my experience, as the lawyer for John Walker and one who deals with many who have suffered the effects of stress at work, teaching appears to be one of the more stressful professions.

The causes of stress

Stress at work can have many causes. Most lists refer to:

- impossible deadlines and targets;
- lack of support from others;
- harassment;
- lack of job security;
- poor communication;
- lack of involvement;
- changes and new technology;
- poor training and, particularly, lack of control and frustration.

In relation to claims for damages it is also necessary to consider the causes of stress outside work. Perhaps these are also a matter of common sense. However, the British top 10 causes of stress are said to be:

1. Unemployment or fear of losing employment.
2. Financial worries, especially debt.
3. Single parenthood.
4. Relationship problems such as divorce.
5. Other family problems such as children in trouble or parents who are ill.
6. Moving house.
7. Death in the family.
8. Having a baby or infertility.
9. Serious or terminal illness.
10. Retirement.

The point is that employers cannot deny the existence of other stress factors. They will add to the problems of stress at work. Employers should not expect teachers to be working at 100% of capacity for long periods and blame staff for suffering when a bereavement pushes someone over the edge.

Inevitably complications arise in legal cases when outside factors come in to play.

Stress and injury

Some even promote a stress model involving a concept of 'positive stress'. The Health Education Authority Stress Conference in 1995 provided delegates with a 'positive stress at work' manual.

Even in concepts of stress at work that do not involve the possibility of stress being considered to be beneficial, it is accepted that 'stress' does not equate to 'injury'. This can be particularly important in legal cases. Claims can generally only be pursued for damages, which are payable for injury but not for stress. Stress can result in injury. Symptoms can develop from stress. They may well be transient. They may become entrenched.

A list of adverse physical consequences from workplace stress would include:

tiredness, exhaustion, insomnia, indigestion, ulcers, bowel problems, high blood pressure, heart problems, headaches, migraine, anxiety, depression, panic attacks, feelings of frustration and helplessness.

Some lists include boredom and lethargy. Others inevitably include 'nervous breakdown'. A 'nervous breakdown' is a term that can be used to refer to a loss of control and simply an inability to cope with many aspects of life.

Stress at work can lead to a reduced resistance to illness and disease generally.

There are a number of explanations as to why it is that stress leads to injury, but broadly most explanations involve the physiological responses to a threatening situation, otherwise known as the 'fight or flight' syndrome.

Walter Cannon, a physiologist, first described this response in the 1920s. When human beings (and many animals) are threatened the body prepares them to respond by confronting threat, or escaping from it and repairing any injuries. The responses are triggered by the sympathetic nervous system, which stimulates a discharge of stress hormones, in particular adrenaline and noradrenaline. The changes that follow include:

- near shutdown of the digestive system;
- improved visual perception and muscle response;
- high blood pressure, blood sugar and cholesterol levels;
- increased breathing and heart rate.

It is believed that ultimately the injury caused by stress at work is based on the same principles and the same processes, which can become entrenched. Prolonged response to threat becomes dangerous. This of itself is important to the nature of the law's approach to the issue and particularly in the context of attempting to pursue a case successfully.

The basic legal duties

There are various obligations to take account of the health and safety of employees. These obligations apply to the adverse effects of workplace stress. This includes physiological and psychological damage.

Here we look in particular at:

- Management of Health and Safety at Work Regulations 1992;
- the contractual obligation;
- negligence;
- Disability Discrimination Act 1995.

Management of Health and Safety at Work Regulations 1992

A lot of people were familiar with the duties of employers (and also employees) imposed by the Health and Safety at Work Act 1974 (HASAWA 1974). Unfortunately, they were broad and largely unenforceable by a toothless and under funded HSE. Failure to comply with the obligations was a crime. Fines were small and prosecutions rare. The possibility of suing an employer for damage caused by a breach was expressly excluded. In the context of stress at work the law might as well not have existed at all perhaps.

However the Act and the obligations remain. There are potentially significant powers for safety representatives, which have, if anything, been strengthened by other laws and a change in attitudes. There can be no doubt that the obligations apply to all risks of injury, including that from stress at work, but it is probably that no one thought of that in 1974.

The HASAWA 1974 was also used as the enabling Act to effect the introduction of the safety legislation introduced in 1992 to comply with the requirements of European Directives. The most important regulations in this context are the Management of Health and Safety at Work Regulations 1992. The concept of 'risk assessments' was introduced and enshrined in the round of legislation in 1992.

Regulation 3 of the Management Regulations provides that 'Every employer shall make a suitable and sufficient assessment of the risks to the health and safety of his employees to which they are exposed whilst they are at work' and this includes psychological injury and the effects of stress.

Regulation 5 states that 'Every employer shall ensure that his employees are provided with such health surveillance as is appropriate having regard to the risks to their health and safety which are identified by the assessment'.

Regulation 8 is also worth quoting here: 'Every employer shall provide his employees with comprehensible and relevant information on the risks to their health and safety'.

Regulation 11 is, in my view, one of the most important in relation to the issue of stress. It states that 'Every employer shall, in entrusting tasks to his employees, take into account their capabilities as regards their health and safety'. This means that an employer cannot just provide for those who are 'of reasonable robustness' and blame those who suffer because they are not. It is necessary to consider the individual's capabilities, including the capabilities of those who have already shown that they may be vulnerable and so on.

Civil liability is still excluded, which is to say that a claim for damages cannot rely on a breach of a provision under the Regulations. However, for example, a failure to produce and act upon an assessment may be evidence of negligence (see below).

Consideration can also be given to the comments and recommendations in the Approved Code of Practice made under the regulations and produced by the HSE.

The HSE has also drafted guidance specifically relating to stress at work. The guidance is not prescriptive – the intention is to raise awareness of the key issues and offer a basic framework on prevention and control. It follows the trend towards encouraging risk assessment and subsequent action. The booklet *Stress at Work – A Guide for Employers* was published in 1995. As far as the law is concerned the courts would assume that most employers, and certainly employers of teachers, would be aware of the contents of such a publication and so they would be expected to pay heed to it.

Perhaps it is also worth noting here that the Management of Health and Safety at Work Regulations 1992 did not apply to John Walker as he was injured before that law came into effect on 1 January 1993.

The contractual obligation

It is an implied term of every contract of employment that the employers will take care of the health and safety of their employees.

Perhaps one way to explain this is by reference to the case of *Johnstone v. Bloomsbury Health Authority* [1991] 2 WLR 1362. Mr Johnstone was a junior doctor. He claimed damages for the injury caused to him as a result of the pressures put upon him and in particular the requirement to work as many as 88 hours per week. In this reported decision, the Court of Appeal considered the employers' application to strike out his claim for damages because, they argued, it was specified in his contract that he was obliged to work such hours if they required him to do so. However, the Court of Appeal accepted the argument put on Mr Johnstone's behalf that there was an implied duty to take reasonable care for his safety. This was so, despite any express term in the contract that he could be required to work so many hours.

After the decision in *Walker,* Mr Johnstone's case was settled before a hearing on the main issues.

Negligence

Most claims for damages for the effects of stress at work will rely upon negligence. At common law, an employee has the right to sue an employer whenever the employer exposes the employee to a foreseeable risk of injury, when it was practicable to take steps to avoid or substantially reduce the risk of injury. This applies to the risk of injury due to stress.

Further detailed consideration is given to the issues involved and the practical problems later in this chapter. It should be noted, however, that there are generally three years from the date of injury in which court proceedings should be started otherwise the court can prevent a case proceeding at all, but the application of the law in relation to occupational diseases is quite complex and apparently late claims can be pursued in some circumstances.

Disability discrimination

Of increasing importance will be the provisions of the Disability Discrimination Act 1995, which came into effect on 3 December 1996.

The definition of a disability is sufficient to cover injury caused by workplace stress in my view. The definition is 'a physical or mental impairment which has a substantial and long-term adverse effect on a person's ability to carry out normal day-to-day activities'. Among other things it is illegal to discriminate in relation to dismissal or to cause anyone suffering a disability to suffer detriment without 'justification'. The obligations on the employer require consideration of changes to an employee's duties or reallocating some work to another person.

Employers who fail in their duties under the Act in this regard could be taken to an Industrial Tribunal. Unlike in cases of unfair dismissal, for example, there is no limit to the compensation that the tribunal can award to make up for the losses caused by the employers' breach of the provisions of the Act. There are three months from the date of an act of discrimination within which an application should be made to a tribunal, but some later claims will be accepted.

It will be interesting to see what effect the Disability Discrimination Act 1996 will have in this area and generally. However, I have to say that most applications to a Tribunal under the Act have not been successful to date, although I have seen decisions by tribunals that show, in my opinion, that there has been a failure to understand the issues and to apply the legislation correctly. Such errors should be clarified in due course when cases are taken to appeal.

Claims for damages

The basic issues

We have seen that employers have a duty to take reasonable care for the health and safety of their employees. Employers must take reasonable steps to avoid foreseeable risk of injury. Evidence is required to prove failure to do this as well as the fact that the employers' failure caused damage. The burden of proof is against anyone seeking to claim damages.

This does not mean that cases on behalf of those workers who have suffered from workplace stress are easy, in the sense that damages are likely to follow. Far from it. Many will not involve a claim for damages. Some may not involve obtaining medical evidence, when the prospects are poor. Obtaining medical records may enable a decision to be made. More files will be closed after medical evidence has been obtained.

It may be helpful to draw analogies with repetitive strain injury or other industrial disease when considering issues in claims for damages – see Table 11.1.

Table 11.1: Stress compared to other industrial disease (for example dermatitis)

Dermatitis	Stress
1. Prevent contact with, for example, unsafe chemicals, contaminated oil, etc.	1. Reduce stress by distribution work load, job training etc.
2. Personal protective equipment (gloves etc.)	2. Stress training
3. Washing facilities and rehydration creams in the event of contact	3. Stress counselling for victims
4. Susceptible people (e.g. atopic or older people)	4. Some are predisposed or more vulnerable

Knowledge

The issue of 'knowledge' is especially important. By this is meant proof of the fact that the employers knew (or ought to have known) of the risk of injury. This will involve consideration perhaps of previous similar problems suffered by others and complaints. Cases that are likely to succeed may involve written complaints by the individual concerned. In other cases confirmation of the problems from work colleagues will be crucial

Surprisingly, 'knowledge' in the general sense may not be a problem in many cases. This is also important in the context of the law. It can be said that it has been 'known' for a very long time that work and in particular certain types of work cause stress that can result in injury. Thus, it may be difficult for defendants to find a psychiatrist who would be able to say that this is not so.

Charles Turner Thackrah (1775–1833) was one of the first to associate stress at work with disease. He wrote about medical practitioners when he said:

> Anxiety of the mind does more, I conceive, to impair health than breach of sleep or nocturnal exposure, or irregularity of meals. The body suffers from the mind. That sense of responsibility which every conscientious practitioner must feel, – the anxious zeal, which makes him throw his mind and feeling into cases of a special danger or difficulty, – break down the frame, change the pace of hilarity to that of seriousness and care, and bring on premature age. (Quoted in a letter from Professor ACP Sims to Thompsons solicitors in the Walker case dated 14 February 1989)

The 1936 edition of Henderson and Gillespie's *Textbook of Psychiatry* says:

> General problems – for example, of business – may be an adequate cause of anxiety state by displacement or at least by a

diffusion of affect as was well shown in a commercial traveller . . .
(Henderson and Gillespie 1936, p. 434)

Professor ACP Sims wrote in relation to the *Walker* case that:

> In general therefore it has been known for a very long time that
> stress is related to the onset of reactive (neurotic) symptoms. The
> person with vulnerable personality is more likely to produce
> symptoms, but increasing symptoms in a normal person would
> eventually lead to mental illness. Work is one possible area of
> stress. A secure family life is a protective factor, but increasing
> stress at work will eventually lead to breakdown even in a person
> of normal personality and contented family background. This
> should be generally known and would be difficult to dispute.
> (Letter to Thompsons solicitors dated 14 February 1989)

Another document brought to the attention of the court in the *Walker*
case was the Health Education Authority publication *Stress in the Public
Sector – Nurses, Police, Social Workers and Teachers* (1988) which had a
significant contribution from one of the Editors of this book, Dr Jack
Dunham.

Identifiable injury

It should be noted that compensation will only be recoverable for identi-
fiable injury and consequential loss. This may be important to consider
in relation to some mental or emotional effects of stress at work. It will
be insufficient for somebody to be depressed in the sense of being 'fed
up'. They will have to be clinically depressed. This is to say they will have
to qualify in terms of the psychiatric definition of depression.

Normally, it will be sufficient initially to consider with the injured
person what treatment he or she has received and what diagnosis has
been made by doctors involved.

It is worth noting, however, that many people who suffer from the
effects of stress will be reluctant to admit the problems to themselves, or
consult their doctors or advise their employers. There remains a popular
perception that 'lunch is for wimps'.

'Causation'

This is another issue to be considered in all occupational disease cases.
Even if employers are liable, for example, because they have been negli-
gent, they will only pay compensation for damage shown to be caused
by that negligence. Causation is always likely to remain a problem (as
would be anticipated from consideration of the issues above).

In common with other types of cases, responses to some of the issues are a 'double-edged sword'. The most important, perhaps, in workplace stress cases is that relating to previous history. On the basis of his findings Mr Justice Colman would not have found in favour of John Walker had he only suffered from one breakdown (I will comment more on this aspect of his judgment below). Further it was of importance to the judge that Mr Walker was of a 'normal robust personality'.

However, the questions that interest the law include: 'Can the injured person show he or she has suffered their injury due to the work?' and 'would the injured person have suffered injury following some other problems anyway?'

Mental illness is commonplace. The incidence of psychiatric illness is approximately one in four of the population. Of course this does not mean that 25% of any group of people are currently ill. We all have a history of mental illness in our families.

Patently, employers must take more care of those with a personal history of mental illness. This to is based on another old principle of law – see, for example, *Paris v. Stepney Borough Council* (1951) AC 367. This is the case of the one-eyed worker. The employer's duty to take steps to avoid injury to his good eye was greater than that duty to one with good sight in both eyes.

Reference can be made to the 'checklist of issues', a copy of which is appended to this chapter.

The cases

Psychological injury

Psychological consequences of injury at work have been recognised for many years. In 1905, Mr Eaves, a collier was injured by a stone falling on his foot. He was awarded additional compensation for the period after his physical injury had healed, when he continued to believe himself unable to work (*Eaves v. Blaenclydach Colliery Company Limited* [1909] 2 KB 73).

Other cases concerning psychological injury generally associated with trauma are strictly outside the scope of this chapter.

Stress cases before *Walker*

The first reported cased concerning workplace stress is dated 1991. In *Gillespie v. Commonwealth of Australia* (1991) 104 ACTR 1, the plaintiff was not successful. Mr Gillespie sued his employers for causing him a nervous breakdown by posting him to Venezuela, where the conditions were difficult. He alleged that they failed to inform him of the problems and failed to relieve the stresses. The judge found that the possibility that someone like the plaintiff would suffer psychological problems beyond the problems that most officers would be ordinarily prone to in these circumstances were such that a reasonable defendant would give no more than a general warning. It was considered that Mr Gillespie had suffered an extreme reaction. He was ambitious, so that such a warning was unlikely to have deterred him. Thus, Miles CJ concluded, his employers were not liable.

The case of *Johnstone v. Bloomsbury Health Authority* (1991) 2 WLR 1362, is referred to above.

The only other case was that of *Petch v. Customs and Excise Commissioners* (1993) ICR 789. Mr Petch was a litigant in person. He worked as a civil servant but had a mental breakdown in 1974.

Mr Petch returned to work in 1975. He was transferred to other duties, but in 1983 he fell ill again and was retired on medical grounds in 1986. There was a finding of fact that the Plaintiff was a manic depressive who was not showing signs of impending breakdown in 1974. His workload did not carry a real risk that he would have a breakdown in 1974. In relation to the second breakdown the Court found that the employers had to take reasonable care to ensure that the duties allocated to the plaintiff did not bring about a repetition of the breakdown of 1974. On the facts the Court found that the defendants had done their utmost to dissuade the plaintiff from going back to work and, in the circumstances, he failed.

The *Walker case*

In *Walker v. Northumberland County Council,* John Walker became the first person to establish, in court, that he had suffered workplace stress resulting in injury in circumstances where the employers were liable to compensate him. Quantum (or the amount of compensation to be awarded) was to be decided later. Meanwhile, the defendants appealed.

John Walker worked as a social worker from the early 1970s. He became an area social services officer about 15 years prior to his first breakdown. He did not work overly long hours – probably about 50 or so per week. He was not a front-line social worker when he had his breakdown.

However, the defendants were obliged to accept that it is known that social work is a profession that gives rise to stress and that stress can give rise to injury. As a social work manager, Mr Walker not only had responsibility for the front line social worker, but also had a responsibility for chairing and making decisions in relation to child abuse cases, among others.

During the relevant period there were five areas within Northumberland. Mr Walker's area, Blyth Valley, had the largest population and was the most urban area. In fact a new town was built in his area during his period as area officer.

Mr Walker had made complaints for some time, as had others, and it was accepted that Mr Walker's workload and responsibilities were greater than other area officers.

Blyth Valley, which was Mr Walker's area, was said to be 'beleaguered'. Other similar phrases and words were used to describe the pressures in Blyth Valley. There was a significant increase in problem cases, such as those involving child abuse. These had to be prioritised. Other work effectively had to be abandoned.

Ultimately, Mr Walker fell off work in 1985 with a 'nervous breakdown' (on his first sick note it said that he had a back ache). After about three months off he returned to work and the defendants promised to take steps to alleviate pressures, but promises of assistance were not honoured and later in 1986 he had a second breakdown, which will keep him away from social work permanently. He was 50 years of age.

I believe that the defendants' approach to the case seemed to be coloured by the view that they were not likely to lose, because the judge would be so reluctant to find in favour of the plaintiff and 'opening the floodgates'. We had approached the case from the outset in anticipation of judicial conservatism.

At trial the defendants spent a long time arguing that a local authority had limited resources and could not be expected as a matter of law to have applied additional resources. We argued that such an approach was wrong in law and, in any event, it was not necessarily a question of resources, but one of reorganisation.

Mr Justice Colman refused to accept that the plaintiff's first breakdown was foreseeable and, in particular, said that the plaintiff's superior did not know that the plaintiff was about to breakdown. However he accepted that the defendants were liable in respect of the second breakdown. Failing in relation to the first breakdown probably only had limited consequences in terms of quantum.

The judge's decision in relation to the first breakdown was not surprising in the light of 'judicial conservatism' and the fact that this was effectively the first case of its type to succeed. However, his findings of fact would arguably have enabled him to decide that the first breakdown was foreseeable. In addition the legal test about knowledge is to decide whether the employers knew or ought to have known of a risk of injury in circumstances where they could be expected to do something about the problem. It is not necessarily relevant to answer the question about whether or not the injured person's immediate line manager knew that injury was about to occur.

The defendant's appeal was primarily based on an argument in relation to resources. See, for example, *Roberts v. Dorset County Council* (1976) 75 LGR 462. Susan Roberts' claim to be provided with temporary housing pursuant to the local authority's statutory obligation failed when the local authority argued that insufficient resources had been allocated to the temporary housing budget to enable her to receive any benefit from that.

However, it was considered unlikely that the defendants would succeed in establishing that a lack or resources can be argued in an employer's liability claim in such a way. The defendants also sought to argue on appeal that the judge was wrong in finding that they were in breach of a duty owed to the plaintiff by continuing to employ him after his apparent full recovery by March 1987.

A cross appeal was lodged on behalf of John Walker in relation to the first breakdown. We were to argue, in the light of the comments by the judge, properly based on the evidence, that there was a risk of significant injury at the time of the first breakdown, which the defendants knew of or ought to have known of, and the employers failed to consider the steps that they could take to remove or substantially reduce the risk.

The appeal was set for 20 and 21 of May 1996. About a month before the defendants increased their offer to settle to one of £175 000 plus costs and the plaintiff chose to accept.

Meanwhile, the Law Commission Consultation Paper No 137 (28 February 1995) had said (at p. 34):

> A primary victim can recover from a psychiatric illness foreseeably caused by the Defendants' negligence . . . the most important decision here is *Walker v. Northumberland County Council* . . . this is a landmark decision and, if upheld on appeal, is likely to lead to other successful claims by employees against their employers for psychiatric illness suffered through work.

(at page 86)

> We see no valid reason to object to such a development. More specifically, we see no good reason why the 'Walker' case should be regarded as incorrectly decided. On the contrary, the reasoning of Colman J seems to us to constitute a logical and just application of the law on safety at work to psychiatric illness.

After *Walker*

Perhaps consideration of the law and the cases involving claims for damages for such injury is not complete now without reference to two other reported cases.

The first is *Page v. Smith* [1995] 2 All ER 736. Mr Page was a 53-year-old teacher, who had suffered for some years from Chronic Fatigue Syndrome (CFS). He was off work from school, because of a relapse in his condition, when he was involved in a road traffic accident. It was on the 24 July 1987. A car pulled out in front of his Volvo. Its bumper and wing were damaged, but Mr Page was able to drive it home. He had been hoping to return to school in September, but was unable to do so. The trial judge found that his CFS condition had been improving before the accident but then became much worse in consequence of it. He did not suffer any physical injury.

The defendants both challenged causation and denied that the injury sustained was foreseeable – it would not have occurred, they said, in a plaintiff of reasonable fortitude. They succeeded in the Court of Appeal on both issues. However, the House of Lords returned the case to the Court of Appeal, and the issues were determined (finally) in favour of Mr Page (on 12 March 1996).

The House of Lords had allowed the Plaintiff's appeal from the original decision of the Court of Appeal by a majority of three to two. It was established that:

*   physical and psychiatric injury are not different 'kinds of damage';
*   although a recognised psychiatric illness must result, the 'eggshell personality' may recover; and
*   the principal test for a primary (participant) victim is 'can the defendant foresee that his or her conduct will expose the plaintiff to a risk of personal injury?'

Reading the *Walker* judgment carefully will show, perhaps, that Mr Justice Colman therefore applied too strict a test when asking if the plaintiff was (as he found him to be) a man of reasonable robustness: this probably enhances the *Walker* case as a precedent.

The second case – and the most recent at the time of publication – is *Frost & Ors v. The Chief Constable of South Yorkshire Police & Ors* [1997] 1 All ER 541. The case is not strictly on the point for us here, but it nevertheless provides some further and much needed clarification of the law relating to post-traumatic stress and the classes of those who can recover.

I have also heard of other cases that have settled. June Ballantyne accepted an offer of £66 000 on the 11 June 1996. She had suffered anxiety and depression, caused by the attitude of a new officer in charge appointed in 1991. The officer in charge was said to be abrasive and he ignored and humiliated staff.

Broader issues and the future

As representatives of those who may be suffering the effects of stress we will also need to consider the effect on employment of an individual who complains or is absent from work as a result of a stress-related disease. This is not intended as a detailed consideration of the association between dismissal and personal injury cases, but it may be appropriate to discuss this further.

Following the publicity surrounding the *Walker* judgment, one lawyer was widely reported as putting forward the argument that employers ought to dismiss members of staff who suffered symptoms of stress due to work.

He appeared to think that it would be cheaper for employers to dismiss employees rather than endeavour to keep them employed. He referred to the maximum compensatory award for unfair dismissal (being £11 300), as compared to more substantial damages which would be payable following a successful claim for damages.

There are many flaws in this argument. Not least that anyone who is dismissed can still bring a claim for common law damages. Further, the act of dismissal may well result in a far more expensive claim than would otherwise be the case. Employers who follow the advice would also expose themselves to easier subsequent claims by the individuals who remained or replaced the dismissed employee. The employers would further damage 'industrial relations' and add to the stress of others by increasing insecurity as well as adding to the workload of those remaining.

Some negative responses have referred to the possibility that employers will consider 'weeding out' potential employees or those in work who may not be able to cope. However, as the Department of Health points out in *Mental Illness – A Guide to Mental Health in the Workplace* (DOH 1995):

> Depression and anxiety are so common that if we excluded everyone who suffered from either just once in their life there would be very few people left to chose from.

Even though some employers may demonstrate an enthusiasm to dismiss, in circumstances where claims would be difficult to pursue on behalf of the injured person, there can be no doubt that the cost of the occasional successful case, particularly when coupled with the harm to productivity and profits from the effect of damage caused by stress will far outweigh the apparent short-term 'advantage' of dismissing a certain employee.

Some others have endeavoured to promote the effect of the *Walker* case on practice in the workplace so that:

> Employees involved in collective bargaining will find it easier to make sure staff are not subjected to unreasonable levels of stress. The case can also be used in arguments over the level of redundancies. Employers must be concerned that heavy redundancies

do not put too much of a burden on remaining staff. (Brian Langstaff QC – *The Lawyer* 24 January 1995)

Industrial tribunal cases and particularly sexual and racial harassment cases will inevitably involve stress and sometimes serious injury and damage. I have referred earlier to disability discrimination.

Unfair dismissal cases can often involve 'bullying' at work, which may, for example, result in time off work and injury. Other cases may involve promotion beyond the level of competence, perhaps associated with a lack of training. Bad management, work overload, long working hours and bullying often feature in 'constructive dismissal' cases – see, for example, *Leech v. CRS Limited* (Case No. 00630/92 unreported). Mrs Leech was a checkout manageress and her employers wanted her to take on the role of cash office supervisor as well. She was given no training and minimal support. She found herself the focus of police suspicions in respect of cash shortages, which she had been expected to monitor in her new role. She was utterly demoralised and frustrated, she suffered a depressive illness and resigned. The tribunal agreed with Mrs Leech that her employers failed in their duty towards her and were in breach of the contract of employment, so that her dismissal was unfair. It appears that Mrs Leech could have brought a civil case for compensation for the injury and associated loss, which the tribunal remedy would not satisfy. (See also *Whitbread PLC t/a Thresher v. Gullyes* [1994] IRLIB 509.)

In another tribunal case, *Cheall v. Vauxhall Motors Limited* [1979] IRLR 253, an employee was awarded £50 for stress. The award was made, because Mr Cheall was denied union representation at a grievance hearing. Arguably there is no limit for such an award.

Consider now also the Working Time Directive, which should have become law by 23 November 1996 but has not been implemented at the time of writing. Teachers may be affected and could use the law to ameliorate the effects of stress.

Conclusions

The answer to the problem is not to go to law. The answer to the problem is to work towards prevention. If employers comply with their legal obligations in a reasonable manner, I am confident they will remove workplace stress. My experience in the field of industrial injury teaches me that most employers will not comply with their obligations.

If more efforts are made towards treating people with respect as a result of drawing attention to the legal obligations and the risks of being held to account then I, too, will be the happier. The unions with which I have worked are keen to support various approaches to reduce stress at work to acceptable levels and this includes the pursuit of legal action whenever the prospects are sound.

Perhaps I can leave the last word to David Shillaker, liability manager with one of the big players in the field of employers liability insurance – those who will pay out when damages are awarded – who said in a conference on personal injury at the Kenilworth Hotel on 28 January 1997:

> The legal boundaries of what is reasonably foreseeable will expand, so there are no grounds for complacency or adopting minimal standards of safety . . . My aim is to offer practical direction to employers to avoid litigation . . . In today's . . . world many staff feel under pressure . . . Union representatives are well placed to offer a solution and enforce a culture change to adopt new safer working practices . . . the marginal cost of a few extra staff . . . must be contrasted to the sharp increase in employers' liability premiums and other costs that flow directly from a stressful environment.

References

Cannon EB (1929) Bodily Changes in Pain, Hunger, Fear and Rage (2 edn). Boston: Branford.

Department of Health (1995) Mental Illness – A Guide to Mental Health in the Workplace. London: Department of Health.

Health and Safety Executive (1995) Stress at Work – A Guide for Employers. London: Health and Safety Executive.

Health Education Authority (1988) Stress in the Public Sector – Nurses, Police, Social Workers and Teachers. London: Health Education Authority.

Health Education Authority (1995) Positive Stress at Work Model. London: Health Education Authority.

Henderson I, Gillespie F (1936) A Textbook of Psychiatry (4 edn). London: HK Lewis.

Kennedy A (1995) Put the stress on leadership. Independent (18 January).

Langstaff B (1995) Report concerning work stress. The Lawyer (24 January).

Law Commission (1995) Consultation paper no. 137 (28 February). London: Law Commission.

Appendix—stress and injuries at work: checklist of issues

1. When did the client first start working in the area of work that he or she found stressful?
2. When did he or she start to experience stress at work?
3. When were the first symptoms experienced and what were they?
4. How did the symptoms develop?
5. Did he or she communicate with anyone in authority about the problem and specifically about the symptoms that he or she was experiencing? (If so, obtain details.)
6. What is it about the work that was found to be overtly stressful?

7. What could or should the employers have done to reduce the stress upon the client?
8. When did the client first seek medical help and in what circumstances?
9. What was communicated to the employers about any absences from work (on sick notes or otherwise)?
10. Has the client had more than one episode of illness due to work? (If so, obtain details.)
11. In relation to each episode or breakdown obtain details of the steps taken by the employers to confirm that he or she was fit to return to work.
12. In respect of each episode, obtain details of the measures taken by the employers (if any) to reduce or diminish the stress of work (before and after the client's return to work as appropriate).
13. If the return to work was followed by a further episode why were the measures taken by the employers not sufficient to avoid the second and/or third episode or breakdown?
14. Seek full details of any other evidence and information that can point to the employer's knowledge of the fact that the client was about to 'break down' or was likely to suffer injury.
15. Did any other employees, particularly those involved in similar work, suffer symptoms of stress? (If so, obtain full details.)
16. Did the employers have or produce any documents such as reports or memoranda concerning the problems of stress at work referring to the client or more generally? (If so, obtain details and copies if possible.)

Other factors

17. Have any members of the client's family (to the level of grandparents) had any reason to seek psychiatric advice from a doctor or psychiatrist? (If so, obtain details.)
18. Prior to the client's present illness, has the client had to seek psychiatric advice or treatment? (If so, obtain details.)
19. What other pressures could be thought to have caused or added to the stress suffered by the client during the material period? (Obtain details and comments.)

Index